JANUARY

Marie Corbett

JANUARY

A WOMAN JUDGE'S

SEASON *of* DISILLUSION

a memoir

BROAD COVE PRESS

Cataloguing in Publication data available
from Library and Archives Canada
Broad Cove Press

ISBN 978-0-9949248-0-3 (print)
ISBN 978-0-9949248-1-0 (ebook)

Cover and text design by Jennifer Griffiths
Cover and title page illustrations reference engravings by
Jacob de Gheyn II, courtesy of the Rijksmuseum
Author photograph by Mike Peake

Lord of the Dance
Words: Sydney Carter
Music: Shaker melody; adapt. Sydney Carter
© 1963 Stainer & Bell , Ltd. (Admin. Hope Publishing,
Carol Stream, IL 60188).
All rights reserved. Used by permission.

Every effort has been made to contact the copyright
holders for work reproduced in this book.

Printed and bound in Canada

16 17 18 19 20   5 4 3 2 1

For
Darrell and Edward
Duncan and Sandy

A thing of beauty is a joy forever:
Its loveliness increases; it will never
Pass into nothingness; but still will keep
A bower quiet for us, and a sleep
Full of sweet dreams, and health, and
*   quiet breathing.*

JOHN KEATS, from "Endymion"

CONTENTS

JANUARY

ACKNOWLEDGEMENTS

I THANK FELLOW AUTHORS Angela Jackson, Ann Ditchburn, Tom Moore, Patrick Boyer, John Parry, and Paul Butler and former colleagues Rose Boyko and Elaine Krivel, for supporting and encouraging this work. I thank Trena White and Megan Jones for their expert assistance in producing this book.

Most special thanks go to my talented and immensely competent editor, Gillian Kendall, without whom this memoir would not have been completed. She never tired of asking "But what was Marie feeling?" to help me express the emotions to accompany the events.

In Anne's memory, I thank Fran Blake, Libby Burnham, Joanna Campion, and Susan Lang.

NOTE: The criminal trials described in *January* were re-created from notes in my bench books made during the trial proceedings. While most names and some identifying details have been changed, the facts remain.

Week One
Monday

BREAKFAST

Vitamin pill

French toast with maple syrup—really
soak the bread

Real orange juice—not orange drink

One sausage

Chapter 1

JANUARY 11

IT ROSE FROM NOWHERE. As I put the phone down, it was nearly midnight. Had I really told Anne I'd pick her up at six-thirty in the morning? Why I would do this was beyond me. She had another lift, I had no car that day, and I hate hospitals. Somewhere deep inside me I must have known I had to be there.

At six-thirty, I was standing on her front doorstep and Anne was making her way out into the January morning, her breath visible in the chilling air.

Her face was ashen and puffy. "Marie," she said, "I'm terrified. I couldn't sleep at all last night." She pulled up the hood of her coat over her peppered light-brown hair. Behind her, Willie the boxer and the two Yorkshire terriers scampered to follow. I shut the door quickly.

Leaning on a cane, Anne walked slowly. I stayed close, holding her arm and steering her across the ice that crunched under our feet. "You're good to pick me up this early," she said. "It's not even daylight yet." Small white blotches were visible on her tongue as she spoke. Glancing along the driveway, she observed, "That's not your car."

"No, the nanny has my car, so I asked my friend Barbara to take us." I opened the front door and helped Anne get seated in the front.

"Hi, Barbara," she said, extending a soft hand. "I'm sorry I got you up too."

"Not at all, Anne—I'm at work by seven every morning. Nurses are used to early hours."

As Barbara drove, I sat in the back seat listening to Anne ask Barbara how she liked living in Toronto and how it was different from Montreal. Barbara chatted about her family and her neighbourhood, and Anne seemed as relaxed and cheerful as if she were at a dinner party. How like Anne, I thought, not to dwell on herself and to focus on the other person.

"It's a big adjustment, and I still miss Montreal, but my family is here," Barbara said. Looking to her right, she added, "I see you don't have a bag. I guess you're not staying long at the hospital?"

"No, I'll be home later today. It's only a biopsy."

A few minutes later Barbara dropped us at the main entrance to the Princess Margaret Hospital, and Anne and I walked slowly into the admitting office. The morning bustle had not begun, and a heavy-set nurse looked up as we entered.

"Good morning, Mrs. Gibson," she said, flipping through files on her desk. "I see your chart hasn't arrived." Disappointment crossed Anne's face, and the nurse hastily added, "But you can go on into your room, 439. Your friend can come back later for your file."

The assigned room had a single hospital bed, a small bedside stand, and a solid chair for visitors. The smell of pine disinfectant was strong. Anne stuffed her purse in a drawer, and I helped her out of her coat.

"Thank you for coming with me," she said. "Doug used to do this kind of thing. I never realized how much he did."

Anne's husband had died the previous year. It had been sudden and shocking, but Anne had moved through her grief with considerable grace. And, I privately observed, like many widows, Anne seemed to love Doug more after his death. It was not that she or others had taken their partners for granted, but rather that they had been oblivious until then about the many domestic chores that person had invisibly undertaken.

Modestly turning her back to me, Anne slipped into the blue hospital gown. I too turned away, putting Anne's clothes in the small locker and setting my own coat on the chair.

"I love that coat," Anne said. "Such a pretty turquoise. Wherever did you find a hat the same colour?"

"It weighs a ton, but it's warm. When the boys ask me if it's real, I look horrified and say, 'Come on, you've never seen a blue beaver, have you?'"

Anne smiled, and I put her sweater round her shoulders. "Where are they taking the biopsy today?" I asked.

"There's a small lump near my ear. It came just before Christmas, but I couldn't face the procedure during the holidays. Oh, and they're doing a bone marrow extraction also."

"Ouch. I'll get your file and be right back." The *ouch* was sincere. Besides hating hospitals, I had no tolerance for pain. Even after giving birth to two children, I still required a general anaesthetic at the dentist's office to endure the ordeal of having my teeth cleaned.

I returned with her "chart"—a twelve-inch pile of records. "Anne," I said, "I can't get over how much paper there is!"

"The entire file is over four feet high," she murmured. Then, looking down, she pressed her stomach and grimaced in pain. "I'm so bloated."

I couldn't deny that her abdomen looked swollen, that her face was tired, or that she was going to undergo another difficult procedure that day. Silently, I took Anne's free hand.

"Marie, I can't die. I simply *can't*," Anne said. A fog of despair engulfed her. Looking into her mournful brown eyes, I could think of nothing to say. I knew she was terrified about the results of the biopsy: the lump almost certainly meant the cancer had returned. She sighed, sitting down on the bed. "I have to stay alive for the boys."

"You will," I said, with hope. "What did your doctor say?"

"Simon said there may be a new treatment in California." Anne paused. "It's not a sure thing."

"Anne, if you want to go there to try it, I'll go with you. Say the word and I'll take a leave of absence. I can be with you whenever you want." The intensity and sureness of my sudden commitment surprised me. Anne wasn't one of my closest friends, or hadn't been before then. Yet I felt the commitment as surely as I spoke the words.

"You're always so kind," she said. "Still, even if there is a treatment, it might take months or years in the hospital. How could I leave Duncan and Sandy for that long?"

I had no answers for her questions and no antidote for her worries. I was glad when a nurse entered, greeted Anne, and then efficiently started the regular checks, first taking her temperature.

As soon as the thermometer was removed from her mouth, Anne continued talking to me, even while the nurse took her blood pressure. "Who's going to take care of them? It's not as if I haven't talked to them about the future, but they're so young, and it doesn't sink in. They think every time I go to the hospital will be like all the other times, and I'll be coming home when it's over."

Not sure how to navigate this difficult terrain, I asked, "You and Doug must have talked about who'd look after the boys?"

"Oh yes." Anne sighed. "We agreed that Fran and Tim would be the guardians. We prepared the papers."

I'd met the couple—Tim a prominent stockbroker and Fran a stay-at-home mom. As I pondered what it would be like for them to adopt the boys, Anne said, "I trust them, but I can't bear the thought of Duncan and Sandy not living in the house. It's all they've known."

"What about your brother? Wouldn't it be better for the boys to be with a family member?" I was unaccustomed to the idea of friends as guardians, and Anne had so many relatives.

She shook her head, and I could tell by way she spoke that she'd considered the prospect. "I don't want my brother," she said. "We don't have the same views on anything."

The nurse returned to take a blood sample. After considerable prodding, she finally found a vein and began to draw the blood.

"I have no veins left," Anne commented dispassionately, watching her dark red blood flow into the plastic vial.

I looked away, queasy. "Doesn't that hurt?"

"Not really. Not anymore," Anne said. And then, absently, "Maybe Simon would be the best."

"Simon, your doctor?" I asked. My eyebrows lifted, although I knew that Anne's oncologist had become a close friend. "Have you talked to Simon about this?"

"No. Not about taking the boys."

I realized that Anne was reviewing any and every conceivable arrangement, realistic or not. As I saw her imagining a life she would not live, not knowing what would happen to her own children, I began to see the horror of picturing one's children with another person, in another home, living another life.

"What about Mark?" I asked. "He's been living with you for a while now." Mark was one of Doug's six children from his first marriage. All were now adults, some married with children of their own.

"Yes, Duncan and Sandy like him. I don't know. I'm worried— there might not be enough money for them to stay in the house." She sounded tense, and then started to cough. Quickly I poured a glass of water, but she shook her head. "I can't have anything to drink before the operation. They could take my house if there's not enough money to pay Mark's mother's alimony."

"I doubt a court would deprive your sons," I said. Although my experience with family court was limited, I felt confident that no judge would put alimony payments for someone's ex ahead of children's well-being. "It's hard to believe that two estate lawyers like you and Doug could have such complications."

"Doug left a mess," Anne despaired.

In the small silence that followed, I wondered where my responsibilities lay. Should I offer to take Duncan and Sandy?

Did Anne want me to offer? After all, my sons were the same ages as hers, and they'd all known each other for almost ten years. We lived in a large house, big enough to accommodate the two brothers.

Yet the prospect terrified me. My life was full as it was, actually overfull—with children, career, husband, in-laws, social commitments, and more. How could I take on two more children?

Hesitantly, I began, "Have you talked to your brother or the others about being guardians?"

"No. I haven't talked to anyone."

"I would be inclined toward family members," I said. "Being with family will give Duncan and Sandy more continuity. They're old enough now, so you know as well as I do, a court will take their views into account. And remember, anything to do with their custody can always be changed if it's not working out. It's hard to make children stay where they don't want to—especially when there are suitable alternatives."

"I just don't know anymore." Anne turned onto her back and stared at the ceiling.

"You're fortunate, Anne, that the boys aren't younger. Imagine if they were even two years younger. Duncan's doing really well in boarding school, and Sandy has matured a lot over the last year."

She didn't seem especially comforted by this assurance— after all, who would be? Then the atmosphere changed and the air bristled as the surgeon arrived, a tall man with powerful shoulders and a head of grey hair. The anaesthetist, a surgical nurse, and an orderly followed at his heels, a small committee of people taking my friend off for another operation. I stood aside.

After Anne was helped onto the gurney, her face fell into a death-like repose, and I watched from behind as she was rolled down the corridor.

———

THE TWENTY-MINUTE WALK from the hospital to the court-house on University Avenue gave me time to think about the hospital, where the ill and the injured sought health and recovery, and the courthouse, where the wronged and the accused sought justice and truth. Two hives of dis-ease: one physical, the other social. I was moving from one pathological environment to the other: from doctors to lawyers—from white to black—from cancer to crime. The bracing, frigid air gave relief.

At the Armoury Street entrance to the courthouse, people stood outside smoking, getting their nicotine and waiting for the official day to begin. Some smiled or said, "Good morning, Your Honour." I returned the greetings to those I knew and nodded to those I did not.

Inside, on the ground floor, the morning mix of lawyers, witnesses, relatives, members of the press, and police officers met, conferred, and checked the trial lists to see where their cases would be heard and who their judges would be. With one hundred judges, the Toronto superior trial-level court was the largest and busiest in the country.

After inserting my pass in the slot at the judges' elevator, I entered the "secure" area of the courthouse. That part of the building contains the judges' chambers, and a corridor on each floor provides access to courtrooms for judges, court personnel, and sometimes prisoners as they are escorted in handcuffs or leg irons to and from the holding cells in the basement.

In my commodious chambers on the third floor, the large windows overlooked City Hall's square and Osgoode Hall. Following custom, I had been assigned the chambers of the judge I'd replaced. It still contained a wall of books and a large desk, but I had redecorated it to reflect a woman's presence—*my* presence—adding blue and white wallpaper with lavender flowers, a blue velvet sofa and wing chair, and some of my paintings and small sculptures. My quiet, pleasing chambers helped relieve the tension that built up inside me during days in the acrimonious, windowless courtrooms.

I walked into the closet next to the bathroom to dress for court, thinking of the line I used to tell my friends: "It's a great job, but I hate the clothes."

Off came my thoughtfully chosen street attire. On went a wingtipped white shirt with French cuffs, requiring cufflinks. I struggled with the flat shell buttons on the starched shirt, especially the top one. Dry cleaners were unable to resist starching the formal shirt, despite repeated instructions. I loathed anything tight around my neck and ordered my shirts an inch wider there. I fastened the tabs under the wing collar as loosely as possible. Next came a pinstriped skirt or trousers and the prescribed black long-sleeved vest, and finally the judicial gown. The long black robe had, draped over the right shoulder, a hideous scarlet sash, which required considerable dexterity to fasten under the opposite arm. The elaborate judicial garments, designed for men, never felt comfortable, even though I ordered fine cotton shirts from Hong Kong and had vests tailor-made in cotton, wool, and satin.

In my daily life outside the courtroom, I enjoyed dressing well, usually adding well-made hats to my designer outfits. Coordinated shoes and purse were a given. Why did I need to be impeccably turned out when I removed my street clothes from head to toe within minutes of arriving at work? Same for the luncheon recess: some women judges simply removed the robe and tossed on a jacket over their court attire when going out to eat, but I would take off the court clothes and completely re-dress, then don the court gear again before the afternoon sessions. This undressing and re-dressing was repeated when court adjourned for the day. Then, twenty minutes later, as soon as I arrived home, I'd put on something comfortable. Altogether, I routinely dressed and undressed up to ten times a day, in each instance portraying my role to perfection.

I'd regarded the standard male suit as monotonous and colourless until I read *Three Guineas*. In that book, Virginia Woolf marvels at the "dazzling" clothes worn by the educated man in his public capacity—attire that served to advertise the social, professional, or intellectual standing of the wearer like "labels in a grocer's shop," with every button, rosette, and stripe having significance. Woolf describes a judge chiding a woman litigant for imprudent dress while he himself is wearing a scarlet robe, an ermine cape, and a vast wig of artificial curls. He lectured the woman without any consciousness of sharing her "weakness."

I finished garbing myself and glanced in the mirror. Woolf's concept notwithstanding, there I was—in men's clothes, ready to administer men's laws.

At ten o'clock, my deputy knocked on the door and entered. For some time, I had refused deputies' offers to help me with my gown and had declined their offers to carry my bench book. This one, an older man who'd been at the court for years, knew not to offer.

Quietly, he preceded me down the corridor to the courtroom where I was to deliver my decision after a two-day sexual assault trial that had concluded the previous Friday. We passed a prisoner being escorted, in handcuffs, his leg irons clanging. His guards paused and stepped in front of him, halting him, to let us pass. As a new judge, years before, I had looked directly at the prisoners as I passed, acknowledging their presence. Some had glowered at me; mostly they looked abandoned and pathetic. These days, I lowered my eyes to the floor.

In the provincial courts of Canada, sexual assault cases are typically tried without a jury, unless the accused elects to have a trial by jury. In that event, the trial takes place at the superior court level, like the court where I served. At the superior trial level, the accused can change his or her mind and "re-elect" to have a trial by judge, without a jury. Such re-elections are common depending on the nature of the case, and they often occur DOJ, "depending on judge." Savvy defence counsel gauge the degree of favour a particular judge might show in a particular case. Inexperienced criminal trial judges tend to attract more jury trials until counsel become familiar with a particular judge's rulings and tendencies.

In the case at hand, the accused, Jerry Bigley, had re-elected to be tried by me rather than by a jury on three charges of sexual assault. Such a choice was common in child sexual assault cases. As two of the charges had occurred when the accused had been over eighteen years of age, Bigley was being tried in adult court. The charges alleged that he had sexually assaulted the complainant ten years earlier. To prepare my verdict for that morning, over the weekend I'd reviewed the notes in my bench book, to bring the details of the trial back to me.

The previous week, the complainant, Alma, a solid girl with neat black hair and glasses, had taken the stand. Jean Walsh, a young, haggard-looking Crown attorney, stood and began her examination of the witness. "Alma, how old are you?"

"I'm seventeen." Alma looked up at me with a half-smile. "Today's my birthday."

I wished Alma a happy birthday, grateful that she was old enough to give evidence under oath. Otherwise, I would have had to conduct an inquiry in order to be satisfied she knew the consequences of lying under oath. "What happens if you lie under oath?" I would ask by rote, mindful of the complexity of such a question. Coached children might reply, "God will be mad" or "I'll go to hell." Others might answer, as I myself might have, "I don't know."

To receive the testimony of younger children, I had to be satisfied that the child knew truth from lies. I might ask a child, "If I told you it was dark in the courtroom, would I be telling the truth or a lie?" The child might be puzzled, recognizing the absurdity of the question. Such legal bells and whistles are of little real import, but they are steeped in the legal tradition that holds that what children say is inherently unreliable. Until recently, the evidence given by children required corroboration before a judge could accept a word of it.

"How many brothers do you have?" continued the prosecuting attorney.

"Three."

"How old are they?"

"I don't know how old Delray is." She paused, counting on her fingers. "Kyle is fourteen and Burke is seven."

"Do you know the man in the box?"

"He's my cousin, Jerry." Alma pointed to the slight, thin-faced man in the prisoner's box.

"Are your families close?"

"Yeah. We lived in the same house for three years."

"Tell the court what happened the first time."

"My brother Kyle and me, we were playing in the basement. Jerry touched my vagina and breasts."

"How old were you?"

"I don't remember."

"Do you remember what grade you were in?"

Alma looked down and pursed her lips and forehead. "It happened sometime between kindergarten and grade two."

"Do you remember how old you were in grade two?"

Alma seemed to struggle, gazed upward, and answered, "About eight."

"Who was in the house at that time?"

"My brothers."

"Were there any adults?"

"No. Jerry was living there then."

"What happened when you were in the basement?"

"I'd be playing with my brother in the furnace room. That was where we played. Jerry was in the room."

"What did Jerry do?"

"I think he placed me on top of him."

"Were you both wearing clothes?"

"Yes."

"What happened next?"

"He touched me. He put his hands in my pants."

"Did he penetrate your vagina with his finger?"

"I think he did... ," Alma stammered. "Oh, actually, it did happen." I looked at the spectators in the first row of public seating. One woman was moving her head but I couldn't tell if she was shaking her head in belief or disbelief. Probably disbelief, as she was sitting in a row behind the defence counsel table.

"Did you say anything to him?"

"No."

"How long did it last?"

"One half-hour to one hour."

"How do you know this?"

"I'm guessing."

"How did it end?"

"I think I tried to leave or someone called me."

Obtaining the evidence-in-chief from young witnesses is typically laborious. Children are rarely forthcoming in the courtroom. Aside from the formality of the environment, any narrative flow is constantly interrupted by counsel's questions to establish the exact time, place, and details of the contact.

Children present special challenges. Some children may be unable to recount details, even when, like Alma, they are older. Young witnesses don't recall dates with precision, since a child's sense of time differs from that of an adult. Incidents of sexual abuse may last a brief time yet appear endless to a child. Defence counsel are quick to emphasize such vagueness and other "weaknesses" to discredit children's testimony. Such "frailties" are often insignificant; children are not mini-adults and should not be judged by the standards applied to adults.

The testimony of children is further complicated if an assault took place at an age when the child lacked the appropriate vocabulary for what happened. The first disclosure of an assault may occur only after the child acquires the language to describe the nature of the acts. Typically, this occurs as a result of sex-education classes in school.

Evidence might be required about the first time a victim told someone what happened. In Alma's case, no evidence was given as to the time of first disclosure, nor to account for why the prosecution was taking place ten years after the alleged incident. And in Alma's case, as in all cases, lawyers present the case, and judges cannot conduct inquiries on their own into matters not called by one side or the other.

Crown counsel continued. "Alma, tell the judge about the second time."

Alma described that when she was in kindergarten, she was at her aunt's house with her cousins and brothers, and "it was the first time we had intercourse." The act had taken place in the living room behind the loveseat. She had been sleeping in the living room with one of her brothers and a cousin. The accused, Jerry, kept calling her over from behind the loveseat. When Alma described the loveseat being in front of the balcony, two women sitting in the body of the court shook their heads from side to side, as if they knew better. Alma testified that Jerry took off her pyjamas—a yellow sleeper—kissed her, and "proceeded with intercourse." She said it lasted "a while, I'm not sure, an hour or an hour and a half." When he removed his penis, she felt something wet. Afterward, he told her to be quiet. She had a burning feeling and went to the bathroom, and then went to sleep.

Throughout Alma's testimony I took notes, recording the witness's words. It was important that I get down the facts, and my shorthand had reached the point that I could transcribe almost verbatim what a witness said.

Alma's affect was wooden throughout. Perhaps she had repeated what happened so often to relatives, police officers, and child welfare workers that this retelling was simply another stale recitation. Or perhaps numbness was her technique to cope with the traumatic events.

"When was the next incident?" Crown counsel continued.

Alma sighed, looked at the ceiling, and finally responded. The next time had been in the bedroom when she was nine or ten and in grade three. She was in bed with her brother Kyle when Jerry, the accused, got in between her and her brother. Jerry kissed her and "fingered" her, she said, "the same as before. I was scared, and I tried to get away and pushed his hands off. He laughed like it was a joke." He left "after intercourse," she went on, straight-faced, her voice flat. "It was the same as before. His penis was in my vagina. It lasted the same amount of time—one to one and one-half hours." Afterward, her vagina was burning, and he told her not to leave. He went to the bathroom and got Vaseline and rubbed it in. She went to the washroom and then to sleep. She thought her brother was sleeping, and she wasn't sure if or when the accused left the room.

Alma testified that the last time the abuse had happened was when she was twelve and her cousin came to babysit. She was downstairs with her brother Kyle, playing Nintendo. Jerry came down and turned off the lights. He called her to the corner, pushed her against the wall, and moved against her with his penis. She asked him to stop, but, she said, "he thought it was a joke. He laughed when I said I'd tell my parents. I kicked him in the groin." Shortly after that, her father came home. Her brother had been just three or four metres away that time, but it was dark.

The Crown concluded her examination. I looked at Alma, her head bent. I thought of all the girls who had been abused, the many I'd seen in court, the many in other courts, the many who never made it to court for any number of reasons, the many in other times and places unable to be heard. Of course, there were boys too who were victims, but from where I sat, most often the face of violence was male.

When Alma had finished, I turned to the accused's counsel, a fair-haired criminal defence lawyer about my age. Peter Block rose from the counsel table and approached the witness box to begin his cross-examination. "What grade are you in at school?"

"Grade eleven."

I started to make a chart in my bench book, working back from her present age of sixteen/seventeen in grade eleven. Alma had been five or six in kindergarten in 1983–84, while the accused would have been about seventeen.

"You don't really know what happened in the furnace room, do you?" the defence counsel charged.

"I have an idea what happened."

"Jerry was playing with you, isn't that right?"

"It wasn't playing. He had me on top of him and I told him to stop and I tried to get away."

"How did you try to get away?"

"I tried to take my hands off."

"Did you scream?"

"He said not to. I was afraid. I was down there by myself."

"Didn't you just tell the court that your brother Kyle was there?"

"He was back and forth."

"Did your brother see what was happening?"

"One time, Delray did. Jerry was on top of me. Delray said, 'If it happens again, let me know.'"

Alma testified that she did not tell her brother that it happened again, but she told her mother two years later, when she was twelve. She waited because Jerry told her not to tell and she was "kinda scared." One time, she said, her aunt and another cousin had been there and they had "an idea what he was doing." Although she liked her aunt, she didn't tell her because the children were "supposed to be sleeping. I was really small, possibly five." She didn't tell her mother because she "didn't know how." She didn't tell her friends because when she was younger, she didn't have many friends and hoped it would go away.

"You were seeking out love from your cousin, weren't you?" continued defence counsel. Though I refrained from rolling my eyes at the ludicrous question, I peered hard at the lawyer over the granny glasses I wore in court. Nearsighted, I'd had the top half of my prescription distance glasses cut out so that the bottom half served for close-up work.

"No," said Alma, eyes downcast.

Expressionless, the defence counsel picked up a transcript and continued. As he did, he kept up his irritating habit of jingling the coins in his pocket. I'd had enough. "Mr. Block, would you please not put your hand in your pocket? The noise of your coins is distracting." He apologized and said it wouldn't happen again.

"You told the court the first time he touched you was in the furnace room," he said. "When you testified at the preliminary inquiry, you told the judge the first time was when you were roller-skating."

"Now I remember. The first time was roller-skating." Roller-skating seemed a far cry from playing in the furnace room. And Alma had said he touched her vagina the first time.

"The second time was in the living room?"

"Yes."

"How long after the first time was that?"

"About two months later, I guess."

"You told the judge earlier, you were nine or ten. We can't rely on your timing, can we?"

Alma sighed like a much older person, and said, "I'm really tired."

IN CONTRAST TO the questioning of a lawyer's own witness, in cross-examination counsel may ask leading questions, questions that suggest an answer, such as "You wanted him to touch you, didn't you?" as opposed to "Did he touch you?" They may frame questions to expose frailties in the testimony, such as "How could you remember, when it was so long ago?" Counsel may suggest that the witness is lying by saying things like "You've told lies before today, haven't you?" And, most importantly, they may point out inconsistencies in the testimony given during the trial: "Didn't you just tell the court he touched you when you were in kindergarten? Are you now telling the court it was in grade one?"

Fuel for cross-examination is also provided by statements made by the witness on prior occasions. Typically, these are statements that were made to parents, teachers, or the police, and the Crown is obliged to disclose the contents of any such statements to the defence.

Prior statements also include the testimony given under oath at a preliminary inquiry, which may have occurred a long time before the trial. Such an inquiry takes place before a provincial court judge, who determines if there is sufficient evidence for an accused to stand trial. At the trial itself, defence counsel has a copy of the transcript from the preliminary inquiry and, using the prior statements, confronts witnesses with inconsistencies between the evidence given at trial and the evidence given at the preliminary inquiry. The greater the number of inconsistencies, especially on significant matters, the less reliable the witness. Adult witnesses, unlike child witnesses, study the transcripts of their earlier testimony to avoid exposure to discrepancies.

In real life, consistency is the mark of truth. The law turns this common-sense principle on its head: in court life, inconsistencies are pounced upon as badges of untruth. Witnesses are prohibited from telling the court what they told about their experience on prior occasions. Such consistent statements are excluded as self-serving. Alma is not allowed to tell the court that she told her mother or others her story, notwithstanding that statements made after the occurrence are fresher and more reliable than remembrances rehashed years later. Alma testified that she told her mother what happened when she was twelve; her mother could not be called by the Crown as a witness to tell the court what Alma said unless the defence agreed.

Defence counsel continued. "At the preliminary inquiry, Alma, you told the judge the incident in the living room happened before the incident in the bedroom. You said that you had intercourse two times?"

"Every time he saw me, he touched me some way or other. Intercourse is not important when a cousin molests you."

"You testified at the preliminary inquiry that Jerry woke you up when you were in the bedroom. Today you told us you were talking."

"I can't remember."

The coins were jingling again.

"Mr. Block?"

He looked up, realizing what I was about to say. "Your Honour, I'm sorry. It's a habit. I'll take them out." With that, he removed enough coins to fill a piggy bank and noisily put them on the counsel table. He continued with aplomb. "At the preliminary, you told the judge you went to the bathroom first. Today you told the court that Jerry went to the bathroom first. What really happened?"

"I get mixed up."

Defence counsel continued to cross-examine the girl on a host of inconsistencies between her evidence at trial and her evidence at the preliminary: whether she or her cousin left the bedroom first, whether her cousin's talking or his actions awakened her, whether she said anything or whether she didn't, whether she tried to wake up her brother or not, whether Jerry got under the covers in the living room or not, whether Jerry was on the loveseat or not, whether she was asleep on the floor or not, whether her sleepwear was a nightgown or not. Less trivially, defence counsel asked if she had noticed any bleeding after the intercourse, but Alma didn't recall blood. He concluded by asking, "You can't really remember what happened, it was so long ago; isn't that right?"

"I reported it at age fourteen. It's fresh. I was shy then. I'm not shy now."

I noted Alma's answers and the inconsistencies. Cross-examination is brutal, particularly in sexual assault cases. A robbery victim would rarely be subjected to such scrutiny, but because the crime alleged is sexual in nature and the scope of cross-examination is vast, the questioning is intensely personal, and often it's a devastating experience, especially for children. Even though I might squirm internally or feel angry or sympathetic, there was little I could do legally. Cross-examination is the main weapon in the search for credibility in law.

"I have no further questions, Your Honour."

Alma stepped out of the witness box and walked past the Crown attorney's table to the court worker, who escorted her out. The Crown called no further witnesses, and I asked Mr. Block if he was calling any defence evidence.

If the defence at this point had elected not to call evidence, I would have heard submissions from the lawyers and then ruled whether the Crown had proved beyond a reasonable doubt that Jerry Bigley assaulted Alma as charged. In that event, I would have found the accused guilty, as Alma's evidence was uncontradicted and the inconsistencies were not significant enough for me to find she should not be believed. I would also have had to decide the nature of the assaults. At that point, I would have concluded that there was insufficient evidence to establish sexual intercourse, but I would have found sufficient evidence for touching and fondling.

"Yes, Your Honour, I'm calling my client, Jerry Bigley."

A dark-haired young man walked from the prisoner's box to be sworn. That action told me that Jerry Bigley didn't have a criminal record (or at least he didn't have a criminal record that was similar to these charges), or he wouldn't be taking the stand.

Jerry Bigley testified that he was twenty-eight years old. Born in Spain, he had come to Canada when he was seventeen. He graduated from a mechanics program and worked for four years before getting laid off. In relation to the matter of the trial, he said, "The allegations are insane. Nothing like that happened."

As Jerry spoke, Mr. Block reached for a glass of water on the table, and the heap of coins fell to the floor with loud pings. There were titters of laughter throughout the court. I bit my lower lip so I wouldn't join in the levity. Mr. Block looked askance. "Excuse me, Your Honour," he said, bending over and noisily replacing the coins on the table.

At such moments, I would adhere to the advice a senior judge had given me when I was appointed to the bench. "Marie," he said, "it's a serious business. Don't laugh at either side's jokes. It's always serious for someone." I took this advice, and to maintain a serious demeanour even when humorous incidents arose, I would secretly press my lower lip between my teeth. No one else could tell and it kept me from laughing.

Mr. Block continued questioning his client. "Did you ever touch your cousin?"

"I could have been horsing around with them."

"Did you rub against Alma?"

"No. I could've been playful with her, but I didn't do those things."

He testified that the children slept in his mother's bedroom but would sleep in the living room if his cousins from the United States were visiting. He denied ever sleeping in the living room, and said there was a loveseat jammed against the balcony door. He added, "There's no room between the wall and the loveseat."

"Did you have intercourse in the living room?"

"No. I wouldn't do that with my mother in the house. I'd have to be a nutcase to do that with my mother and brother there."

"No further questions, Your Honour."

I turned to the Crown attorney. "Cross-examination, Ms. Walsh."

"Were you ever alone with the children?"

"I could be alone with the children with my brother."

"You played with the children?"

"We were just horsing around."

"Did you horse around with Alma in the furnace room?"

"It's possible. She might climb up on me or would jump on me."

"Did this happen often?"

"Not a lot."

"No further questions, Your Honour."

That was a pretty feeble cross-examination, I thought.

Defence counsel called Alma's brother Delray to the witness stand. Delray testified that he lived in New Jersey, that he had never seen Jerry mistreat Alma, and that Alma never

complained to him about Jerry and did not ask him to look out
for her.

Crown counsel's cross-examination was brief. "How long
have you been in New Jersey?"

"One year."

"When was the last time you had contact with the family?"

"I've had no contact for two years."

It was notable that Crown counsel declined to ask Delray any
questions that might have bolstered the evidence given by Alma.
While lawyers are trained not, in cross-examination, to ask questions to which they do not know the answer, in this case such
questions could have elicited more information about sleeping
arrangements, Jerry's babysitting, Delray's observations of the
relationship between Jerry and Alma, and the like. Alma herself
had testified that her aunt and another cousin had had an idea
about what was going on, so possibly Delray had as well.

The defence submitted that the allegations were not supported by the evidence and that there was no physical or medical
evidence. There was no "air of reality" that intercourse occurred,
the defence said. The evidence of the complainant stood alone,
and that evidence was vague, unspecific, and inconsistent—too
unreliable for a criminal conviction. The Crown agreed that
there were inconsistencies in Alma's evidence but submitted that
her general description of what happened was consistent. Crown
counsel asked me to find that Alma had told the truth when she
testified that intercourse occurred.

All of that trial had taken place the previous week. This Monday, I had to give my verdict; I began my reasons by reviewing
the evidence on the charges before the court and continued with
the law to be applied.

"The law is clear. The degree of proof required to establish guilt in a criminal trial is proof beyond a reasonable doubt. As I instruct juries, any doubt must be reasonable and based on the evidence. It's not a mathematical certainty. Rather, when the jury is sure of the guilt of the accused person, proof beyond a reasonable doubt has been established.

"The law is equally clear that I cannot decide guilt or innocence merely by deciding if I believe the complainant or if I believe the accused. Contrary to popular belief, a criminal trial is not a credibility contest between the victim and the accused. It's a three-step process.

"First, when an accused person testifies in his own defence and I believe him, I must find him not guilty. In this case, I did not believe Jerry. His evidence amounted to a bald denial of the charges. As well, his descriptions of Alma climbing up on top of him and playing with him were consistent with her evidence of touching. In this case, the evidence of the accused did not raise a reasonable doubt.

"Second, even if I didn't believe his testimony, if the defence evidence raised a reasonable doubt, I must acquit him. In this case, Delray's evidence had raised a reasonable doubt. Alma said clearly that Delray stopped the accused's actions and asked her to tell if it happened again, but Delray denied any inappropriate behaviour. Cross-examination elicited no reason for Alma's brother to come from New Jersey to support the accused over his sister.

"If the defence evidence had not raised a reasonable doubt, I would have to be satisfied that Alma's evidence was credible beyond a reasonable doubt. However, the many inconsistencies in Alma's evidence in the face of Delray's evidence rendered her evidence insufficient for proof beyond a reasonable doubt. Specifically, I doubted that sexual intercourse took place, although I found that the accused probably engaged in a pattern of touching Alma sexually. 'Probably' means it's more likely than not, but that standard is not proof beyond a reasonable doubt." For those reasons, I dismissed the charges.

Though my manner as I gave my decision was as professional and calm as ever, I was angry at having seen yet another trial where there was no evidence beyond the testimony of the child. How tired I was of the obvious reality that eyewitnesses to the sexual assault of children are rare! Why walk through the charade of justice? What about finding other supporting evidence that could give credence to the child's narrative? The Crown could have fleshed out details about the nature and frequency of the contact between the complainant and the accused, any other inappropriate behaviour toward the child, sleeping arrangements, and babysitting patterns. Where were the mother, the aunt, and the other brothers who could provide circumstantial corroboration of Alma's narrative? There seemed to be an ample number of relatives in court.

Why do we parade children and young people through the criminal justice system with nothing more than their young voices? The criminal justice system is a blunt instrument for social resolution in one-witness child sexual assault cases.

Of course, my anger included frustration, and I questioned my own role. I wasn't sure sexual intercourse had occurred. If I could find sexual touching probably occurred, did I lack the courage to be sure Jerry sexually assaulted Alma from kindergarten to age twelve? What had I become in men's clothes, with men's laws?

I expect that Alma, like the others, would be told by the Crown attorney or the caseworker that the judge believed her but that there wasn't enough evidence to find Jerry guilty. How could she make sense of the fact he was "not guilty"?

After years of such trials, I no longer thought that the pursuit of criminal justice was a search for truth. It wasn't an inquiry either. Ours was the Anglo-American adversarial system, not the European inquisitional system. It wasn't the job of the trial judge to investigate, to have all questions answered. I was the impartial referee, the decider of facts on the evidence that the lawyers brought before me. No, not a search for truth. *Happy birthday, Alma,* I thought. A hard lesson for Alma; a hard lesson for me.

———

BACK IN MY CHAMBERS, I detached the red sash and hung up my gown. I remembered how thrilling it had been almost ten years ago, when the judge's garments were put on me at my swearing-in ceremony, presided over by the Chief Judge of the District Court with two Chief Justices also seated on the dais. The large grand-jury courtroom had been filled with some fifteen judges, most gowned. Family, friends, and colleagues filled the body of the court. I entered wearing my Queen's Counsel gown, as lawyers wore silk robes after being appointed a Q.C.

How irked I was at that time to be addressed in a letter as "Mr. Corbett" by the vendor of legal gowns! I promptly wrote them on my legal letterhead commending "Dear Sir/Madam" as a more fitting salutation.

On the day I was sworn in, the Sheriff of the county was on hand to help me take off my former robe and to don the purple-trimmed robe of the District Court, which later would merge with the Supreme Court of Ontario. The oaths of office as a District Court judge, a local judge of the High Court, and a Surrogate Court judge were administered, and after I had taken the oath of allegiance, the Sheriff led me to the vacant chair on the dais. I walked up the steps to take my seat, giddy at the height, overwhelmed by the power of judging. I couldn't wait to begin.

The Chief Justices of Ontario, the Chief Judge of the District Court, and the Senior Judge of Toronto welcomed me in turn. Representatives of the federal and provincial attorneys general and of seven legal societies gave tribute. Throughout the addresses, I kept my eyes on Darrell and Edward, then age six and four, hoping they would not become too restless. They were seated with Alex in the grand-jury box. Edward kept rolling a truck along the box railing, unimpressed, mesmerizing some in the audience.

At the reception afterward in the Lawyers' Lounge, we all felt such an air of celebration. Ten years ago, at forty-three years of age, I'd felt I had it all—a renowned legal career, including an enviable record of service to the profession and to the community; a gentle, intelligent, handsome husband; two sons who were the joy of my life; and then, a judicial appointment. Why wasn't I as happy now as I had been then?

I finished dressing and took a taxi to the hospital at four. Anne was lying on the bed, gazing out the window. Impulsively, I kissed her on the forehead. "I see you're dressed, so you can go home!" I said, cheered. She did not respond, and I asked, "You're not relieved?"

"It's not good." Anne looked into my eyes. "The cancer metastasized. The bone marrow transplant didn't work."

I sat down, my pleasure replaced by fear. "Oh dear. What happens now?"

"More chemotherapy," said Anne, her shoulders drooping. "But they told me I can go to the hospital each day for the chemo and go home after."

Here, then, was a tangible way I could help. "When do you come back?"

"On Monday morning."

"I'll take you and be with you every chance I get." It certainly wouldn't make anyone else happy, but helping Anne seemed as good a thing as I could do.

Week One
Monday

LUNCH

Chunky tuna sandwich—cut in·half

Two chocolate chip cookies (*Kids'
Cooking*, p. 63)

One drink bottle

Celery stuffed with peanut butter—make
enough to last all week—keep in fridge
in cold water

One apple

Chapter 2

JANUARY 16

ON MONDAY, another grey day, I rang Anne's doorbell early. She came to the door with her son, saying, "I told Sandy he could stay home and come with me to the hospital."

Sandy was beaming, happy as children are when sprung from the grind of school. I grinned at him, saying, "I'm sure you'll help your mom feel much better," and he nodded hard. My own sons were allowed to stay home if they had a temperature, so sometimes, at breakfast, they'd been known to dip the thermometer in hot tea.

I was feeling happier, too. The trial coordinator had said that my trial had been postponed and wouldn't start until tomorrow. I hadn't volunteered for other work, as was expected of judges, but the quick twinge of guilt was quickly rationalized: I'd done my share of helping out at the courthouse, and it was more important to be with Anne.

In the assigned room on the ninth floor of the hospital, Anne changed into a cotton gown to await the chemotherapy. I hung up her grey wool slacks and folded the matching sweater in the drawer. I set her cardigan around her slim shoulders. There wasn't much to do, as she expected to go home later in the day. Anne lay fitfully on the bed. She had difficulty breathing and coughed frequently. Her swollen stomach protruded under the thin bedding.

Sandy sat on the bed close to his mother, seemingly oblivious to her discomfort, demanding her full attention. "Mom, the science project is due tomorrow. I'll lose ten percent if it's late. I need you to help me set up the graphs."

"The one with the different detergents in the plants, or is this another?" Anne asked in a raspy voice.

"Yes, that one, and I still have a trillion French verbs to memorize. Do the French really talk that way?"

"I'll help you this afternoon, dear. I'm going home after chemo."

A nurse entered to take blood, walking round the bed to Anne's side, and Sandy watched with interest.

"I have no veins left," Anne said, raising both arms and turning them to display the pale skin underneath. Not a single vein was visible.

"I know, Mrs. Gibson," sighed the nurse. "I'll be as gentle as I can." The oncology nurses seemed to exhibit genuine compassion, I thought as the nurse slowly turned each arm, squeezing and tapping, looking for a place to draw blood. After a minute, she said softly, "Let's try here."

The nurse held an eight-inch needle, more suitable for a horse than a human, and tried to insert it into a vein on the back of Anne's hand. Sandy grimaced and turned away. I couldn't watch either, but I held Anne's free hand and gently massaged her head to provide some distraction.

The nurse stopped and said, "That's not working—sorry. Let's try here." On the third try, the nurse tapped a vein in Anne's right thumb.

"When will I be getting a Port-a-Cath?" Anne asked as the brown-red blood slowly filled the large vial. She was referring to the surgically attached device that would permit blood to be taken directly from the heart. The risk of infection from the open line was well worth the obviation of prolonged, painful probing for a vein.

The nurse looked doubtful. "We won't be able to insert one until Thursday."

Suddenly, Anne took a deep breath, and then began to cry. "It's so long to wait." A glance at Sandy and she quickly resumed her previous calm disposition.

Later in the morning, as soon as Sandy had been picked up, Anne returned to talking about her sons' future. "There'll be enough in the trust for the boys to have a good education. I've always kept my life-insurance policy high. They could even go to school in Europe; we have relatives in England." She was speaking candidly, somewhat musingly. Yet I knew how hard it must be for her.

"Anne," I said, "you can use me as a resource in any way you want."

"I was thinking I'd like you to be my executor. I seem to remember some rule that judges can't be executors?"

"It's more a policy than a rule, frowned upon but not prohibited." It was a little like not offering to do extra work when a trial was postponed—it was not *de rigueur*. But I was getting to the point that I no longer cared so much about doing everything exactly as legal custom dictated. "I'll do whatever you want. Don't you already have an executor?"

"Yes, two business friends of Doug's, and Libby."

"Great, she's very down-to-earth." Libby was a lawyer I'd known for twenty years. I had no desire to be an executor in such complicated proceedings, but if Anne asked, I would agree.

Another nurse or technician appeared, this time a pleasant-looking Asian woman. "Time for your X-ray, Mrs. Gibson."

"I'll be back after lunch, Anne," I said.

She smiled, and I knew she was glad I'd return.

———

I WALKED TO a crowded restaurant near the courthouse. It took a few minutes for me to locate my friend, a provincial court judge, who was already seated. I hardly recognized her as she'd lost so much weight since I'd last seen her; petite and small-framed, she couldn't have weighed more than a hundred pounds.

Like mothers everywhere, we talked about our children first. One of her three had bronchial pneumonia. Her family was still feeling the excruciating effects of ongoing, acrimonious divorce proceedings. Her estranged husband had fired his third lawyer, and her being a judge exacerbated matters because his allegations, no matter how ludicrous, made news. The strain had sucked the flesh from her face.

Walking back to the courthouse, I wondered if there were any women—anywhere—having fun. Certainly none of the women judges I knew, including myself, were.

Family litigation is a quagmire. The stuff of human emotion infects the so-called logic of the law. Other than child custody cases, family law held no appeal for me, either as a judge or as a lawyer. I could never understand why spouses and parents paid vast sums of money in legal fees instead of settling. During one trial, fed up with the haggling and ill will, I asked both parties directly why they wanted to litigate further instead of spending the money on their children.

There were rarely sensible reasons for such choices. The essential nature of litigation is adversarial, and it provides every imaginable tool to enable a vindictive spouse to spin out proceedings, grinding down the ex-spouse and depleting everyone's assets. There's every reason for spouses to settle quickly, but often little incentive for lawyers to settle. The longer the legal dispute takes, the more money lawyers earn. The professional joke, sadly true, is that parties settle when there's no equity left in the matrimonial home.

When I called Anne from my chambers, she told me she hadn't had chemo yet and didn't know if she would get it that day. "I thought I'd be home by now. I didn't bring anything to stay overnight," she said, and I remembered her promise to help her son with his homework. I told her I'd pick up what she needed, and she gladly accepted, saying she'd call her house to have someone get some things together, including her pillow and a warm blanket. She added, "You know how cold I get."

On the way to Anne's house, I stopped at a flower merchant on Avenue Road and bought eucalyptus branches to bring their clean fragrance to the hospital room. After picking up Anne's things, I returned to the hospital as the winter afternoon light started to darken.

"Hi," I said, looking at her face for signs of how she was feeling. "What's happening?"

"I'm still waiting for chemo." The circles under her eyes made her look even gaunter. "It looks like I won't be going home today."

I put the eucalyptus in a vase and rubbed the leaves to release more of the fresh scent. "Here you are. I also brought a blanket my aunt in Newfoundland crocheted for me. I know you don't want wool next to your skin."

"It's pretty, such a cheery yellow," she said.

I draped the blanket over the hospital bedding at the end of the bed. "How are you feeling?"

"Getting okay. I've had an Ativan."

"I saw one of your mother's nurses while I was at the house. How is she doing?" Anne's mother, herself very ill, had moved into Anne's house the previous year, and Anne had hired nurses to help keep her comfortable.

"Sometimes she knows me," Anne said, sadly. "She can't really talk since the stroke. Still, I feel so much better now that she's living in the house."

"Does she realize how sick you are?"

"I don't think so. I don't even think she realizes Doug is dead." I pictured Anne's home with her mother and her nurses in the basement that Anne had refurbished for her, with the busy household above, and I wondered how she had managed so well without Doug. What an extraordinarily hard time she'd had in recent years—tending her mother, losing her husband, and still being a good mother, keeping up a law practice, and founding the cancer centre! "You look sleepy," I said. "Go ahead and nap."

She soon closed her eyes and dozed on and off, while I phoned her nanny and friends to tell them she was staying in the hospital.

After a while, she woke up and smiled. I asked her if she would like something to eat.

"I don't think I can eat the cafeteria food," she said.

"How about if I pick up some bread, jam, and peanut butter and make a sandwich?"

"I'd like that," she said.

Upon my return, I lifted the plastic lids from the small containers and spread the peanut butter and jam on the soft bread. Anne chewed slowly, sometimes with her eyes closed.

Later, a young woman Anne engaged as a companion for Sandy paid a visit, and after she left, Anne was drowsy.

The lights hurt Anne's eyes. I turned most of them off, leaving the upturned lights over her bed on low. Anne's vision had never been the same after radiation. As she rested, I gazed at her exquisite face, so at odds with her ravaged body, and remembered when we met, eleven years earlier.

———

ANNE SPOKE TO me for the first time in the parking lot as we left Branksome Hall kindergarten, having dropped off our sons. (Although Branksome Hall was a girls' school, boys were accepted in kindergarten. There were few boys.) Anne's long, dark mink coat and matching headband gleamed in the sun of the bright winter morning. Blond curls framed her face—an angel in fur. I marvelled that Catherine Deneuve had engaged me in conversation. Her brown eyes were warm and attentive; her lips, bright pink and cherubic.

"My son Duncan is in junior kindergarten," she said.

"So's my son Darrell."

"I thought there would be more boys."

"Me too. But Darrell seems to be enjoying it, especially the swimming. The coach is terrific."

"Yes, Mrs. Lumsden's son coached Marilyn Bell," said Anne, referring to the first woman to swim across Lake Ontario. Chatting briefly, we ascertained that we both lived close to the school; that she had another son, who was almost two, and I also had a two-year-old son; and that we were both lawyers on our way to work—Anne to a large law firm and I to my own practice. We laughed that we had so much in common.

Opening the door to a sleek Jaguar, Anne said to me, "We must get together. I'd like to talk about our boys and compare notes on schools." Years later, another friend of Anne's remarked that Anne had carefully picked her close woman friends, each for different reasons. I was flattered that she was interested in me.

We were both overachievers, successful lawyers engaged in many activities well beyond the parameters of our employment. While our goals seemed similar, the paths of our lives had little in common. Anne was born in Toronto. I was born in Avondale, an ocean village in Newfoundland, then not part of Canada. Anne attended a private girls' school, while I went to a one-room schoolhouse.

Anne studied in New York and Switzerland. My plan to study in France was thwarted by my own naïveté. I trustingly lent a handsome blond sergeant my earnings as a waitress at the USAF air base in Goose Bay, Labrador, and when he didn't pay me back, Paris was no longer an option.

Anne came from a prominent background. She was the niece of Bud McDougald, a member of Canada's business establishment. I, on the other hand, was the daughter of a World War II widow who had struggled to raise three children. My path to law school was forged with work as an A&W carhop, a ballroom dance instructor, and a cocktail waitress. I was an adult before I ever laid eyes on a lawyer.

Four years after we met, Anne was diagnosed with non-Hodgkin's lymphoma and told she had five years to live, more or less. By January 1995, she'd lived for seven years.

After her initial diagnosis, Anne had told me how she'd first known about the disease. She was getting dressed to go out with Doug and her sons for a festive dinner before the Christmas holidays.

"Hurry up, Mom. We're all ready," Duncan had called from downstairs.

"Two minutes," said Anne, tucking her blouse into her pantyhose. Then she felt a lump, and thought instantly, "How could it be so big and I never felt it before? Oh God, please don't let it be cancer." She put on her skirt and jacket and went downstairs.

"You're flushed," Doug noticed.

"Just hurrying, that's all," she said, but she didn't eat a thing at dinner, and Doug kept asking if she was all right.

Later, undressing for bed, she felt all over her stomach, legs, and breasts for more lumps. No more were evident, but the first one was undeniable, and she remained tense, sleeping little that night.

First thing in the morning, she called her doctor, who told her to come right over. "Marie," she'd told me, "I was too scared to go.

I postponed going three times and finally went to his office at four-thirty." Within minutes, she had an appointment with an oncologist at the Princess Margaret Hospital, and the next day, she underwent all the tests: CAT scans, angiograms, ultrasounds.

"And the day after that was Christmas Eve," she said. "As I was wheeled in for the biopsy, it was absolutely freezing. I could see my breath in the operating room. I guess the heat had been turned off over the holidays. I was shaking all over. I was so frightened that they couldn't get a vein to put the IV in. I remember the surgeon frowned at me and said, 'Pull yourself together.'"

Right after the procedure, Anne dressed and was standing alone in the corridor. The oncologist walked up to her and abruptly said, "It's malignant. You've got non-Hodgkin's lymphoma."

Anne's mouth fell open and she stammered, "What exactly is that? What does it mean?"

He looked her directly in the eye. "I'm sorry I can't discuss it. I have to go to a Christmas luncheon. Besides, it's not my kind of cancer." With that, he turned and strode down the corridor.

Christmas Day was a blur. She couldn't take it in, couldn't grasp the new reality. Doug told her to have another test, to be sure. On Boxing Day, she went back for another biopsy to make sure it was the right diagnosis. Again, the ward seemed deserted, and she remarked on the emptiness to a nurse. "Oh, yes," the nurse said, "only the terminal patients are left." With that, Anne sank even lower.

When Anne told me, back in 1988, that she had five years to live, I replied that I would do anything I could for her. The glibly spoken offer masked the depth of my commitment to her. I wasn't sure what that commitment would turn out to be. I wasn't family or a best friend, and Anne had other, closer friends of long standing. Our social circles sometimes overlapped but were not the same. Yet I knew I would do whatever presented itself and, oddly, I wanted to be with her as much as possible. With my undertaking, our friendship gradually intensified.

The spring after her diagnosis, we sat having lunch in Anne's kitchen at a small table overlooking the garden. A light drizzle fell on the new crocuses and the yellow, blossoming forsythia. That day, she'd worn a matching pale blue sweater and slacks, and even her shoes were the same lovely colour. I felt alive to and warmed by her beauty, even as I asked her the difficult questions. "What do you have to do at this point, Anne?"

"Right now, nothing. The doctors don't know where the cancer will metastasize. When it does, I'll have aggressive chemotherapy and radiation."

"Are you able to work?"

"Oh yes, I can still practise law."

"Have you considered doing something completely different? Writing a book?"

"I have written a book," Anne said simply. She set a plate of spinach quiche and tomato salad before me.

"That looks delicious. Yes, you wrote on estate law, but I was thinking something more personal."

"I don't know. I still edit the *Estates and Trusts Journal*. I'm working on a paper to give in June."

"What about a memoir? Maybe you'd like to write something for Duncan and Sandy. This is delicious, by the way."

"Mm, yes it is," she said. "It's a new recipe. Actually, I've been thinking about doing something for people like me who are diagnosed with cancer. When that doctor told me in the hospital corridor I had cancer, I was so frightened. I couldn't think of any place to go for support and information."

"Anne, your cat. She's on the counter." A sleek beige cat with large green eyes was eyeing my quiche.

"The Siamese go where they want," Anne said without looking up.

"I hope she doesn't want to jump on me," I said, glancing away, genuinely fearful—I have an almost phobic aversion to cats.

"I want to do something for the families," she continued. "I know we were turned inside out, and it's a crisis for everyone."

"Are there really no support groups?" I kept the cat in the corner of my eye.

"There are, but there's no central place, no central resource with research, practical help, and emotional support. There's a lot more to cancer than the disease."

Anne never did anything by half-measures, whether she was gift wrapping or planning a dinner party or organizing a seminar, and I could hear the earnestness in her voice. She was thinking about something. "I can't see you sitting in a support group talking about your problems," I said.

"Marie, you have no idea how lonely you become when you are diagnosed with cancer. All of a sudden you have nothing in common with everyone around you. I wanted to talk to others like me. Not in a hospital, in a relaxed setting."

"Are you sure you want to take on a new project at this time?" And I wondered, *Why do we tell people who are ill to take it easy? Maybe they need the activity.*

Anne cleared the lunch plates and set out a platter of fresh fruit for dessert. "Well, the first thing I'm going to do is find a first-rate doctor, someone I can trust. I refuse to have an indifferent doctor. "

"You must have lots of contacts through Genesis." Five years before her own diagnosis, Anne had co-founded the Genesis Research Foundation, to support research into women's health care. Even after she became ill, she continued as a director and trustee.

"Yes. I'll see you at the Genesis breakfast next week. Thank you for getting a table."

And so, in her own efficient, effective, lovely way, Anne made the decision and chose her path. She would continue to fully pursue her life as mother, wife, daughter, lawyer, and community leader; it was an affirmation of the values she'd always lived by. If it had happened to me, I doubted I would have continued in law. I would have done something different, maybe written a book. A continuation of the life I was living wouldn't sustain me after a diagnosis of cancer.

———

THE CANCER METASTASIZED early the following year, 1989, and Anne began rounds of chemotherapy and radiation. One day early in her treatment, I peeked into her small room and saw several people, including doctors, crowded into it.

"The meeting's almost over if you don't mind waiting," said Anne from her bed.

I thought for a second she was joking, but fifteen minutes later, they filed out and I realized not all of them were hospital or medical staff: she really had been conducting a meeting from her sickbed. As I entered, Anne was tired, but her eyes were alive.

"Anne, you're crazy. How can you keep doing all these things? Shouldn't you be resting, taking it easy?" Her bed was littered with papers.

"This keeps me alive."

"I thought *I* did a lot, till I met you." I put my coat over a chair.

"It's really starting to happen. We were discussing the structure of Wellspring."

"Wellspring?"

"That will be the name of the cancer centre. I'm giving the money to get started. I'll incorporate it. We'll have to raise funds and start looking for a place." Anne moved some of the files on the bed into a briefcase on the side table. "My doctor, Simon Sutcliffe, is enthusiastic, and he's head of the hospital."

"I don't know where you get the energy. How are the chemotherapy and radiation going?"

Anne looked at her watch. "I'll be having chemo soon. It still frightens me. I've always had such bad reactions to drugs. Now the nerves in my hip are gone. The last time, the radiation burned my throat so badly, I couldn't swallow and couldn't speak. I was frightened I'd stop breathing."

"I don't know how you cope."

"You can't imagine how dehumanizing the treatments are, as if all there is to cancer is the disease. Wellspring will treat the whole person, not just the disease. And after today, I'll be done with chemo for a while."

I kept thinking, *How does she do it?* Not only was she enduring the horrific treatments, but as she was awaiting her own chemo, she was thinking about what she could do for others— and not just thinking, doing it.

A nurse entered the room, all peach-coloured scrubs and clip-board efficiency. "We're ready for you now."

I stood up to leave, and Anne looked at me with a smile. "I need to celebrate. This Christmas, Doug and I are having a party. We're calling it a survival party. What a year we've had!"

———

AT THE "SURVIVAL" GALA, the York Club had never looked better. Red, white, and gold floral arrangements gleamed against the intricately carved oak walls. After cocktails, 130 guests were seated at tables of eight decorated with scarlet red drums, gold drumsticks, and holly. I kept the drum and have made it part of each Christmas since.

Anne was resplendent in a rose-pink taffeta ball gown. A ruffle framed her shoulders and décolletage. Doug—tall, handsome, fair—wore a kilt in the red plaid of his ancestors, the colour made more dramatic by the profusion of roses and poinsettia in the room.

At our table sat Anne's son Duncan and his stepbrother Peter, a charming tuxedo-clad Tyrone Power, with twinkling eyes. The party could have been a scene in a 1930s movie. Pipers in Scottish dress heralded the arrival of the flaming Christmas pudding, and we partook of the feast and the wines in good spirits.

After dinner, the orchestra enlivened the pace and dancing began. I danced throughout the soiree with Alex, Peter, and Duncan. As always, I had fun dancing. Like we say in Newfoundland, "Sure I loves the floor!" I had put my brief ballroom dance career to good use and had taught Alex a smooth foxtrot. Like Anne and Doug, we made a handsome couple.

It was 1989, a year after the diagnosis. The party was indeed a celebration. Thinking the worst was over, we rejoiced with Anne.

TRUE TO HER WORD, Anne made things happen. The following year, Anne gave me a tour of the three-storey coach house she'd found on Wellesley Street east of Church Street, where she planned to base Wellspring, the centre for people with cancer. "There's nothing institutional about this place," she said.

"Anne, you've made it look like a comfortable townhouse! I like that it has a front veranda—so welcoming." I could have been in a well-appointed home. "I can tell you must have selected the chintz—it's lovely."

"Yes, that was the fun part. I still have to get curtains. Here, this will be the library, with computer hookups and Internet access."

"I see some of your watercolours on the walls. Hard work must agree with you. You look well."

"It's so rewarding! I'm getting lots of publicity and support now. Come in here and have a cup of tea."

We sat in the kitchen. Anne plugged in the kettle and took down a teapot and dainty cups. "Will you have Earl Grey? What's happening in the court today?"

"Oh, the usual murder and mayhem," I said. Even though I spoke lightly, I liked being a judge and was well aware it was serious business.

"I sometimes think I should apply to be a judge."

"You'd like the intellectual challenge, but you'd lose a lot of flexibility. You wouldn't be able to participate in all the organizations you do. Plus the schedule is so rigid."

"You do get a lot of the summer off."

"Yes, that part's good—even if we have to do a slew of paper divorces."

"Well, my becoming a judge is on the back burner for now. Simon, my doctor, says I should have a bone marrow transplant. I'm a good candidate, he says. Try one of these cookies. A volunteer brings them in."

"What's involved in the operation?"

"They collect cells from my bone marrow and grow new cells. Then after radiation and chemo, the marrow will be transplanted. I'll do it over the summer."

I sat up, puzzled. "I thought you were cancer-free now?"

"Yes, but it's still 'wait and see.' This will give me a better chance that the cancer won't return."

I looked around at what Anne had accomplished—while enduring cancer and its treatments—and could well appreciate the pride she felt. Being a judge didn't give me that kind of satisfaction, even though I was a good judge. There wasn't the same sense of service, of creating something that wasn't there before. Founding the Canadian Chapter of the International Association of Women Judges hadn't been very fulfilling. Well, I could count my work in getting a stamp to honour the first federally appointed woman judge in Canada. Yet none of it seemed to compare. As a lawyer, I had had a more direct sense of service— solving problems for clients and spearheading law reform. A judge, the more powerful figure, was more removed.

———

THAT SUMMER, the collection of marrow cells did not go well. When I phoned Anne at the end of June before heading north to my in-laws' cottage, she was sobbing. After making forty painful punctures to her hip and shoulder, the doctors had extracted only half of the bone marrow needed for the transplant. I wished I couldn't picture the process so vividly, her delicate body covered with bruises and sores. Over the summer, the doctors were going to give her an experimental growth drug so that she would grow more bone marrow.

"If my blood count is high enough with the drug, I'll have five days of extraction using needles in my neck. I feel like a guinea pig."

I refrained from saying, *Maybe you are.* And what if she was? Surely, I'd do the same. Or maybe not, if I didn't have children.

"My summer is ruined," she said, still crying. "And now all I want to do is go to the lake with the boys, and Doug doesn't want to go."

"Why not?"

"He's going to Europe on Tuesday and wants me to stay in Toronto with him."

"Why don't you go anyway?"

"He told me if I went he'd walk out on me." Anne gulped and then blew her nose.

"You're kidding," I said, thinking that Doug's departure might not be a bad idea. "Have you talked to Doug about this? About whether the procedure is worth doing?"

"I haven't seen him for days." Anne was still sniffing and gasping. She declined my offer to stop by her house on my way out of town—another friend had come by. I drove north worrying about Anne. She wasn't often that distraught. I called again as soon as I arrived at the cottage, and that time, Doug answered, saying Anne was not there.

"Not there?" I asked, blankly.

"No, she's gone to the charity auction the choir is having this evening," he replied.

"Doug, I can barely believe it. She was so upset when we spoke two hours ago. She told me she hadn't seen you."

Doug hesitated, and then said, mysteriously, "I've been around."

"She told me she felt like a guinea pig with her treatments. Have you talked to her about it?" I asked this bravely; Doug wasn't one to invite intimacy.

Doug paused again, emitting a slight sigh of exasperation. "Anne hasn't wanted to know the whole truth. She won't talk about the odds."

"The odds?"

"After the first bout of chemotherapy and radiation, she had maybe five years. The transplant will give her two or two and one-half years, about half the time again."

"No wonder she's so distressed. Maybe you could talk to Anne about the growth drug to make sure she thinks it's worth it." I felt nervous telling Doug what I thought he should do with his wife. I sensed that he'd not been treating her well, or perhaps that was Anne's perception. Either way, he should be aware how distraught she was.

"I think she knows it's worth it, but I'll talk to her."

So it seemed that Anne had had little choice: if it was going to give her two and a half more years with her boys, there was no question.

We'd never discussed half-measures or entertained the notion that she wouldn't be cured. I'd want to know the odds and thought Anne would too. Then again, maybe if I were the one with cancer, I'd choose the path of limited acceptance.

I hung up, astonished again at Anne's resilience. I'd thought she was on the verge of a nervous collapse, yet she'd rallied to attend a charity auction. I shouldn't have been surprised. I'd seen her rise to any occasion, conducting meetings from hospital beds, instantly changing her mood when her sons were around, and doing whatever had to be done for others no matter how awful she felt.

———

THE FOLLOWING MONTH, Anne invited us for the weekend to their cottage at Lake of Bays in Muskoka. I was reluctant to go, since Anne had entertained so much company all summer and I felt she could use some quiet time with the family. "The boys want to see Darrell and Edward," Anne insisted. "And we can belatedly celebrate your birthday and Duncan's birthday." Duncan and I shared a July 14 birthdate. "Don't bring anything," she said. "It's casual."

It wasn't my idea of casual. On Saturday morning I helped Anne put food in picnic baskets—a feast of homemade fried chicken, sandwiches, fruits, and sweets. Alex and Doug brought the baskets down from the large cottage perched on rock to the boathouse and docks below. We loaded Doug's vintage wooden cruising boat with the lunch, swimming gear, children, another houseguest, and dogs, and we cruised to a nearby falls for a swim before lunch. Back in the boat, we motored to an unoccupied island Doug owned. "The boys will love exploring after lunch," Anne said. She made everything an occasion. Nothing was too much trouble.

Back at the cottage, our four young blond boys, looking like sets of twins, pumped water guns, shouted across the water, and dove from the high board. At one point we all panicked when Willie, the heavy boxer, fell into the water between the boat and the dock. All four boys yelled, "Mom, he can't swim!" as if expecting Anne or me to save the dog from where we sat on shore. We cheered when my husband dove in and managed to lift Willie from the deep water.

I sat beside Anne watching the boys play. It was the first time she'd sat still all weekend, though she was exhausted from the effects of the growth drug. "For a week," she confided, "I felt like I was having a heart attack, constantly. Then, after two days of inserting needles into my neck, they gave up."

I couldn't bear to picture it. I could hardly handle having a blood test and always asked for the baby needles.

She had to go back the following Thursday for the surgeons to try to extract more bone marrow from her hip. I offered to pick her up and take her to the hospital so she could stay overnight in the city, at home, and then I would take her back to the cottage. Strangely, Doug refused to let Anne stay over in the city. Instead, he drove her to the hospital and they returned immediately after the procedure, all in one long, exhausting day. Accompanied by a nurse, Anne lay in pain on a makeshift bed in the back seat of the car for the three-hour trip back to the cottage. I never understood why Doug insisted on the jostling journey, and I knew Anne was in no position to argue.

———

ONE EVENING in September 1991, I stopped by to see Anne on my way home from work. She was sitting at her little desk surrounded by cookbooks, the dogs lying on the sofa under the wall of windows. Again I noticed how well she looked in the colour she wore: she was dressed in a soft pink cashmere sweater and tailored slacks.

"Hey, you look good," I said. "What's happening?"

"Getting organized for the transplant. I'm writing out the menus for when I'm in the hospital. I want Duncan and Sandy to have the food they're used to and the food they like. I want them to be the same as if I were here. Tea's ready. Let me pour you some."

I peered at the typed loose-leaf lists with Anne's handwritten additions. She must have written them out for her secretary to type.

Week One
Monday
Breakfast
Vitamin pill
French toast with maple syrup—really soak the bread
Real orange juice—not orange drink
One sausage

I was moved as I read, thinking of the love that Anne was putting into such detailed preparations. At the same time, I wondered how likely it was that her housekeeper would actually follow the precise instructions.

Anne returned with two china cups of tea on a tray. The dogs snuggled next to her on the sofa.

I faced her in an armchair and said, "I don't know that I'd trust the nanny to take such trouble with meals. You have more faith than I would. So, you must have got enough bone marrow?"

"Yes. And I'm ready. I've been in and out of the hospital all week having tests. They inserted a Hickman catheter. Look."

Anne showed me the line extending into her heart. "Ouch. Does it hurt?"

"No. It makes everything easier—no more needles to draw blood. The transplant itself is the easy part, takes about two hours. The hard part is the heavy chemo and full-body radiation before."

I glanced up to see one of the Siamese cats walking toward us on the kitchen counter. "The cat won't jump on me, will it? You know how I am about cats."

"No. They only jump on Doug."

"I admire your attitude. About the treatment, I mean. Not the cats."

"I'm scared to death, but I feel lucky. The success rate is high, about eighty percent. Then the fun begins. I'll have no immunity and I'll be in isolation for two or three months. I don't know how I'll manage without seeing Duncan and Sandy." Anne looked sadly into my eyes. "That's the worst part. They aren't allowed to visit."

"Have you told them?"

"We've talked about it. I'm not sure they know how long it will be. They feel more involved because they've been part of the good press with Wellspring. It's become a family venture and a bit like a science experiment. I hope it's okay—I told the principal and the teacher you would liaise if there were any school issues."

"Of course. No problem at all. It's good Edward and Sandy are in the same class."

"My therapist will be on deck to help the boys emotionally." Anne walked to her desk and handed me an envelope. "Take this letter. It sets out what will happen and gives you names and phone numbers."

———

WHEN I WENT to the hospital the day before the transplant, Doug was visiting. He offered to hang the paintings Anne had brought from home, all of which were still resting on the floor. "Do you have hooks?" Doug asked.

"Yes, I'll get them," Anne replied, leaping from the bed.

"Anne," I protested, "tell us where they are. You shouldn't get up."

But Anne rushed to find the packet. She couldn't do otherwise. Such wifey deference appalled me. It reminded me of my husband, who on occasion would decide to make a cold lemon soufflé and would begin the task by bending over the cookbook and, surgeon-like, ask me to hand him "four eggs, at room temperature."

On the day of the transplant, when I approached her room for a quick visit, the door was closed. A large notice was posted that no one could enter without taking precautions not to contaminate Anne, who was in isolation. Those with contagious diseases could not enter. I hesitated, fearful I might be transporting some unknown contaminant. After remembering that I had not been around anyone ill, I sterilized my hands as directed, using the solution on the wall, and put on a surgical gown and mask. I took a deep breath and opened the door.

The room was dark; the figure lying on the bed was still. Five intravenous lines extended from her motionless body. She was sedated with morphine. Her eyes were encrusted and her skin looked flushed. Anne was charred outside and inside. Her burned throat made it impossible to eat or drink. When she tried to speak, the constant spitting up of mucus scorched her throat anew.

She saw me and roused slightly but could hardly say a word. Her hands and feet were blistered, and huge red bruises covered her legs.

I picked up an ointment from the side table and asked if I should rub her skin with it. She nodded, silent, and gingerly I placed the salve on her raw skin without rubbing. She cringed at even the lightest pressure.

Her condition seemed interminable. It was three weeks before she could eat or drink; all that time she was fed through a tube. The effects of radiation burn would change in intensity from one area to another. Some days she could tolerate light touch; at other times, her grimace showed me she could tolerate no pressure at all. Going to the bathroom was an obstacle course in which we wormed a path through the maze of tubing and poles.

One day, a few weeks after the transplant, she was holding a pair of scissors when I entered. "Marie, I need you to cut this dead skin from my lip. I can't do it with my left hand." I looked at the hanging piece of skin at the edge of her mouth. Feeling sick, I washed my hands again and then picked up the small pair of scissors. Reluctant to proceed with the gruesome task, I asked, "Are you sure?"

She nodded, and I managed to cut off some of the dry skin. It was as brittle as paper. When I had removed some, I held up a mirror for her to look in. She said, "A little more."

"I'm afraid I'll cut you."

"You won't."

Occasionally the morphine made her delirious. "You look nice today," she greeted me once.

"Do you think so?" I smiled under my mask, all too aware of my hospital cover-up. Even in a stupor, Anne's graciousness was evident.

"I look forward to meeting your children when I leave here," she said.

"Yes," I said, drawing a quick breath. "We'll make an occasion of it."

Gradually, over the weeks, Anne became more lucid, and she could talk more. "The pain is excruciating," she said. "I've stopped thinking about survival. I only think about surviving the pain, surviving the day. It's all I can think about. Can I get to dinner? Not that I'm eating. Can I get to the next morning?"

Diarrhea was a constant problem, and Anne was embarrassed by the indignity of her body's afflictions. "Marie, I'm so sorry you have to see this, but I couldn't get to the bathroom in time."

"Anne, it's perfectly fine. Don't worry," I replied truthfully, though I turned my head to avoid some of the stench. When I could, I helped Anne move to the bathroom. I certainly had never wanted to be a nurse and invariably gagged at body odours. Yet with Anne, I felt as I had while changing my sons' diapers and wiping their vomit: I could easily manage it with those I loved. Not everyone that I loved—only those I wanted to touch. As she rested in the chair, I said, "I'll call the nurse to help you clean up and change the bed."

The nurse briskly changed the sheets and brought fresh clothing. Anne returned to bed looking relaxed, saying, "Marie, thank you for coming so often. I always feel better and more relaxed. A lot of people don't come because of the fear of contamination."

"I can understand why. There are so many cold and flu germs this time of year." A wave of guilt swept over me. That morning, I'd sneezed once or twice, and feared I too might be coming down with something contagious.

"I have this terrible nausea at the same time as the diarrhea. The doctors want to do an exploratory rectal examination."

"In your condition? You can't be serious," I said, aghast. I continued to wonder if cancer patients were unwitting guinea pigs.

"I don't want to do it. I think the diarrhea is a side effect of the drugs, and I'm frightened of rectal bleeding from the surgery."

Still, she later acquiesced to the futile procedure.

That night, Anne called to tell me she thought she was getting a virus. I felt responsible and ashamed of my selfishness. Chastising myself for putting Anne's delicate health at risk, I fretted for days. When I remained germ-free and Anne told me she did not contract the feared virus, I was ecstatic.

And even better, after what seemed a long time, Anne gradually began to improve. At one point she was allowed to go home, for her first visit in months. Although she was allowed to stay only forty-five minutes, the visit did her good. And as she told me about it, I pictured it clearly.

———

AFTER WORK, Doug picked Anne up from the hospital. She was wheeled downstairs to the front door, where he had parked the car. Doug kissed Anne and lifted her into the front seat, commenting, "You're so light."

"I feel light today," she said, smiling, as the attendants put the wheelchair in the trunk. Describing the evening to me afterward, she said, rejoicing, "Marie, he carried me into the house!"

As soon as he opened the door, the dogs barked and jumped all over the place. Sandy raced downstairs. Doug laid Anne down on the sofa and brought a blanket.

"Mom, you're home, you're home! I'm not going to choir practice."

"Yes, you are," ordered Doug. To Anne he said, "I'll get you some tea."

"Oh Sandy, darling, I can't stay."

"But Mom, it's been such a long time!"

"I know, but this is a first visit to see how I do, and I'll be back soon. Tell me what you're doing in school."

Sandy didn't leave her side the whole visit, talking fast and excitedly about his homework and school. "It seemed like I'd missed a lifetime," Anne said to me. "And then it was not even an hour before Doug carried me out to the car. I was brave for Sandy. I told him I was getting better and would be back soon. You can't imagine how horrible it was to leave Sandy."

Anne looked into my eyes. "Marie, they carried me back, but I know I'll get another chance to go home, maybe soon. It's a tremendous turning point for me, knowing I can get out and go home. It will keep me going."

———

BY THE END of October, almost two months after the transplant, Anne had improved to the point that she could sit up in bed, and she was painting a watercolour.

"How nice to see you up and looking well," I said, meaning it heartily.

"Yes, I feel better. Look, Marie, my eyes have turned almost turquoise."

"They're a beautiful colour."

"Yes, I'll have to get a turban that colour. I'm still not seeing that well, and look at this: my nails are falling out. Maintenance will be easy—no haircuts, no manicures."

"One thing about hair and nails, they do grow back." I stroked her tiny hand. The stubs of nails looked raw and sore.

"And I'll be home for Christmas," Anne said, and smiled.

———

I'D BEEN THINKING back on Anne's life as she slept in the hospital bed, but my reverie ceased when Reverend Doug Stoute, Dean of St. James Cathedral, entered the dark room. Anne immediately awakened and made introductions. He asked her if she'd like to pray, and she said she'd like it very much. Stoute laid his hands upon Anne's forehead and prayed aloud. I sat quietly, thinking that I wouldn't have liked it at all. Religion didn't soothe me, but Anne was soothed, and that's what mattered. Soon two more ministers arrived. One of them thanked me for being with Anne. It struck me as odd to be thanked for doing something so natural and inevitable. Not wanting to spend more time with three men of the cloth, and knowing she was in good hands, I kissed Anne goodnight, saying, "I'm going now. Call me if you want me to return."

I stopped at the nursing station, left my number, and asked the nurse to call me if Anne wanted me. Pressing my number into the nurse's hand, I made sure she understood that I meant it. "I live five minutes away. I can come back at any time. It's no trouble at all."

Week One *Monday*	DINNER Spaghetti with meat sauce (*Casserole Cookbook*, p. 120)—sometimes do meatballs Walnut orange salad (*Creative Cooking*, p. 5) Carrot sticks—make enough to last all week Milk Frozen bananoids (*Kids' Cooking*, p. 64) Make brownies for next day

JANUARY 17

A FEW MINUTES before ten o'clock, my deputy knocked on the door of my chambers and entered. Deputies are assigned to judges on a weekly basis or for the duration of a particular trial. For them, the judges' court personalities and trials are an ongoing source of gossip. Deputies had tended to be retired men, but those with whom I'd worked for years were gradually being replaced by slightly younger employees. The lanky, grey-haired man greeted me warmly. "Counsel may want a little more time. Do you want to go in?"

"Yes. If they want more time, all they have to do is ask." I chose to be an "on-time judge," one who entered the courtroom when the case was scheduled, as opposed to when counsel advised the deputy that they were ready for the judge.

My respect for punctuality was well known. I rarely faced an empty courtroom or tardy counsel. Court staff appreciated my punctuality, knowing I ordinarily took the morning break promptly at eleven-thirty and the luncheon recess at one, and rose for the day at four-thirty. Reasonable adjustments were made to accommodate witnesses.

I stood up from my desk to put on my gown, which hung in the small closet beside my washroom. As I walked out, the deputy asked, "May I help you, Your Honour?"

Shunning the institutional intimacy, I replied, "No, thank you—I'll get it. Is my chair in court?" After bouts of severe back pain and shoulder spasms, I had bought an ergonomic chair and required that it be brought wherever I presided. I had also learned to exercise to prevent backache.

A judge's back bears the daily grind of justice. Day after day, I sat hunched behind a large dais, writing almost verbatim what each witness said in a large, red leather-bound bench book. Contrary to popular misconception, judges do not rely on a court reporter's transcripts in making decisions. Most decisions are made at the conclusion of a trial, and transcripts are rarely available during the course of a trial—they are generally prepared only if there is an appeal after the judge has rendered a decision. In coming to a judgment at the end of trial, we rely on our own notes.

While court is in session, a judge's range of motion is limited. Seated, as I was all the time, I could turn my head to the left toward the witness and the jury or I could look straight ahead toward counsel and the accused in the prisoner's box. There was rarely a reason to look to the right. And no matter how much I might want to, stretching in place would be unseemly.

This rigidity of posture is exacerbated by the stress of continually making decisions, large and small, in an arena of confrontation and while under public and professional scrutiny. In any trial, two dramas are playing out simultaneously: the immediate drama of the trial itself—the ongoing process of finding

guilt or innocence where none of the players knows the ending—
and the re-enactment of the drama of the past: a story that has
already occurred and that is relived as the evidence unfolds.

With my gown arranged, I picked up my bench book.

"May I carry your book, Your Honour?" My deputy had his
hands outstretched.

"No, thank you. I like to carry my own book."

He opened the door for me and walked beside me down the
third-floor corridor. "I've never forgotten that case we had, Your
Honour. Remember Beck Taxi, where the son wanted to set aside
his father's will, and the lawyer wanted you to watch videos of
fish in an aquarium to show he was crazy?"

I nodded slightly, thinking, *Spare me from chatty deputies.*
At my instigation, we took the stairs up to the fourth floor rather
than using the judges' elevator, which was busy at that time of
the morning, and always slow. The deputy preceded me into the
judges' entrance, saying loudly, "Order. All rise." He stood aside
as I walked up one step to the deputy's box and then five more
steps to the judge's dais.

On the wall behind me, presumably arranged for the benefit of the people in the courtroom, was the Ontario royal coat
of arms with the motto *Dieu et mon droit* ("God and my right").
Over the rampant lions was *Honi soit qui mal y pense* ("Evil be to
him that evil thinks"). It wasn't my choice to have the motto of
the British Order of the Garter overhead; it was in every courtroom, and the mottoes, like the clothing and the language, came
with the territory.

The deputy took his post, sitting on my right in a box similar to the witness box on my left. Nodding off was irresistible
for some deputies, but I drew the line at snoring. After so many

years as a judge, my sense of hearing was extremely acute, and my ears reacted to every auditory distraction.

Being heard may well be the essence of justice: the ear is the divining rod of truth. Observation is less helpful. In most courtrooms, witnesses tend to face the jury or the counsel who is questioning them. Generally, judges have a view of only the right side of a witness's face. Justice might be blind, but it must never be deaf.

As a judge I had to decide, in every non-jury trial, who was telling the truth and who was not. In ordinary life, we take people at face value by and large, there being no need for such scrutiny. At first I had been stymied. How was I going to tell when someone was lying? With that object in mind, I learned to pay close attention to what was said, how it was expressed, and in what context.

The Registrar, seated below me, opened court by intoning the prescribed greeting. "Oyez. Oyez. Oyez. Anyone having business before the Queen's Justice of the Ontario Court of Justice, attend now and you shall be heard. Long live the Queen. Please be seated."

"Good morning." I made it a point to speak loudly and clearly so that all in the courtroom, not only the participants at the front, could hear me. Criminal trials attract reporters, students, and members of the public, many of whom are regulars.

"Good morning, Your Honour," counsel replied.

My court list for the day consisted of one entry: *Regina v. Davidson*. *Regina*, Latin for "queen," refers of course to the Queen of England. That fact that the Queen of England is the Queen of Canada is overwhelmingly evident in the Canadian criminal justice system. Her Majesty, the Queen of England, through her local agents, the Attorney General for Ontario or the Attorney General for Canada, prosecutes those in Canada accused of crimes.

When Prince Charles assumes the throne, all proceedings will be carried out in the name of the King of England and will begin as *Rex*. This trial would then be *Rex v. Davidson*. Perhaps the required change to the doglike "Rex" will trigger the initiation of criminal proceedings in the name of and on behalf of Ontario and Canada. Canada could be no less a monarchy if we maintained criminal proceedings in our own name.

I knew nothing in advance about *Regina v. Davidson* except the particular charges against the accused, as set out in my copy of the indictment. It showed two counts of sexual assault while using a knife.

"Your Honour, Kathleen Barker for the Crown." The Crown attorney introducing herself was a solid, no-nonsense woman in her early thirties who began matter-of-factly, "Mr. Davidson has re-elected to be tried without a jury and the Crown has consented."

"David Mather for the defence, Your Honour," said the defence counsel, a handsome, experienced criminal defence lawyer in his fifties. His gown was rumpled as if it had been scrunched in the back of his car for days.

"How long do counsel expect this trial to last?" I asked.

"About six days, Your Honour."

"Are counsel ready to proceed?"

"Yes, Your Honour."

"Are there any preliminary matters?"

"No, Your Honour. We thank you for the indulgence yesterday. The additional time granted will help to expedite the trial."

"Very well. Madame Registrar, arraign the accused."

"Will the accused please stand?" began the Registrar. A slim, clean-shaven man stood up in the prisoner's box.

"Mike Davidson, you are charged that you, on the twenty-fourth day of August in the year 1993, at the Municipality of Metropolitan Toronto, unlawfully did commit sexual assault on Kathy Y. while using a knife, contrary to the Criminal Code.

"You stand further charged that you, on or about the fourth day of September in the year 1993, at the Municipality of Metropolitan Toronto, unlawfully did commit sexual assault on Kathy Y. while using a knife, contrary to the Criminal Code.

"Upon this indictment, how do you plead, guilty or not guilty? Count one?"

"Not guilty," replied the accused.

"Count two?"

"Not guilty."

"Please be seated."

At the beginning of trial, Crown counsel may make an opening statement to describe what the case is about. Opening statements are made in jury trials to help jurors understand the evidence as it unfolds. I find them helpful in judge-alone trials as well, and certainly would have appreciated an outline in this case. However, none was made.

Crown counsel called the first witness, and a young uniformed officer stepped into the witness box, looking solemnly at the Registrar as she administered the oath. "Take the bible in your hand and raise your right hand. Do you swear that the testimony you are about to give touching the matters before the court shall be the truth, the whole truth, and nothing but the truth, so help you God?"

"I do."

"Please be seated."

"I prefer to stand." Police officers almost always stood, and many other witnesses did as well, perhaps to have a better view, to feel more in control, or to appear more formal. Sitting didn't seem to have the same air of integrity.

The Crown attorney began her questioning, looking at her notes on the lectern in front of her.

"You've been a constable with the Metropolitan Toronto Police for two years, is that correct?"

"Yes."

"Officer, you were on duty on August twenty-fourth, 1993?"

"Yes."

"Please tell the court what happened in relation to the matter before the court." Pulling out a small black book from his breast pocket, Constable Bowen asked if he could refer to his notes.

"No objection, Your Honour," defence counsel interjected. This was a routine concession. Defence counsel would have had access to the officer's notes before trial and would know what they contained.

"On August twenty-fourth, 1993, at 4:10 a.m., in response to a telephone call, I arrived at 1556 Victoria Lane and went to the third-floor apartment. I observed a female who was tied up. Two ambulance attendants were on scene."

"Will you describe the female for the court?"

"I saw a gagged female seated on the side of the bed. Her hands and feet were tied in front. A phone was by her feet and the receiver was off the cradle."

"What was she tied with?"

"With velour belts from a robe. The ambulance attendants untied her."

As I made rapid notes, I pictured Kathy on her bed. My mind runs to the graphic, and I never had any difficulty appreciating the reality of testimony that was presented before me.

I remembered the advice I received as a new judge, when a senior woman judge had suggested to me not to "take the work home" with me. I had replied that the day I didn't take it home was the day I shouldn't be a judge. It wasn't that I let emotion play a part in judging, but I felt an immediate empathy for those who suffered at the hands of others, especially when the victims were children. Over time, my emotion and empathy became intellectualized, moving from the heart to the head.

"Did you observe any injuries?" counsel asked.

"I observed marks on her wrists and ankles," the officer said.

"Did you see any other injuries?"

"No. I asked her if she wanted to go the hospital and she said no."

"What was her condition?"

"She was upset."

"Could she communicate with you?"

"Yes, she was lucid. She wasn't intoxicated. She sat at the table and I took a statement. She said it had to do with a debt collection involving her boyfriend."

Such a statement would be hearsay and inadmissible at trial. However, because the victim would be called later as a witness, the officer could tell the court what she had told him. The victim could expect to be cross-examined on any of her testimony that contradicted what she told the officer, as the defence would hold up any inconsistencies as evidence of untruth.

"What did she say?"

"At two a.m. she was lying down, expecting her boyfriend. A man entered, pushed her down, and tied her up. He insulted her, pulled out a blade, and ran it up and down her arms and legs, telling her he had a message for Fred, her boyfriend."

"Did she give you a description of the assailant?"

"Yes. She described her assailant as a white male, thirty-six years old, five feet ten inches tall, with light brown shoulder-length hair, a goatee, and numerous tattoos on both arms but mainly on the left arm. He had a scraggy, biker appearance, wore a beige T-shirt and jeans, and had a bad, musty smell."

I looked at the accused seated in the prisoner's box. He was clean-shaven, with short neat hair, which meant nothing as he could have shaved and had a haircut at any time. I couldn't make out whether he had any tattoos.

"What did you do next?"

"I left when she felt okay, and I went to talk with her boyfriend at the address she gave me."

"No further questions, Your Honour."

"Cross-examination, Mr. Mather?" I turned to the defence counsel, who walked from his counsel table toward the witness.

"Officer Bowen," he began abruptly. "Did you see any knife marks?"

"No."

"Did you preserve the cords?"

"No. I should have preserved the bindings. It was inexperience on my part."

"Did you take photos or take fingerprints?"

"No."

"Did you call for an officer to take fingerprints?"

"No."

"Were there signs of forced entry?"

"No."

"No further questions."

"Your Honour, the next witness is Kathy Y.," said Crown counsel.

I was interested in hearing from the victim. Typically the victim is the first witness, and I wasn't sure and wasn't told why the police officer had been called first—perhaps it was a scheduling issue. A thin woman wearing jeans walked to the front of the court. Her long, red-brown hair was tied in a straggly tuft on top. In contrast, her painted fingernails were perfectly manicured.

Crown counsel began her questioning. "How old are you?"

"Thirty-five."

"Are you married?"

"I'm separated."

"Do you have children?"

"Yes, I have two children, age sixteen and eleven."

"Do your children live with you?"

"No."

"Do you know Fred Clark?"

"He's my boyfriend. I've been with Fred five years."

"Do you live together?"

"No."

Although these preliminary capsules of information were usually not relevant, I always appreciated the introduction to the witness.

"Tell Her Honour about the events of August twenty-fourth."

"I paged Fred at midnight and waited for him to come over, but there was no sign of him so I went to bed. I heard a knock on the door and thought it was Fred, so I opened it, but it wasn't Fred."

"What were you wearing?"

"A T-shirt and nightgown."

"What happened next?"

"The man grabbed me and pushed me to the bedroom. I struggled a bit and he went to the closet. He took the pink and black ties to my housecoat. He gagged my mouth with my housecoat. He pushed me on the bed and fondled me a bit. He had a knife, like a switchblade, and ran it up and down my body and called me names, 'slut' and stuff like that." Kathy frowned, twisting the rings on her fingers.

"What parts of your body?"

"My breasts and private area." She hesitated, looking at the accused. "He played with my rectum with his finger. He peed on me. I think he peed on me."

"Why is that?" the lawyer asked, sounding startled.

I wondered the same thing: she *thought* he peed on her?

"Because after, my housecoat was wet on top on the belly part and it was urine."

"Did he say anything?"

"He asked for money—forty-six thousand dollars—and asked where Fred was."

"Did you sustain any injuries?"

"I had scratches." Kathy lowered her gaze. "I was cut in my private area."

"Did you tell the police about the scratches?"

"No, I didn't know until later. I had a shower after the police left and I felt stinging from the soap and when I was urinating."

"Was there any blood?"

"No. I was menstruating at the time."

"Had you seen this person before?"

"No."

"Do you see the person who came on August twenty-fourth in court?"

"Yes," said Kathy, pointing to the accused. "He doesn't look the same today. He had a goatee around his chin then and his hair was different. It was untidy."

"What else do you recall about the assailant on August twenty-fourth?"

"He had a bad odour—possibly from being a mechanic. I saw tattoos on his arms, a rose tattoo on the inside right arm."

I began to wonder why it would take six days to try this case. Either the accused had a rose tattoo, or he didn't. He must have *some* kind of tattoo.

Judges learn to be patient. We never know as much about the matter as the lawyers who decide what evidence will be put before the court. More importantly, we learn to keep our mouths shut and wait for the case to unfold. Only judges on afternoon television take charge and ask pointed questions. In real life, and as we tell jurors, judges are neither advocates nor investigators.

"How tall was he and how much did he weigh?"

"I'm bad on height and weight. He was over two hundred pounds and six feet something. I can't tell height or weight or age even when I'm looking at them."

Interesting, I thought. The officer said she told him he was five feet ten inches tall.

"How tall are you?"

"I'm five feet two inches and weigh eighty-seven pounds."

"How long was he there?"

"I don't know. I blacked out. When I came to, I dialled 911. It took a while because the phone was above the bed. I used my head to pull it down to the floor."

"Your Honour, with the consent of defence counsel, the Crown is tendering in evidence the tape of the 911 call made by Kathy on August twenty-fourth, 1993, at three-thirty a.m."

The 911 recording of Kathy's call was played and marked as an exhibit. Crown counsel continued questioning her.

"Did you tell the officer you were fondled?"

"No. I was too embarrassed."

"Did you ever see the intruder again?"

"Yes, I saw him again on September fourth. I had a big fight with Fred. We went for a drive and then he left. When I came back in, two men followed me inside and shoved me into the kitchen and shut off the lights."

"What did they say?"

"They were looking for Fred. That was puzzling because they knew where to find him. He's been in the same house for thirty-six years."

"Did you recognize them?"

"One was the same man from August twenty-fourth."

"What happened next?"

"One guy got a beer. He pushed things off the couch table onto the carpet. He lifted my top over my head and scraped my legs. He fondled my breasts and cut my jeans."

"Who did that?"

"I'm not sure which one was doing it because my shirt was over my head. The accused was on the couch."

"What was he wearing?"

"He wore jeans and a jean jacket and cowboy boots. He had a goatee. There was no odour like before."

"What happened next?"

"They drank four beers. They wanted me to get Fred, so I called his friend Rob to get him."

"Why didn't you call Fred yourself?"

"I don't call him directly because he's married and lives with his wife and his parents."

Why would this woman continue to be in such a relationship? I thought. It didn't matter legally, so I relegated the thought to my mental file marked "Well, go figure."

"How long did they stay?"

"They left after a half-hour, and I called 911."

After the tape was played and marked as an exhibit, Crown counsel continued questioning Kathy, saying, "Did the police arrive?"

"Yes, the police and Fred arrived together. They took fingerprints off the beer bottles."

"You also participated in a photo lineup?"

"Yes. I identified a photo of the accused."

"Your Honour, I am tendering as the next exhibit Kathy's ripped pants and photos of her legs showing scratches," Ms. Barker said. "I have no further questions, Your Honour."

"Cross-examination, Mr. Mather."

The lawyer addressed the victim point-blank. "You've had major problems over a few years."

"Yes. The police know about it. They were all reported. Someone broke into my basement, and my car window was smashed. I had to take my daughter to and from school. Notes were left on my door. My house was trashed."

"Do you know why they were looking for Fred?"

"Fred owned a bar with Denise G. in the eighties. He owed her five thousand dollars from when they owned the bar. With interest it came to forty-six thousand dollars. Denise had assigned the debt to Satan's Choice. They had a garnishee. I didn't think it was legit."

"You didn't mention to the officers on August twenty-fourth or September fourth that you thought it was Satan's Choice?"

"No, but I thought they were connected."

"Why?"

"Because of their appearance, manners, and ignorance. No one else would know about the garnishee."

"You laid charges against Denise, didn't you?"

"I reported I was assaulted by Denise. She was charged and pleaded guilty to some charges. I think this is a personal vendetta by Denise."

"Did you tell Constable Bowen about this?"

"No."

"To go to the incident on August twenty-fourth, what time did the intruder arrive?"

"About twelve-thirty or one-thirty."

"How long was he there?"

"I don't know. I passed out. It could have been fifteen minutes or three hours."

"You've already said you are not good at heights and weights?"

"Yes. I can't tell height or weight or age even when I'm looking at people."

With that answer, it made it more difficult to accept her identification evidence on those issues. Still, I was mindful, many people would have answered similarly.

"After the incident on August twenty-fourth, Fred arrived later that morning?"

"Yes, I told him the bastard pissed on me, and he helped me strip the bed. He knew about the victimization. He suspected Mick C. at first because he rented my basement one time. But he was sentenced on August twenty-fifth."

"Did he have a rose tattoo?"

"He has a rose tattoo but not an open rose."

"When you first talked to P.C. Bowen, you didn't say you saw a rose tattoo?"

"I didn't bother telling about the rose tattoo at the time because I didn't want the person caught. I just wanted to be left alone."

"Did you see any tattoos on September fourth?"

"No. I tried to avoid looking at them."

"Did you say anything about a rose tattoo in your statement of September fourth or in your video statement to the police on September eighth?"

"No."

"You were asked if you could describe any of the tattoos?"

"Yes."

"And you said no, you couldn't, isn't that right?"

"Yes, but things are coming back, little things. Unless you were a sexual assault victim, you wouldn't know. You block things out."

"When did you remember about the rose tattoo?"

"I remembered three months ago, and I told my mother."

Curious, I noted. Here was a woman who suspected someone named Mick and noted his rose tattoo but only remembered the other rose tattoo over a year later.

"Did you tell the Crown?"

"No."

"And you withheld information about the sexual assault?"

"All I remember is true. It's all I wanted to remember. I did remember some but thought it was too late to say. I thought sexual assault was a penis and vagina. I didn't want to talk about it. It was disgusting." Kathy continued with tears in her eyes. "I didn't want to think about it and I blanked it. I've only had two men in my whole life. Some things are not anyone's business. I think I did pretty damn good."

"No further questions, Your Honour."

———

THE IMAGE OF Kathy as victim stayed with me all day. As I pictured her in her bed in the dark of night, I could see Anne in her hospital bed. I felt for each of them—lying helpless, their bodies tormented by knives at the hands of strangers. For Kathy, the victim of crime, the disease was social. For Anne, the victim of cancer, the disease was physical.

Was Kathy's social well-being any better protected than Anne's physical well-being? Was I really helping either one of them? We expect redress for social injustices; we demand that wrongs be righted. We look to the judge to right those wrongs. On the other hand, we don't demand or expect health or longevity. We seem to have a greater tolerance for the inequity of our physical ills than for our social ones. We're more accommodating of the limitations of medicine than of those of law.

Why do the expectations vary? Perhaps it's the notion of intentionality. No one deliberately gave Anne cancer, but someone definitely did intentionally assault Kathy. We want someone to be accountable for social ills.

Would the law serve Kathy any better than medicine served Anne? Doctors and lawyers do what they can, but the law might no more provide justice for Kathy than medicine might provide health to Anne.

What was my role in righting social wrongs? "Dispensing justice" or "finding truth" are responses too wide of the mark. I was realizing that my function was narrower and more modest: as a criminal trial judge, my job was to ensure that an accused person received a fair trial. Certainly, a fair trial is part of the goal of justice. Increasingly, I concluded that justice meant ensuring a fair trial for the accused, not necessarily redress for the victim, not necessarily the protection of others, and not necessarily the prevention of crime.

———

THESE THOUGHTS PREOCCUPIED me as I changed into my street clothes and drove home. I opened the door to my calm, serene home and began to think of Anne again. Her suffering and chaotic life were so at odds with my orderly, organized routines. But Anne's life always had been more chaotic on the outside than mine was. In the months after her bone marrow transplant in 1991, I had often been surprised by her ability to cope in a home that I considered stressful and demanding.

———

BACK IN 1991, Anne did indeed go home before the holidays. One icy evening the week before Christmas, when snow had not yet softened the cold, I went to call on the family. Anne's housekeeper, Gloria, let me in, saying, "Mrs. Gibson's in bed."

I went up the circular stairs to Anne's bedroom. One of the Siamese cats and two dogs were on the bed. Anne cuddled one of the terriers. Willie, the boxer, lay snoozing at her feet. A nurse was just leaving.

I called Gloria and asked if she would take the cat out of the room. I could tolerate the dogs, but I couldn't handle the cats. The frisky Siamese cats pounced high and low. I'd seen them jump onto Doug's shoulder and curl around his neck like a collar. The prospect filled me with dread.

Anne was in the middle of the bed surrounded on all sides by hot water bottles.

"What are you doing with all those?" I asked, laughing slightly. It looked like some kind of sitcom set-up.

"I can't get warm," she lamented.

Horrified, I said, "But they'll get cold, and someone will have to change the water. What if one of them leaks?"

"That's happened. One of them leaked, and I couldn't get out of the bed to change the linen. I don't like to wake up Gloria late at night. I got so cold."

"Why don't you get an electric blanket?" I asked, placing my lotions and creams on the nightstand.

"Doug doesn't like them. They're too hot for him."

Who cares what Doug wants? I thought, but said, diplomatically, "You can get a king-size blanket with separate dials."

"Maybe." She turned, looking out the window briefly. "How good of you to come in this weather. I didn't think you'd still be in town."

"It's fine. No one's at home. Alex and the boys flew to Orlando. I'll meet them on Saturday, and we'll drive from there to Key West."

"Your facials are wonderful." Anne managed a slight smile. She lay on her back without moving.

"Are you able to move closer to the edge of the bed?"

"It hurts too much to move. I have shingles and the pain is unimaginable."

"That's okay, I'll be able to do it this way." I would half-sit, half-lean over the bed, and reach her face from the side.

Facials had become my gift of touch after the first round of radiation burned Anne's throat, a countermeasure for the wounds of treatment. I had paid attention to how Olga at the Skin Care Centre did my own facials. This study had required concentration, as I could barely ascertain what Olga's soothing hands and fingers could possibly be doing to make me so relaxed—not that Olga thought I ever relaxed.

I went to the bathroom adjoining the bedroom. "I'll get your towels and a facecloth."

I gently lifted Anne's head, spread a towel on her pillow, and then placed a clean, steamy facecloth gently over her face to let her breathe in the moisture. Sandy quietly entered the bedroom, lay on the bed, and began to draw on his sketchpad. It was a little distracting, but I knew Anne enjoyed his presence.

Before the cloth was cool, I cleaned Anne's face and then applied a light moisturizing mask. Her dry skin soaked up the cool cream. After wiping off the mask, I put moisturizing lotion on her face and neck and began the massage. I started by rubbing her forehead and gradually moved down the sides of her face, under her chin. My thumbs moved up her nose and around her face. I applied light pressure points to her head. Too much pressure was painful, particularly near her ears. I took my time and concentrated on sending my love and strength through the soft pillows of my fingers. Every now and then, I reminded her to take deep breaths, to help her relax, and it worked well: within minutes, Anne was asleep.

Finishing, I gathered my things and tiptoed out, whispering, "Sandy, please stay quiet so your mama can sleep. I'm going to unplug the phone so she won't be disturbed. When she wakes up, be sure to tell her the phone is unplugged."

No matter how ill she was, Anne rarely disconnected her phone. She would hear the phone ringing in the house and wonder why no one was picking it up. She always wanted to know what was happening, or who needed her.

The next day, still indignant at the idea of Anne surrounded by cooling, leaking hot water bottles, I drove to the department store on Bloor Street in search of an electric blanket. The king-size blankets were sold out, so I purchased a double. Also, for the boys, I bought Nightmare, the game of the moment, hoping it was not too morbid.

When I returned to Anne's to drop off the blanket, Doug answered the door and invited me in for a drink. Anne was downstairs on the sofa with a blanket on her lap, cuddling the small dogs. Yet again, I marvelled at her ability to rally.

"Marie, that was wonderful. I slept until six-thirty," she said. "Don't sit on that chair. Tiger Lily has messed, and I have to get new chintz." That the small dogs were not completely house-trained didn't seem to bother Anne.

Doug prepared a gin and tonic for me and a Scotch for himself. Anne didn't drink alcohol. We discussed our sons' schools, concurring that Sterling Hall boys' school was pressurized and stressful. The conversation was relaxed, and all seemed well. Doug sat attentively beside Anne, and there was no indication that one week earlier, Anne had described him as a "sonofabitch."

When she'd come home from the hospital, she said, the house had been truly filthy. The laundry hadn't been done; the litter boxes were dirty. Doug told her she was useless, couldn't control the children, and couldn't run the household. She told him she was too sick to deal with it. Hearing this had made me angry: I didn't know how Anne was supposed to oversee her home from her hospital bed, or how Doug could expect life to go on as it always had been before. Surely, her husband must understand that she lacked the wherewithal to wash stacks of clothing or clean up after pets.

Even now, Anne's housekeeper's husband was quitting his job at the end of December and already Gloria wouldn't help out in the evenings. A string of calamities had persisted in Anne's house as long as I'd known her. Commotion bubbled close to the surface, spitting chaos. Nanny turnover was high. Furniture was scratched by cats. The chintz regularly had to be replaced.

By comparison, my own life and household seemed utterly organized and smoothly uneventful. Whenever I walked through my front door after being at Anne's, I marvelled at the tranquility.

Was I really so different from Anne? Was my life so different? I always fulfilled my husband's expectations. I remembered my friend Barbara saying to me, "It's like Alex doesn't know you have a demanding job. You run the household as if you were a full-time housewife and mother. His cocktail is ready when he walks in the door, dinner is prepared, and you deal with the children."

Yes, not so different, I thought, but I didn't have a terminal illness.

Week One
Tuesday

BREAKFAST

Vitamin pill

Pancakes—add sliced bananas, peaches, or apples when you are ready to cook

Warm maple syrup

Sliced melon—remove rind

One slice bacon

Milk

Chapter 4

JANUARY 18

ON WEDNESDAY MORNING, I entered the courtroom at 10:00 a.m. to continue the *Davidson* trial. Crown counsel called Police Constable Mullen to the stand, and the lean, uniformed officer was sworn. He testified that he had been the attending officer on September fourth and arrived at 11:20 p.m. He talked to the victim, obtained a brief description of the perpetrators, and broadcast it to the other units. He described the victim as quite upset, withdrawn into herself, not forthcoming.

"What did she say?" asked Crown counsel.

"She told me she was home and her boyfriend, Fred, arrived around 9:50. They left and drove around in his car. They argued and Fred left. As she opened the door of the apartment, she felt a push from behind and it was two men. They turned off the lights when they entered."

"What did they do?"

"The first man asked for Fred, saying he owed money."

"Did she give you a description?"

"Yes. She said the first one was the same as before. He was five feet ten inches tall, with long brown hair, a goatee, wearing a blue jean jacket with cowboy boots."

"Please continue."

"The second male grabbed her, put her to the ground, and held her head. The first one had a knife in his hand and cut her pants. He grabbed her crotch, saying dirty things. The first one took out his penis and said, 'Do you want it before I cut your pants?' He asked her to phone Fred and she paged him. They left and she called 911."

"Did she give you a description of the second man?"

"Yes. The second was shorter, five feet eight inches, a thin build with a baseball cap, short black hair, clean-cut."

"Did you do anything else?"

"I called forensic identification for prints and photos."

"No further questions, Your Honour," said Crown counsel, returning to sit at her table.

"Cross-examination, Mr. Mather," I said turning to defence counsel.

As usual, he began with no preliminaries. "Officer, did you follow up on the second man?"

"No, though I've seen him before."

"Were any prints found?"

"A palm print was checked."

"Were there any matches?"

"No."

"No further questions, Your Honour."

Such a brief cross-examination was unusual. The questioning in identity cases can be quite laborious, asking about the lighting at the time of the event, the accuracy of a witness's memory, and a myriad of other details, all in attempts to cast doubt on the accuracy of the identification. I knew there must be more to the defence.

After nine years as a trial judge, little surprised me. Before I was appointed a judge, I'd been a voracious reader of fiction. Now, after years on the bench, I hadn't read fiction in ages; there was no need to.

"Your Honour, the next witness is Fred Clark," said Crown counsel. A tall, stocky man with a ruddy complexion and an impressive moustache took the stand. I was interested to hear from this man who had a wife and whose girlfriend, Kathy, had been terrorized, evidently on his account.

"I understand you're thirty-six years old, married, with two children?"

"Yes."

"Do you have a criminal record?"

"No."

"Do you know Kathy Y.?"

"Kathy has been my girlfriend four or five years."

"Do you know Denise G.?"

"She's my ex-girlfriend. I was with her fourteen years. We owned a restaurant together in 1981. She was bitter when I married someone else in 1989." He fingered the wedding band on his left hand, answering with the assurance of one who knows his way around women. The fragrance he was wearing was a little overpowering, but I admired his pale yellow shirt and matching pocket handkerchief.

"Did you have further relations with her?"

"She wrote threatening letters and put a lawsuit on me. She started bugging my wife. Then the bike gang showed up. My van was destroyed, and they ransacked Kathy's house when she was out of town."

"Did you know who did this?"

"No, but they left a card from the collection agency, which I found out was Satan's Choice."

"What did you do?"

"I tried to get to the bottom of it. I went to a strip joint where the Choice hung out. I saw Mike, the accused, there, but there was no problem with him. I seen him before after Kathy's tires were slashed. I called the police, but he'd gone by then."

"Have you experienced any problems since September 1993?"

"There have been no problems since."

Well, that figures. Everyone would have been on their best behaviour after the arrest.

"Your Honour, I've concluded my examination of Mr. Clark. Mr. Mather and I would like to take the afternoon to review Crown disclosure and to check some evidence. We are requesting that the trial be adjourned until tomorrow morning. We're confident the adjournment will expedite the hearing of the trial."

"That's agreeable to the court," I said, not letting my voice betray just how agreeable it was. "Court is adjourned until ten o'clock tomorrow morning."

———

AT TWO-THIRTY, I took a taxi to the hospital, where Anne's friend Joanna was sitting on a chair in Anne's room, gazing at a magazine. Joanna was a slender, pretty woman in her forties with short blond hair. She was a churchgoer, with a puppy-like eagerness.

"Hi, Joanna." I looked at the empty bed. "Where's Anne?"

"Hi, Marie. She's in the X-ray room now." Joanna put her head in her hands. "Her kidneys have failed."

"What does that mean?"

"I'm not sure. I'm waiting to hear something... " She trailed off, and then sat up and started again with what was obviously on her mind. "Marie, I've been talking with Anne about the boys. I'm afraid Anne's going to ask me to look after them."

I put my coat on the back of the other chair and sat on the edge of the bed. "I know. I feel the same way. Has Anne asked you to take the boys?"

"No. But if she does, I don't know what I should I say. I'm really not in any position to look after Duncan and Sandy along with my own family."

"That's perfectly understandable. There's no need for you to say anything right now, Joanna. And you don't have to explain why it's not possible for you." I continued, "As you probably know, Fran and Tim were named as guardians. The problem is Anne's having second thoughts. She's reconsidering all possibilities."

It was what I'd realized days before: Anne was simply considering every possible option, reasonable or not, for what would happen to her sons if she were to die. I wondered how to help her choose the best option; I didn't even know what that might be.

Joanna left soon afterward, and I waited for Anne to return. I felt powerless to do anything about her sons, her illness, or her future.

As I sat contemplating my own futility, Mary, the family's therapist, arrived, and soon after, Anne was wheeled in on a gurney wearing an oxygen mask. Her stomach beneath the sheet still looked huge. Large tubing and a bag containing pale, bloody liquid extended from her catheter. Looking at anything other than her face depressed me, so I focused on her eyes, which were groggy and half-shut.

As the nurses helped Anne into bed, two more friends, Fran and Sue, arrived. The nephrologist entered, seeming startled by the number of us in the small room. He moved past us unceremoniously and addressed Anne. "I'm Dr. B. I was called in when your kidneys failed."

"What will happen now?" asked Anne. Her voice was barely above a whisper.

"We've put in shunts to keep your kidneys working." He continued in a matter-of-fact tone: "This is a critical forty-eight-hour period, especially the first twenty-four hours. There could be a complete kidney failure."

Anne sighed and closed her eyes.

"You should have someone to make decisions if something happens," the doctor continued. "I understand you have no husband?" There was an air of condescension in his voice, as if she had no business being at the point of death without a significant other.

"No."

"Do you have someone to make decisions if you become incapable of making your own decisions about your health care?"

"No. But I think it should be the three executors in my will. That would give continuity."

"Are they accessible if we need them?" asked the doctor.

"One is here and one is in the Cayman Islands. The other goes back and forth between Toronto and England."

"It's advisable to have someone who can be available during the next forty-eight hours. I can't tell you how important it is to have this done quickly," said the doctor. "I have to leave now, but I'll be back."

The doctor left as abruptly as he arrived. Mary, the therapist, followed him to pick up the legal form.

The atmosphere was charged as each of us began to realize that Anne could die at any moment. My head might have known Anne could die, but my heart still didn't accept it. Anne broke the heavy silence by asking me to bring her her black binder from the closet. "I've put copies of everything in it," she said. "My will, Doug's will, the guardianship papers. I don't want to leave the mess that Doug left." Of all of us, it seemed that only Anne had recognized before then that she might soon die.

Still reeling from the recent round of treatment—and no doubt the latest prognosis—Anne sank low in her bed. "I have to go the whole distance for Duncan and Sandy. But I don't know if I can last like this. I can't go on if there's no point, if it's futile."

Yes, I thought, *you can go on. We can endure for our children if there's any hope at all.*

Anne dozed on and off, finally falling asleep. Susan went home to her two sons, and I remained with Fran, who had been named guardian. How odd that we four—Anne, Fran, Sue, and I—were discussing guardianship and each of us had two sons. Fran appeared anxious and fidgety, clicking her nails together unconsciously. "I really haven't been consulted about being a guardian," she finally said.

How could she not have discussed being a guardian? I wondered. "I assumed from the way Anne spoke that you had been."

"Well, I had—a long time ago. Doug and Anne and Tim and I talked about being guardians to each other's children. But I haven't really talked to her about it lately. I feel terrible. I don't know if Anne expects me to raise her sons. Does she really expect me to?" Fran kept fidgeting, rubbing her knuckles.

"I don't know," I hedged. This was my second conversation in an hour with another woman who, like me, was considering the monumental prospect of being a guardian for Anne's sons and realizing it might be too much of an undertaking. I was beginning to feel that I had become a focal point of the communication, and I didn't know what to say on Anne's behalf. Instead I said, "I know she doesn't seem to want her brother to raise her sons."

Fran, becoming more agitated at the enormity of the situation, stood and looked out the window, then sat down again, glancing at her watch. I kept my composure by breathing slowly, in time with Anne's breaths, even though I too felt nervous and unsettled.

The awkwardness of the situation was relieved when Anne's son arrived with his stepbrother Mark. Sandy hugged me on arriving, and I was moved and comforted by his affection.

Anne immediately woke up and raised herself higher in bed, reaching for hugs from her boys. She looked dreadful and was in considerable discomfort but chatted readily about school and household activities, uttering not a word of complaint. It was consoling that she was still able to rally.

After Sandy and Mark left, I turned the lights off again. As soon as I had done so, a nurse entered, switching back on the bright lights to check the IV.

Anne turned her attention to the nurse, pleading, "Where is Simon? Why isn't he here?"

"Your doctor will be in when you're less groggy. Don't worry. He's left instructions for you."

I re-dimmed the lights, and Fran and I kept watch in the dark. Fran's reddened face was in tears. Our sadness for Anne and her sons filled the room. After a quarter-hour or so, the nurse returned, putting on the lights, once again adjusting the IV.

"Where's Simon?" Anne asked again.

"He'll be in," she said, vaguely. "You're a special patient of Dr. Sutcliffe's."

After Fran's husband came and took her home, Anne became increasingly fitful and announced, "I need to use the potty." She rang for the nurse, who soon appeared. Anne said, "I need you to help me off the bed."

"Why do you want to get up?"

"I need to use the potty."

The nurse looked perplexed. "Mrs. Gibson, there's no need to use the potty." She continued a little sadly, "You've had a catheter inserted."

"I simply have to or I'll explode. Can't you please take out the catheter?"

"Mrs. Gibson, the doctor wants you to keep the catheter in."

I'd never had a catheter and intended to avoid the experience no matter what. I'd even put "no catheter" on a hospital consent form.

When the nurse left, Anne held my arm. "Marie, please help me." We struggled with the tangle of hookups, and I guided Anne to the potty chair by the bed. She sat on it with her head in her hands. "It feels better even if I don't go."

How useless I felt. How wrong it was—a woman with a catheter sitting on a potty trying to urinate.

"Anne, would you like to get a night nurse?" I asked. "Marte was in earlier and she said she could help." Anne's friend Marte owned a health care business, and she had provided nurses to care for Doug at home.

"No, I can't do that. I can't spend the money. I want Sandy and Duncan to have as much as possible. The nurses here are excellent." I refrained from telling Anne that that might not be the best decision because I didn't want to remind her that the current twenty-four hours were critical. Nor was I going to denigrate her putting her sons before herself.

Anne rose from the potty and I helped her make her way to the bed. After she was rearranged, I washed her face and gently applied moisture cream. It seemed a small gesture when I wanted to do something large and bold, like rescue her. As usual, she soon fell asleep with my touch.

Later, as I was talking to her sister-in-law on the phone, Anne suddenly turned her face sideways, gasping as if she couldn't get enough air. I hung up the phone and called the nurse, who quickly brought oxygen. When the mask was on her face, Anne breathed evenly again, and my own heart rate returned to normal.

The kidney doctor didn't come to see her until after ten. He said he'd checked the charts and that Anne's condition was stable.

When her brother's wife arrived, I left, exhausted and hungry, grateful to return to my uneventful home. I called Marte to tell her that Anne did not want any nursing care at this time, and I called Anne's brother to explain how critical this period was.

"It might be a good idea for the boys to see their mother," I suggested.

"No, Duncan is not coming in from Trinity. The children have had enough."

His brutality shocked me. Sadness took root inside me and started to grow.

LUNCH

Sandwich with slice of deli ham, Miracle
Whip light, honey mustard on both sides

One drink bottle

Celery stuffed with peanut butter—make
enough celery sticks to last all week—
keep in fridge in cold water

One apple

Chapter 5

JANUARY 19

IT WAS STILL DARK when I awoke, put on a housecoat, and walked downstairs toward the bright light of the kitchen. The kettle was boiling: Alex and Edward were already up. I smiled at Edward, who was sitting at the counter. "Good for you, getting up so early." No I-have-a-temperature tactics were evident on this day of the swimming competition, and I made toast and instant oatmeal for everyone. As it was for Anne, my joy in the presence of my sons was immediate and warm.

"Let's go, Edward," Alex said. My husband was the first one out the door on any morning, and the boys were required to move at his pace.

"I haven't finished my tea," Edward complained.

"Here, Edward, take this thermos." I poured his cup of sweet, milky tea into it. "I'm sorry I can't go to the meet, but you know Mrs. Gibson is still in the hospital and I'm trying to be with her as much as I can."

"I know, Mom."

I kissed Edward goodbye and wished him luck, grateful that my sons knew Anne and understood my commitment. Alex, however, was never emotive, and he barely responded to the mention of Anne's name and condition. *Maybe he isn't interested in my life, either.* I dismissed the thought; there was no time to think of that.

Day was breaking as I drove to the hospital, the city buildings turning from grey to lighter grey. Anne was still sleeping when I arrived, and I sat watching her, happy to see her at peace and relieved that another uneventful night had passed.

When a noise on the intercom woke her, she opened her eyes with a smile, and even with her burnt-looking skin, she looked sweetly at ease. "How kind of you to come so early," she said.

"I was so worried about you." I put my arm around her shoulder and brushed her cheek, wishing she were strong enough for a real hug.

"I had a very good night," Anne said. "The nurse I like the most was with me."

"I'm glad you turned that corner," I said. The twenty-four-hour "critical" period would soon be over.

Simon, Anne's doctor, arrived on his morning rounds, and I left the room while he met with Anne.

Afterward, he spoke to me in the corridor. He had a soft voice with a slight Australian accent, but his news wasn't soothing. "We're all surprised how fast the cancer is proceeding," he said. "It's important at this time to have a power of attorney for personal care. That way decisions will be made in a consultative manner and not by me alone."

"I agree," I said, making my voice and eye contact stay steady. "I think Anne agrees now, too. I'll do what I can."

He left then, and I sensed that he was relieved that I was there to help Anne. When I returned to Anne's room, Mary, the family therapist, arrived with the personal care form.

Anne, quite lucid, even cheerful, asked me to be an attorney for health care. I knew that meant I would make health care decisions if Anne became incapable of doing so. I certainly had no appreciation that I might actually have to be involved in any life-or-death situation. "Of course," I said. Mary and a nurse witnessed the signatures.

Anne then opened her black binder and removed the copy of the guardianship papers. She said, "Whoever will look after Duncan and Sandy will have to be resolved after. No matter what I say, the decision will be a collective one and will be part of a process." She paused, looking pained and wistful. "The person who wants to do it will do it."

Anne's ability to accept that the guardianship of her sons could be resolved in the future without her controlling influence was a remarkable act of faith, all the more startling because Anne was such a perfectionist, so much in charge of her life and the lives of her children. Although she knew that ultimately a court would decide on or approve the guardianship, she had wanted to name the person herself in advance. I empathized with how concerned she was for their future and how she longed to know they would be in the best possible situation.

Although I'd never had to face the horrific uncertainty of having someone else raise my children, I knew how important it was to be able to at least picture our children's lives. Even as my sons aged, I would like to visit their rooms at university, their apartments. We mothers somehow need to be able to visualize our offspring in their environments. When Darrell first went to boarding school, it comforted me that I could picture him throughout his day—in his bed, getting up, walking to class, in the dining room, studying. It helped to handle missing him.

It would be nearly insurmountable for me to face death while being unable to picture where Darrell and Edward would be. Anne's letting go expressed her faith that others would do the right thing not only for her, but also for her sons. She had always done the right thing for others, and now it was their turn. *"The person who wants to do it will do it."* I suppose her statement could also have been a realization that she was dying, and she'd given up. Yet her tone was more hopeful than despairing. I saw it as Anne's own innate goodness that enabled her to have confidence in the goodness of others.

The doctor and nurse arrived to prepare Anne for the installation of the Hickman catheter, the direct portal to allow intravenous access for the chemo and for blood sampling. Before she was moved onto the gurney, Anne removed her ring and watch. She touched the ring to her cheek and placed it in my hand. "Please keep these for me, Marie." She clasped my fist, wrapped around her treasures, in her own cold, small hands. "The time doesn't matter, but I hate to be without my ring." I felt the warmth and strength of my flesh against hers and wished I could give her some of my own health.

"I'll keep them safe," I said.

———

BY NINE O'CLOCK, I was in my chambers and dressing for court. I threaded the watchband through Anne's ring and tucked both of them in my vest pocket, so I would have them close and couldn't misplace them. As I fastened the tabs around my neck, I couldn't get my head around it. *Why am I not at Anne's side?* She was my friend, I loved her, and nobody else was there. It was obvious that I should take time off to be with a dying friend. Why didn't I call the Regional Senior Justice and say, "I have other priorities. I'm taking a leave of absence for a while"?

When I'd told Anne earlier that I would be willing to accompany her to California to seek treatment, my commitment had been genuine. It wasn't merely a dramatic response engendered by a dramatic situation. What was so important now about my work? Nothing in my life as a judge couldn't be postponed. The muddle of the trial with the tattooed bikers could start again after two days of evidence. A few other cases would have to be rescheduled, but trials are routinely rescheduled for many reasons. In my judicial career, I'd missed only five days of work, and those were in the first three months, when I'd foolishly tried out my sons' skateboard and fractured my elbow. The truth is that accused persons aren't anxious to get to trial, and delays work in their favour. Witnesses move away, memories become dimmer. And then there is the legal dance of seeking adjournments with an unexpressed hope of getting the charge dismissed because of delay in bringing the case to trial.

Devoted to my work, I took pride in being a thorough, fair, and competent judge. Even as opportunities had arisen to visit Anne, I'd felt guilty leaving my chambers without offering to do other work, as if my professional life was more worthwhile than my personal one. Although I was trapped in the daily exigencies of my workplace and my work, I felt it more important to be with Anne as she struggled to stay alive.

I saw that imbalance, yet I couldn't act on it. My lifelong commitment to work and to doing that work well was ingrained, along with some mantras: *Get an education*; *get a job*; *be successful*. In law school, I had added the goals of contributing to social and legal change. I was dutiful to family, career, community. Never could I remember anyone saying that happiness was a worthwhile goal. If they did, it passed me by. Now, having achieved secular success and respectability, I was no longer sure of their value. I was no longer living as I wanted to live.

Still, I entered the courtroom exactly at ten o'clock. I was an on-time judge.

The defence counsel in the biker trial, quietly confident, began his cross-examination of the victim's boyfriend, Fred Clark. He elicited that initially Fred Clark did not suspect Mike, the accused, and that even though he recognized him at the preliminary inquiry, he did not identify him as the attacker.

"How tall are you?" he began.

"I'm six feet."

"How much do you weigh?"

"Two hundred and fifteen pounds."

"You look to be in good condition."

"I work out five days a week."

"How tall is Mike, the accused?"

"Five feet eight inches." The accused was sitting down, so I couldn't gauge his height.

"Are you aware Mike has an alibi?"

So that's what this case is about, I thought. *Identity is secondary. A credible alibi would make identification of less importance.*

"I first heard of it last Thursday."

"Did you see Mike with a rose tattoo?"

"No, I didn't see it."

"No further questions."

———

DURING THE LUNCHEON RECESS, I hurried from the court and drove back to the hospital to check on Anne and to return the ring and watch. The surgery had been successful, the shunts were in place, and Anne was in good spirits.

Anne's friend Fran, who the day before had appeared so upset at the prospect of becoming the boys' guardian, was visiting.

I slipped the ring onto Anne's cool, tiny finger and placed the watch in her hand, which felt soft and limp.

"Thanks, now I feel dressed again," she said. "I can't wait to get out of these hospital clothes and off these harsh sheets."

Fran smiled. "Yes, you can't expect Porthault sheets here. And you'll be back in your La Perla nightgowns soon." Fran, a tall, handsome woman, was always well dressed and well groomed.

"It's fun to talk about clothes with you," Anne said. "You're my two friends who like fashion and like to dress well."

"Since I've been a judge, I like clothes even more," I admitted. "I dress like a penguin and wear the same black and white clothes day after day. Not many lawyers have our fashion sense, Anne."

"I always think of lawyers being well dressed, if a trifle too business-like," said Fran.

I thought back to the many women detectives and officers who came to my courtroom in their civvies. "From what I see," I said, "women police officers wear even snappier clothes than women lawyers. Maybe, like me, they relish being out of uniform."

Fran and Anne both laughed, and Anne seemed a little like her old self. It was a relief to talk lightly for a few minutes about nothing much, instead of having the inevitable discourse about pain, the will, doctors, and death. Maybe she'd get better after all.

———

"YOUR HONOUR, I call Detective Drew to the stand," said Crown counsel after the lunch recess.

Detective Drew gave evidence that a photo lineup of twenty-four members of Satan's Choice had been shown to Kathy, who had identified the accused. After the identification, the detective arrested the accused, whom he described for the Crown counsel.

"He had strong body odour, was about five feet ten or five feet eleven. He looked like he was lifting weights. He's smaller now."

"No further questions."

I called for cross-examination by Mr. Mather. He began, "What is the description of my client on the arrest form?"

"It says one hundred seventy-six pounds; five feet eight; Grim Reaper tattoo on his chest, and a dagger-rose-flag on his right forearm."

"The first disclosure of an alibi was on September twenty-fourth at the bail hearing?"

"Yes."

"Did you ask Kathy about the tattoos?"

"Yes. She could give no details about the tattoos."

"No further questions, Your Honour."

———

AFTER COURT FINISHED that day, I made sure Anne had company for the evening as I had to attend parent–teacher interviews for Edward at Bayview Glen School. I called Anne as soon as I returned from the meetings.

"Hi, Anne, can you talk? I made it through the parent–teacher interviews."

"How did it go?"

"You know how intense it is getting round to all the teachers. I was pretty tired, and by the fourth or fifth one, I entered the classroom not knowing what subject the teacher taught. I was sure I'd figure it out without admitting my ignorance." I paused, enjoying Anne's little laugh of recognition. "So the teacher started talking about grammar and speaking in class. I thought it was kind of odd that he was praising Edward merely for talking out loud in front of other kids. It took a while to figure out he was the French teacher, not the English teacher." Anne laughed. "And how are *you* feeling?" I asked.

"I'm feeling so much better," she said. "I'm watching television and it's even sort of interesting."

"Is anyone visiting?"

"Not right now—I've had lots of company."

"That's good. Do you mind if I don't come down tonight? I'm exhausted."

"You've been so good to me," she said. "Please, have a deserved rest."

"I'm so glad you're feeling better. Sweet dreams, Anne. Call me anytime."

Alex was gone on yet another business trip, and I wasn't sorry to have the bed all to myself—not to mention the lack of snoring. I lay down tired, and a little hopeful for the first time in many days.

Week One
Tuesday

DINNER

Home-baked fish sticks (*Kids' Cooking*, p. 38)

Fresh corn with butter or mashed
potatoes—make enough for two nights

Glazed carrot coins
(*Creative Cooking*, p. 3)

Pineapple upside-down cake
(*Fannie Farmer*, p. 482)

Chapter 6

JANUARY 20

WHAT A BREAK! Both counsel asked that the biker trial be adjourned until Monday, January 30. In the meantime, I would start another trial on the coming Monday. That meant I was sprung from the courtroom for the rest of the day. As I was relishing the prospect of some free hours, my colleague Susan, who was another long-time friend of Anne's, phoned.

"You'll never guess who wants to look after the boys," she said. "Jessica."

Jessica was a well-known lawyer, married to a wealthy older man. Though she was financially able to assume the responsibility, the offer struck me as otherwise quite inappropriate. She wasn't a close friend of Anne or her family. "You're joking," I said, knowing she was not.

"No, I'm serious. She made arrangements to see Anne at lunchtime to discuss adopting Duncan and Sandy."

"She doesn't even know them! She barely knows Anne."

There was a slight pause. "I think it's very sweet of her," Susan said.

"I think it's preposterous, pixilated." It was a strange word to use, and one which carried a special weight for me.

"What's that mean?"

"It means somewhat crazy." The word had become part of my vocabulary after an academic review of a tax case I had litigated on my own behalf while in law school. The legal article had begun, "There is a pixilating air about this case."

Pixilated described how I felt much of that week, and had felt much of the time since Anne had become ill. So much in my field of vision seemed distorted. Jessica's offer to adopt Anne's sons seemed only slightly stranger than everything else.

And yet mundane life went on. My hair was straggly, and the adjournment provided an opportunity to get a haircut. Afterward, happy with the trim, I went to the hospital, arriving mid-afternoon, when the light was starting to fade in the short January days. Anne's catheter had been removed that morning, thank goodness, and she said, "I feel much better."

"You do look more like your old self." At least there'd be no more torturous indignity—sitting on the potty, trying to urinate. "Would you like to freshen up a bit?" I asked. "I can brush your hair and help you."

"I think I can manage that." She sat upright and lifted the mirror from the bedside table. Then she picked up her silver hairbrush and set it in her lap as if it were heavy.

"Here, let me help you," I said. I brushed her hair, now brittle and longer than usual. There wasn't much hair to arrange, yet I enjoyed the feeling of comforting her and making her look pretty, and I could tell she enjoyed the touch and the attention. We didn't speak as I brushed her delicate hair, and I was happy that she smiled when I gave her a light head massage. She leaned back on the pillows and the tendons in her neck relaxed.

She admired the coral lipstick I was wearing. "I'd like to put some on," she said. "My lips are so dry." She pointed to her makeup bag, and dabbed a little of the lipstick on her lips, which were still bright red from the chemo. "Ooh," she sighed. "They're still so dry."

"Let me get some Vaseline."

"There's only the skin lotion."

As she put a little on her lips, I told her I would bring some Vaseline next time.

Then, the personal care treats attended to, I tidied up. There is always something to straighten out in a hospital room. I got a fresh box of tissues and I folded up one of the extra blankets. I hung up one of the bed jackets and took a tray of uneaten food into the hallway so it would be out of sight. I fetched ice chips and offered her some to suck.

"Thanks," she said, putting a tiny sliver of ice into her mouth. "My throat is still raw. I can't believe I'm having more chemo, and then maybe a transfusion, but I'll be okay. It's good having you here."

"I brought some magazines," I said, pleased. "I think you'll enjoy the article about Pamela Harriman in *Vanity Fair*. It's about the legal complications arising in her estate." We had both enjoyed reading Harriman's biography, despite the differences between her life and our own paths. "What a modern-day courtesan she was," I observed.

"A real slut."

Anne's harsh words, though not her view, took me by surprise. I felt glad I'd never told Anne about my own sexual adventures before I was married: I didn't want to risk a similar judgment.

"Well, yes," I said, diplomatically. "Pamela Harriman's path is not one either of us would have chosen. Using men to get ahead."

"I was brought up to give something back," Anne said. "I was brought up to believe that I should try to do good in the world—kind of like the Kennedys!"

"We did more than that," I said. "We succeeded in a man's world." I shook my head, remembering the first words ever said to me at law school. A fellow student looked in my direction with the greeting, "So they let another one in." I told Anne the story of how I had met that former student years later, when he was Premier David Peterson and I was a judge. At a formal gala, I reminded him of his words of welcome. He assured me that in the interim, he'd become a feminist. "Yeah, right," I said to Anne. "I didn't believe him, but I told him, 'That's okay, I have to live down that I go-go danced at the law-school stag.'"

"You didn't."

"It's mortifying when I think back," I said. At the instigation of two classmates, I'd agreed to do it. I put fringe on a turquoise bikini and stuffed the bra with foam rubber under my breasts. As I danced, my fellow students threw pennies. I watched Anne's face, wondering if she would think that "slutty." Changing the subject, I said, "I can read the article to you if you like."

While I was reading, two of her executors arrived, followed by her son Duncan. I invited Duncan to lunch in the cafeteria so the others could talk privately.

Duncan was handsome, with his mother's facial features, thick, straight blond hair, and large, lively brown eyes. At fifteen, he looked like an eighteen-year-old and conversed with sophistication well beyond his years. He spoke with animation about his boarding school, sixty miles from Toronto. He liked the school and the freedom it gave him. As he spoke, I enjoyed our interaction and I soon realized that he wasn't at all aware of how close he might be to losing his mother. For him, it was probably like all the other times his mother had been in the hospital.

Duncan and I walked back into Anne's room as the would-be adoptive mother, Jessica, appeared, and Anne introduced Duncan to her. Sensing that Anne and Jessica needed to be alone, I asked Anne what Duncan and I could bring her, and we set out shopping.

I was agitated, remembering the time Jessica had remarked how well Anne looked after her transplant. I was stunned when she added, "Maybe we should all have a bone marrow transplant to look that good."

We drove to Canadian Tire at Duncan's suggestion to buy the Walkman Anne had requested. On the way back we stopped at the Body Shop on Wellesley for the soap she liked. When we returned to the hospital, Jessica was gone, but two more friends were visiting, and Anne was obviously tired. Grand Central Station wasn't for me, and I wasn't sure it was so good for Anne, either, though she never complained.

When I phoned at five, Anne was sleeping. I returned at a quarter past six with a milkshake from the Yogurty's on Church Street. I sat quietly on the chair by the window until she awoke.

"Hello," I said softly. "I brought you a banana shake."

Anne tasted it. "It's delicious. You're so kind to me. It hurts to eat food."

"I also brought a can of jellied consommé and a can opener. And Vaseline for your lips."

I needn't have worried about interrupting Anne's sleep, because Mary, Anne's family therapist, also stopped by to visit. We spoke in the corridor, where Mary confided, "Anne's brother wants to know how come everybody knows everything before him."

"Yes, the problem is Anne doesn't want him to handle her affairs or to be the boys' guardian," I explained. I wondered if it was really my role to be explaining this and if Mary should be discussing these matters with me.

"He feels someone should be talking to him," Mary pressed.

Still uneasy, I assured her that Anne was perfectly capable of talking to her brother and added, "It's not really my place to tell Anne what to do. I do what Anne asks me to do or what I think she might like."

I appreciated Mary's delicate position as the family's therapist. It was awkward for all of us as there was no relative or partner who spoke with authority on Anne's behalf or upon whom Anne relied to look after her interests. I was a member of a coterie of women who loved her, but I was one of many and it wasn't my place to assume a larger function. I wasn't her executor or lawyer; my role was to comfort and support her.

Still more visitors began to arrive, and despite my wish to be alone and quiet with Anne, I left, after leaving the usual instructions with Anne and the nurses to call me any time I was needed.

That evening, my best friend, Barbara, came for dinner at my house. Over martinis, she asked, "Where's Alex this time?"

"Left early to ski at Whistler before working in Calgary next week." I hadn't even said goodbye to him properly, and I wasn't exactly sure when he'd be back.

"I guess it makes it easier for you, since you're going to the hospital so much."

"It's easier, and to tell the truth, right now, it doesn't matter one way or the other. Ever since he went to New York for the weekend and lied about it, I haven't felt the same."

Barbara nodded, knowing how hurt I'd been when Alex went to hear Pavarotti at the Met with a friend and two women, ostensibly business colleagues. He hadn't told me he was going to the opera; he said he went to a football game and confessed only after I pointed out there was no football game that weekend. He claimed he'd nothing to do with it—his business friend had arranged it.

I was grateful for my best friend's easy and familiar company that evening. Dinner was delicious—Julia Child's beef stew. After a long chat and a little wine, Barbara went home, and I got to bed before midnight.

The phone rang, waking me from a sound sleep. The digital clock showed 1:20 a.m. I was alarmed to hear Anne's voice, and glad when she said it wasn't urgent—she wanted to talk.

"That's fine, Anne. I told you, you can call anytime." I sat up, ready to listen.

"They gave me an Ativan, but I can't sleep."

"What's wrong?" I asked, propping a pillow behind my head.

"I get panic-stricken at night."

Hesitantly, I asked, "Are you afraid that you're not going to get better—that you're going to die?" I hadn't used the word *die* before with Anne, but I didn't want to bypass the topic if that was the source of her panic.

"Yes, that," she admitted. "And I have other fears."

"Sure you do. Of course you do. Anne, you're not going to die tonight. You've passed a big hurdle today. You're going to be fine."

"I used to call Doug late at night and he would calm me." Her voice was soft and she spoke slowly. Thinking Doug probably chatted about everyday matters, I asked if she'd had any visitors.

"My brother came in later."

"How did that go?"

"It was okay." Then, perhaps avoiding her own questions and feelings, she changed the subject again, saying, "I was quite taken aback by Jessica's visit today."

"I'm not surprised. She can be injudicious." Remembering Jessica's insensitive comment about the bone marrow transplant, I felt peeved all over again.

"Jessica told me she had unlimited money, horses, and, you know, basketball hoops and things. I felt odd, as if I were playing a role—the dying widow," Anne continued.

"It does seem preposterous, and she has children of her own. Maybe she thinks it will add to her social cachet." I knew my comment was catty, and perhaps I was a bit envious of Jessica's blithe assurance that she could handle bringing up Anne's children.

"I was even more upset when she talked about Duncan," Anne said. "The boy she described wasn't Duncan! She said he was troubled and had a horrible life and that she would get him any psychological help he needed."

"Good grief, how insensitive!" I said. "Well, maybe it springs from good intentions—the idea of helping orphaned children." It was time for another change of topic. "How did your visit with the executors go?"

"It was great—a welcome contrast to all the women the other day going at me from all sides."

I felt hurt. Was I one of the people "going at" her? "To be fair, Anne," I said, "the doctor had just told us you might die within forty-eight hours. We were all upset."

"Well, the doctors didn't tell me that."

Clearly she felt she'd been besieged, and clearly she was not aware how close to death she'd come. "You're getting better now, Anne. You're not going to die. You'll see. We'll travel together again and do fun things."

"Yes, I'd like that," she began. "Oh, here comes the nurse. I have such a headache. She'll give me a Tylenol 3. Thank you, Marie. I'm getting sleepy now."

It was 2:30 a.m. when I hung up.

———

ANNE'S COMPLAINT THAT she felt the women were "going at" her stayed with me. I shuddered to think that I might be implicated. Anne's feeling that we women acted like harpies reflected differences in our feminism. Certainly, Anne believed in equal opportunity for women, and she had achieved great success in a male-dominated profession. However, fundamentally, Anne was comfortable with the male domination of much of public life (law, medicine, religion) and much of her private life (marriage). Anne didn't view that dominance as inhibiting. She enjoyed the company of men and the advantages her beauty and charm brought to male–female relations. Her values were grounded in middle-class respectability, not rebellion, and she was more inclined to support the status quo than to try to change it.

I, on the other hand, resisted the reality of men's dominance. Having grown up in a relatively poor family in a tiny village, I had become a lawyer partly to ensure my own financial security—something Anne had not had to grapple with. Also, I'd been attracted to the image: being a "woman lawyer" sounded so glamorous. I'd wanted a career, not a job. In my twenties, marriage wasn't anything I wanted or contemplated.

Anne didn't share my view that, at our particular time in history, women were more interesting than men. I was finding my relationships with female friends more satisfying than those with men. Men were doing the same old things, when so much was new for women in public life, with consequent changes and growth in our private lives as well.

A year and a half earlier, at Anne's request, I had spoken about feminism at a meeting of the Junior League of Toronto at the Granite Club, a private athletic and dining club. Neither the audience nor the setting had inspired me, and I'd agreed only because Anne asked me. It was typical of her milieu, that Junior League event, and not a place where I felt particularly comfortable. The subjects of the speeches I'd given as a lawyer, highlighting social injustices with a view to reforming the law, were too controversial to give as a judge.

When I picked Anne up the night of the speech, she was visibly exhausted. Her husband, diagnosed with Lou Gehrig's disease, had been hospitalized after suffering a massive stroke.

"You really shouldn't be coming with me," I told her. "You have so much on your plate with Doug in the hospital." I opened the car door for Anne and she slowly sank into the front seat.

"I want to go with you. It's a break from the hospital."

"How is Doug?"

"Half his body is paralyzed and he can't speak." She spoke dejectedly, staring straight ahead. "He hates being in the hospital. He keeps pulling out his intravenous tubes. He pulled out the feeding tube fourteen times."

I shook my head, picturing it. "How dreadful for you."

"I'm going to take him home where he'll be comfortable. I'll arrange nursing care and have IV and oxygen. And then, when I've got time—that waiting room outside the intensive care unit is so dowdy. I'm going to decorate it for the hospital when I get a chance. I'm tired all the time now."

"I'm drained too," I commiserated. "I've had the most intense trial, and it was all in one day." As we negotiated our way through the inaptly named "rush-hour" traffic, I told Anne a little about the horrific trial—the bearded burly man in a wheelchair, the enmity between two brothers, the social ills I could do so little to remedy.

The gruelling cross-examination had been classic. Defence counsel had calmly demanded of the man in the wheelchair adjacent to the witness box, "Do you use drugs?"

"No," he replied sharply.

"Never?" asked the lawyer, looking at a paper in his hand.

"Maybe I did a little cocaine."

"Did you inject it?"

"Yeah. In my forearm, a fraction of an inch. It was very minor." The hospital report would show he had cocaine in his body and needle-track marks on his arms.

"Where did you do this?"

"At my brother's."

"You were mad at him, weren't you?"

"Yeah, he mixed the coke with water."

"Did you use coke at the Vagabond Club?"

He bristled. "What's that got to do with this?" I instructed him to answer the question, and he said he used to be a member.

Counsel continued: "Where is the club located?"

"It's none of your business," he shot back.

"Your Honour—" counsel began.

Anticipating my reply, the witness interrupted: "It's on Gerrard Street."

"And how long were you a member?"

"What the fuck does this have to do with this?"

"Mr. Ward," I interjected as gently as I could in the face of his increasing belligerence, "defence counsel is permitted to ask many questions on cross-examination that may not seem relevant. Mr. Kempster is allowed to ask questions to show that you are not a credible witness. He's also allowed to ask questions to show that you have a propensity for violence or that you have a violent nature."

Mr. Ward fumed quietly but answered the question. "I was a member for nine years. So what? Humphrey and Hamilton rode with us."

I smiled inwardly, as he was referring to two of my judicial colleagues, biting my lip. By that time the tiny red bruise on my lower lip had become a permanent feature.

"Were you the sergeant-at-arms?"

"I'm not answering that question."

"Mr. Ward," I began again. "Unfortunately it's not up to you to decide whether to answer a question. That's my job. If the question is improper, Crown counsel will object."

"No, I wasn't a sergeant-at-arms," David Ward answered.

"You have a criminal record?"

"Yes," he answered with a measure of resignation.

"You were convicted of break and entry in 1969 and were sentenced to three months imprisonment?"

"Yeah. My brother got me into it."

"You were convicted of possession of stolen property in 1979 and received a suspended sentence?"

"No," he said, glaring at defence counsel.

"You were convicted of possession of a restricted weapon in 1982 and were fined one thousand dollars?"

"Yes."

"What was the weapon?"

"A handgun."

"You were convicted of trafficking in a narcotic in 1983 and were sentenced to one year in prison?"

"I can't remember."

"You were convicted of uttering a forged document in 1987 and were sentenced to fifteen days?"

"I can't remember."

"You were convicted of two counts of assault in 1987 and sentenced to three months?"

"I don't remember."

"You were convicted in 1991 in Windsor of conspiracy to traffic in a controlled drug and were fined fifteen hundred dollars?"

"I was charged with four others, and we all pleaded guilty, but they were members of a different club. I wasn't involved. I pleaded guilty to get away from it. It was costly."

"How did you get along with your brother?"

"I never liked him."

"You were angry when you were there?"

"No, I wasn't," he replied, obviously angry. "My brother is jealous because I have a motorcycle. He wanted me to sell it to him. He said he'd give me the money, but he didn't have any money. So I sold it to someone else and he was pissed off."

"You fought with your brother and you hit him?"

"No. He had no injuries and had no cuts to his face."

"I'm showing you a photograph of Jason which indicates he has a cut to his finger and face."

"I didn't cause those injuries. He gets violent when he gets arrested. I didn't lay a glove on him. Basically, I'm not a violent person."

He concluded his testimony by denying that he'd gone to his brother's to look for drugs and denying that he told the police he was involved in an argument with his brother.

I explained the gist of it to Anne as I manoeuvred around the cars heading out of downtown Toronto. Though I was hungry and tired, I knew that Anne enjoyed hearing about my cases, so I continued telling her about the trial. "As you can imagine, the nub of the case was whether I could believe what Mr. Ward said. Obviously, he told lies under oath—about any number of things. And he hates his brother, but that's understandable. I said if an unsavoury cocaine user with a criminal record could never be believed, justice would only serve the virtuous. His evidence was supported by the existence of blood splatter on the porch at his brother's place and by the fact that his brother's injuries were slight. I believed him and convicted Jason."

"The people you have to deal with! So, when do you sentence him?"

"I did that too, a mere hour before I picked you up. My head's still reeling. His brother was a drug addict with many physical problems and a record of fifty convictions, twelve of which were for assault. I sentenced him to three years."

"That seems lenient, doesn't it?"

"I guess. The Crown wanted five years. I took into account that he'd just started serving a seven-year for robbery." I pulled into the crowded parking lot of the Granite Club and drove up to the entrance behind a couple of SUVs. "Here we are. I'll let you off at the door and park the car."

When I walked in a few minutes later, Anne was being warmly greeted. About forty society do-gooders were seated at the various tables, everyone well turned out and festively chatting.

After a few business matters were attended to, Anne introduced me. I'd decided to use the occasion to re-examine my views on feminism, although I doubted it was a subject of interest to many in the audience. I intended to be honest about my views, but I certainly didn't want to express any disdain for their lifestyle, different as it was from my intense careerism.

Amusingly, a few weeks later I would be dining at the private Rosedale Golf Club with my member husband when a woman who had always known me only as Mrs. Alex Squires would warmly greet me, saying, "That was a great speech. I had no idea you were a judge."

That night, I put aside my tiredness and my doubts about the audience's receptivity and gave the speech, mainly as a gesture of friendship for Anne but also as a self-imposed re-examination of my life and my values.

I am privileged to share my thoughts with you—women who make contributions to our social betterment by helping others in need and by enriching our personal and cultural life. We make these contributions whether we are women who work outside the home or whether we are homemakers or both.

It remains an awkward phrase—"women who work outside the home" or "women who are gainfully employed." We are all gainfully employed. I recall asking the eight-year-old friend of my son if his mother worked outside the home. "Yes," he told me with a wide smile, "she likes to work outside the house. She works in the garden, and every fall she grows me a great big pumpkin."

As a feminist, I have embodied many of the changing social values for women during the past three decades and my attitudes marched with the times.

I graduated from high school in 1960 at age sixteen with four choices: I could go to secretarial school; I could become a nurse; I could go to university to become a teacher; or I might enrol in that intriguing new course in fashion design. Not inspired by this range of choice, I attended university because I knew I wanted a career, not knowing what that career might be.

This was not typical for 1960, but I was raised by a widowed, self-reliant mother who emphasized the importance of education and prescribed these rules: First, if you don't look after yourself, nobody else will. Second, if you work really hard, you can do and be anything you choose. Third, why do you want to get married? There is nothing you have married that you can't have single. With this open-ended programming, I began to live my mother's prescriptions.

At that time, I truly did believe I could do and be anything. If anything, I felt I had an edge over men. After all, I could be a lawyer and give birth.

Early in my career, I applied for a position at a large law firm. I was told candidly by the employment agent retained by the law firm that I was the best-qualified lawyer for the job but the firm did not want to hire a woman. I began to realize that I could not, on merit, do and be everything I wanted and that being a woman had something to do with it. My consciousness was raised.

I was one of seventeen women in the province who were called to the bar in 1970.

When women first entered public life, we wanted to be treated in the same way as those who were already there. We wanted equality with men. To be taken seriously, we felt we had to be the same as men.

The struggle for equality then was more literal. The initial decision made by the first Ontario Status of Women Council in 1973, of which I was a member, was to recommend the repeal of the law requiring employers to provide taxis for female employees working at night. Because we were tired of being treated as feeble dependants, we rejected protective legislation. We resisted pedestals and special favours. We said if we want to be equal on the job, then we must do the same job that men do, without special accommodation. We wanted equal opportunity and equal pay.

At the same time that women were working to achieve equality in the workplace, we worked to achieve recognition of the contribution of wives and homemakers. In *Murdoch v. Murdoch*, a decision of the Supreme Court of Canada in 1973, Irene Murdoch and her husband worked as farm couple for twenty-five years. Title to the farm property was in the husband's name. The Supreme Court of Canada refused to give

Mrs. Murdoch a half-interest in the property because her con-tribution was considered that of an ordinary homemaker.

Wives began to realize that if they did not own property outright, their contribution as homemaker was economically worthless. The so-called pedestal on which wives and mothers were placed could be an economic disaster. As a result, family law reform attempted to achieve a measure of parity in mar-riage by legislating recognition of marriage as a partnership.

In the eighties, we began to realize that being equal did not always mean being the same. Certain realities had to be recognized.

For example, the bulk of child care is done and will, in all likelihood, continue to be done by women. Despite the invita-tion, men are not flocking to assume the child-care function. That being the reality, the male work mode and male-driven work patterns must be modified to accommodate child-rear-ing patterns and needs of working women.

In my own work, judges were asked to volunteer to go out of town for three weeks. I did not volunteer because of family commitments, although three weeks away had considerable appeal. Some time later, I commented to the Senior Judge that women judges were not sitting on high-profile murder cases. He denied this was the case and observed, "It appears as if women want to have it all but do not want to assume their share of less attractive duties. For example, not one woman judge volunteered to go to Windsor." It doesn't take a rocket scientist to figure out that it is not a question of women not doing their share of drudge work or extra work, but rather that most of us are not free to make some job decisions because of the exigencies of our child-care duties.

In my personal life, reality also set in. My husband, Alex, and I agreed to share domestic tasks. He volunteered to do the shopping because I detest shopping for groceries. *How wonderful*, I thought. The following Saturday, the conversation went something like this.

Alex said, "I'll do the shopping. Where's the list?"

I replied sweetly, "I don't have a list, dear. Making the list is part of doing the shopping."

"Okay, get me a piece of paper and a pencil."

I gave him the pencil and paper and then he said, "Okay, what do we need?"

"Alex, when I do the list I have to check."

"Do we need milk?"

"Alex, when I check to see if we need milk, I walk over to the refrigerator and I look in."

I call this the "surgeon theory of husband responsibility." My husband used to make a wonderful Béarnaise sauce and he would say, "Marie, hand me two eggs at room temperature."

We had other sharing discussions when my biological clock was ticking. Our sons were born when I was thirty-six and thirty-nine years old.

"Alex, if we are going to have children, child care has to be shared equally."

"But of course," he replied.

After I stopped nursing, we agreed to take turns getting up at night. For some reason I was the only one who heard the baby stir. I would then make an unseemly effort to awaken Alex from the blissfully sound sleep of contented husband and father. In a climate of equality, disparity again set in. It became easier for me to go to the children at night.

Another significant difference is the reality of the nature of violence. Over ninety percent of violent crime is committed by men, and the victims of violent crime tend to be women and children. In the 1980s, the Status of Women Council may not have repealed the requirement for employers to provide cab rides for women at night in cognizance of the fact that women suffer a much greater risk of harm than male employees in similar circumstances.

Although our social order is evolving, I have very few role models. We are all pioneers. We must share our struggles. My young son used to beg me daily to stay home. When I thought he was old enough for me to be candid, I told him that I loved him and I didn't want to leave him but that I actually liked to work. He sat silently for a while. I asked him what he was thinking and he said, "I want to be a building when I grow up." I looked at his sad face and asked, "But, why, darling?" Breaking my heart, he replied, "If I were a building, you would come to me every day."

My remarks received generous applause, and I wondered if any of my ideas might be shared. Anne and I stayed for tea for the least time politeness would allow. We were worn out.

Later, Anne thanked me for coming and said she'd enjoyed my speech.

"Glad you liked it," I said. "But it's probably not anything they were really interested in."

"And you're so right," she continued. "We women do so much more at home because it seems easier."

"Or maybe we can't stop being in control, except near the barbecue."

Anne laughed. "Yes, and for me, it's weekend breakfasts when Doug's around."

It had been a long day for each of us. I marvelled that Anne and I, and women like us, could pack so much into a day. Yet it was another example of getting my priorities wrong. I derived no pleasure from the evening, other than doing something for Anne and being able to take her to the event. I didn't think my attempts to enlighten the Junior League on feminist issues counted for much. Compared to family and work, the added chore simply wasn't worth the effort and energy.

Week One
Wednesday

BREAKFAST

Vitamin pill

Hash browns

3½ minute boiled egg—mix with salt and
pepper and serve in snowman cups

Slice of brown toast with butter

Chapter 7

JANUARY 21

THOUGH SATURDAY BROUGHT RAIN, at least my morning was a little more leisurely than the week had been. On my way to the hospital, I picked up a power shake and some fashion magazines.

When I arrived, Anne was awake, looking rested. "I've received my last chemo," she said. "The doctors said my condition seems stable again."

"What good news!" I said, starting to think, *Maybe she'll get better, be able to go back home for a long time.* "I have some magazines."

"The only thing is, my head's a little sore." Seeing my gifts, Anne added, "Thank you. I'll have the shake later."

I put the cup on the side table. "I've brought some dry shampoo to use, if you like, and I can massage your head at the same time."

Without talking much, I worked the shampoo into her hair and softly massaged her head as she closed her eyes. I wished I could make her well.

After the head massage, I started reading the Pamela Harriman article aloud. Anne and I had fun talking about that woman's life—so unlike our own—and she drank almost all the shake. It was a short, pleasant visit, and Anne seemed more like her old self. When another friend of hers arrived, I left them to have a visit. "I don't know when I'll be back," I said. "Edward's having a party for twenty of his friends from two until six. I won't be able to leave the house until they're all picked up."

Twenty thirteen-year-olds are beyond boisterous. Still, I reflected, listening to the thumps and distant shouts coming from the third floor, teens' birthday parties were a lot easier than those at younger ages. Over the years, I'd hosted kids' skiing outings at the cabin, a planetarium excursion, a Chuck E. Cheese free-for-all, sleepovers, and a bowling night. "They can't harm anything in a bowling alley," a friend had suggested. Right she was, until I saw one little fellow headed down the lane still attached to the ball. As each birthday celebration approached, reliving the original birth had more appeal. At least at thirteen they liked to be left alone in the playroom to wreak havoc.

At six o'clock, the official end time on the invitations, the party was still going strong. Shrieks and laughter could be heard as I delivered more ice cream cones and candy up the stairs.

I was peevish when I called Anne. "They're still here," I moaned. "I thought all of the kids would be picked up by now. I was careful to specify six o'clock on the invitation."

"You're a good mother," she said. She was breathing heavily.

"How are you feeling?"

"I'm so tired now."

"No wonder," I said. "You have non-stop visitors, especially now that it's the weekend. Why don't you turn off the phone for an hour and try to sleep? I'll come down as soon as I can. Anything you'd like?"

"I'm still cold," she complained. "I need socks and a wrap for my head. Chemo makes me so cold."

"I'll bring them as soon as all the kids are picked up."

Finally, at seven-fifteen, the last parent arrived to take away her offspring. I was barely civil, herding the boy out the door and pointedly reminding his mother that the invitation had said six.

When I arrived at the hospital, there were two visitors: the boys' companion/sitter and Anne's "cancer twin," Lisa. Lisa was a bone marrow transplant survivor with whom Anne was paired for support. They'd brought the movie *Mystic Pizza*, with Julia Roberts, along with a VCR and popcorn. Everyone was festive except Anne, who was trying to laugh and enjoy the film but could barely keep her eyes open.

Though I didn't speak about it, I was irked. I'd seen it before: people decide what another person would like and carry it out without putting themselves in that person's shoes—in this case, without considering if Anne were up to watching a movie. I reminded myself that their actions sprang from good intentions.

Silently, I slipped Anne's size-six feet into the socks and draped the soft cotton scarf around her head. When I left, the movie was still playing and Anne had fallen asleep.

The next morning, it finally snowed, relaxing the day and making it seem more like a real Sunday. Since friends were visiting Anne that afternoon, I waited until five o'clock to see her, when she was alone. I arrived with another milkshake and she thanked me, saying, "It's the only thing I can eat."

I was happy to be alone with Anne, glad to absorb myself in trying to make her feel more comfortable. Anne was tired and still quite cold, so I rubbed her icy hands and feet. After putting a hot water bottle under her feet and tucking the blankets around her, I gave her a facial and gently brushed her hair. Once she was relaxed and warm, I read to her. When she fell asleep, I turned out the lights.

Though Anne was very tired, she seemed to have turned a corner. Apparently the doctors thought so too, since they'd said she was stable. But what did "stable" mean, exactly? After the bone marrow transplant three years earlier, she'd been called "stable" too. Her life had continued as full as before: social engagements, charitable activities, her law practice, domestic chaos, plus monitoring her health. She'd continued to fill several tables with guests at the annual Genesis breakfast. As ever, she overextended herself. Anne would go to every school meeting, tired or not, because the principal insisted. She went even on a morning that she'd had a CAT scan and three other procedures.

In those days, we'd most often meet for lunch, usually at the York Club, where our husbands were members. One Saturday in the lounge there, she sat on a sofa and I sat in a large wing chair. Then as now, I found Anne mesmerizingly beautiful. Her navy blue suit was elegant, the hot pink floral silk blouse matching the lining of her jacket. Only her slow walk and her use of a cane gave a clue to her fragile health. The waiter handed us menus and extended a small notepad and pencil. Anne took it, announcing, "This will be my treat." Although women could not be members of the York Club, we "privileged ladies" could sign on our husbands' accounts. Anne ordered a Perrier and I had a Bloody Mary. We looked at the menu and Anne wrote the orders—liver and onions for both of us.

I admired her suit, and she said, "You know me, Marie, I don't spend money on jewellery, but I love beautiful clothes." Showing off her tan, she said, "I'm just back from a visit to Nassau for March break. We all love it there."

"It must have agreed with you. You look marvellous. Are you feeling good too?"

The waiter brought our drinks. Anne said thank you, picked up her water, and continued. "Well, I still have shingles. The sun aggravated it. I'm taking drugs for the shingles and for the pain in my legs where the nerves were destroyed."

It amazed me that Anne always sounded so matter-of-fact when she described her horrific afflictions. She never whined. I said, "Is there anything else that can happen to you?"

Anne smiled half-heartedly. "I have a ninety-eight percent chance that I'll have cataracts within three years. I have no saliva glands, and that means my teeth are going."

"I don't know how you bear it," I said—a sentiment I'd always felt. Yet I did know: it all came back to the children.

"I try not to think about it." She looked out the picture windows and stared briefly into the distance. "I've been thinking about what I want to do work-wise. I don't want to practise in a big firm anymore."

"I don't blame you. Who would? Especially when you have kids."

Anne took a sip of her water. "The firm's been giving me a hard time. Forbidding me to do work for my clients."

"On what basis?" It seemed untenable.

"Years ago I took out a large disability insurance policy. They say they don't want to jeopardize my insurance coverage. I was thinking, though, maybe I could become a judge."

"Sure, I can help if you like. We've talked about it before." We finished our drinks and headed toward the bright dining room, where the black-suited maître d' showed us to a small table set with linen, fine china, and a spring bouquet. We had a view out the corner window.

Taking my time on the topic of being a judge, I tried to sound Anne out, cautioning her. "I know you. You wouldn't like the rigidity and the lack of flexibility. It's hard to get time off the calendar to do things, like the boys' concerts and sports. The lack of control over your time is the most frustrating part of the job for me. And of course, you couldn't do all the extracurricular work you do. You'd be in a social bubble, in a way."

Anne nodded. "You have good time off in the summer. And you have judgment weeks."

The waiter brought the salad, an appetizing mix of greens.

"Yes, like now, which is why I can have a leisurely lunch. Even in the summer, judges get vacation based on seniority. I lobbied to allow judges with school-age children to choose their summer workweeks first. You know how it is. The youngest judges with the least seniority have young children and want to plan their weeks off around the summer activities of the children."

"Makes sense to me."

"And can you believe it? A couple of my women colleagues told me that children are a 'special need' and other judges have their own equally valid special needs." I could hear the frustration in my voice.

"I guess it sounds to them like special treatment for women."

"Well, it is, in effect, but that's because most of the younger judges are women. The crazy thing is, they finally adopted the policy, only to ignore it in practice. So nothing's changed."

The waiter brought the entrées and I asked for English mustard to go with the liver. I was hungry, and glad that Anne liked to eat early too. By noon I was usually ravenous, so having the judges' lunchtime at one o'clock meant trying to resist the muffins during the morning break. Often I'd eat a sandwich at my desk during the break and then go to a nearby gym at lunch hour instead of heading to the Martin Room—the dining room for judges on the top floor of the courthouse.

Anne looked up from her plate. "Maybe I should leave the firm and set up my own practice."

"I don't think you have the strength for that right now. You'd have to do all the business side as well as practise law. It's too much."

"I guess you're right. I'm headed off to Sterling Hall at four—a big showdown about Sandy," said Anne. Sterling Hall was the new small private boys' school our sons attended.

"Good luck."

Anne looked down at her food, trying to eat a little more. She didn't manage much.

When we put our knives and forks on the side of our plates, the waiter promptly removed the plates and offered tea or coffee. We ordered English Breakfast, both declining dessert.

"I know my children are angry," Anne said. "They act on it sometimes. I was in the hospital for months and months, and they weren't allowed to see me. They asked why I even went through such a process. They don't really understand I was trying to stay alive for them, trying to have a better statistical chance. I don't know how to deal with their anger. I feel guilty because my illness has created an unstable atmosphere for them."

Though dismayed at her ongoing hardships, I tried to reassure her. "You're doing your best. You're plugged into good professionals. The boys know you love them."

"To tell the truth, I don't care what happens at the meeting today. Sandy is very smart. I'm not worried about him."

"Good for you. I think you're right." We both had agonized about the decisions we made about schools and getting the best education for our sons. However, Anne was right—they were smart and they would be fine.

After we finished, Anne asked, "Would you help me up? I can barely get up from a chair now."

That was the marvel always: although had Anne told me about her side effects from her treatment, she didn't say, and I wouldn't have guessed, that she could barely stand by herself. Such beauty on the outside and such disease inside.

———

IT WAS THE same at her house. Whenever I visited after the bone marrow transplant, there was disorder and distress. When I dropped in after work one day, Anne seemed upset, and her son Duncan walked away as I entered. The tension between them and the smell of animals hung in the air.

"Come into the living room," said Anne, lifting a small dog from the table. As we walked toward the living room, I saw poop on the kitchen floor.

"This is a new terrier. She's not trained yet."

Duncan came in, walking importantly toward his mother as we were seated on the sofa. "Mom, Sandy's not sick. He's faking it to get out of choir practice."

"Duncan, he's feverish and has stomach cramps," said Anne, clearly exasperated. "Now please go upstairs and get ready for practice." Abashed, Duncan left, presumably to comply with his mother's request.

"You seem upset," I said.

"Doug and I are not speaking," Anne said slowly. Petting her dog absently, she told me that they had taken their sons and three of Doug's stepchildren to the SkyDome stadium to celebrate Sandy's birthday. "The boys wanted to see the giant truck show."

"Sounds dreadful. You couldn't drag me there." If my boys wanted to attend such an event, I'd make Alex take them.

"It was crowded, and Doug parked far away. It took me forever to walk to the stadium even with my cane. After the game, I told him I'd take a taxi home because it was too far to walk to the car." As always, Anne described these calamities in a soft, modulated voice. "Duncan, bless his heart, said he'd stay with me. It was a cold, rainy Saturday night. It took us two and a half hours to get home."

"Oh, Anne, that's unbelievably cruel."

"Yes, and Doug is angry because I 'deserted' the family. And now we're not talking. So no decisions are being made about schools, the summer, or anything else."

"Anne, you don't have to live like this," I said, shocked by Doug's behaviour.

"What can I do? I can't do it by myself, I'm not strong enough."

I realized no matter how cruel Doug could sometimes be to her, on the whole she needed him. Even with domestic help, she simply couldn't manage alone.

A MONTH LATER, I called Anne from my chambers because the evening before she'd looked ill at an art show where three of her watercolours had been on display. She said she felt terrible and asked me to come over, but I couldn't leave because I had a jury deliberating. I promised to come as soon as they reached a verdict, hoping deliberations would be swift.

When I arrived late in the afternoon, Anne was lying in bed, thoroughly distressed and surrounded by papers strewn over the chintz bedspread. Willie the boxer was noisily chewing a large bone on the floor. One terrier was sprawling on the bed, and a creature I assumed to be the Siamese cat was burrowed under the covers, clawing at the headboard.

"What are you doing?" I asked.

"I've been organizing a fundraising baseball game at the Sky-Dome for Sterling Hall School."

"Why on earth would you take that on?" *And how can you possibly work in such chaos?* I wondered.

Anne looked at my frowning face. "I agreed because the proceeds are going to Wellspring. I planned to work on it over the weekend, but then I had to go to the cottage." As always, it was difficult to find fault with Anne's motivations.

I refrained from saying, *So what? It's too much.* "But Anne, why did you have to go?"

Anne started putting the papers in piles on the bed.

"Here, let me take these," I said, stacking them on the bureau.

"I had to go as a symbol. Doug's son and his family were here from Australia. Doug told me I was a princess, and if I didn't go it would alienate his family."

"I don't know how you can function this way," I said, sitting on the edge of the bed.

"I'm hanging in for two days. Then, Doug's going away for six days. I've rented a place in Cape Cod for the last two weeks in June to be with the boys."

"Have you talked to Doug about what you said to me, about leaving him?"

"No, I'm not strong enough to separate now. I will in the fall. If he doesn't leave, it will kill me."

I sighed, not convinced she would ever get to that point. "Turn around and lie on the end of the bed. I'll give you a facial." I moved some remaining papers to the side and helped her turn around and lie on a pillow. I took off my suit jacket and rolled up the sleeves of my silk blouse, then went to Anne's bathroom. I assembled her cleanser and lotions and brought a towel to put under her head and a warm, moist facecloth. As I returned, the boxer scampered off the bed and went out. Pleased, I sent the cat out too and closed the door.

Putting the steaming cloth on her face, I said, "Slowly breathe the moist air." There was no hurry. I removed the facecloth and cleansed her face and neck. After I put on the face mask, I massaged her hands and arms with lotion while the silky paste nourished her skin.

"It's exquisite," Anne murmured.

"Wait till I give you a body facial. Now, that's exquisite." At the Skin Care Centre, it was two hours of sheer bliss, lying on the heated massage table, looking out the window at the blue sky while Olga replenished every inch of my skin. I wondered if Anne would ever allow such intimacy, but it seemed natural to share my pleasures with her. I gently rubbed her scalp and touched the pressure points around her head. I put warm water in a bowl and removed the mask, cleaning her face with the warm facecloth. Her eyes stayed closed and her lips rested upward in a slight smile.

When her skin was clean, I smoothed on moisturizer with a few drops of lubricating oil over and over into her skin, making each touch last as long as possible. The afternoon light of spring cast a warm glow through the bay windows. Anne's skin was soft, fragile, unblemished. The feather touch of my hands and fleshy pillows of my fingertips absorbed her tension and channelled my stillness and love.

———

SIX MONTHS LATER, Anne was back in the hospital with a punctured eardrum after having got the flu. I visited after work. As soon as I entered her room, the phone rang. Someone was asking Anne for extra tickets to the Brazilian Ball. Throughout my visit, the phone didn't stop. She talked to the dog breeder about a new dog, as one of her little terriers had died. She talked to lawyers about her aunt's estate.

When she hung up from that phone call, she asked me, "What should I do about my aunt's estate? This situation has arisen." Anne went on to ask questions about the huge estate as if I were instantly privy to all of the circumstances.

"Anne," I interrupted, "I'm sorry, but I really don't know enough about all of your relatives to be helpful." It was how Anne was: if she was in the middle of something, she included whoever was around.

The phone sounded again and she looked at me apologetically. "I'm sorry to be on the phone so much."

"That's okay, I know how it is. Your hospital room is now your office."

"I can't be here doing nothing. If I have to be here, I have to do something if I'm able to do anything at all." She picked up the phone, and after that I didn't stay long. Anne was preoccupied, and I didn't want to be a witness to all the demands being made upon her. It made me uncomfortable that so much seemed to be expected when she was suffering, and I had to remind myself that it was Anne's choice: she liked to be engaged, even overly engaged.

———

THREE WEEKS LATER, Anne was still in the hospital. Because she was going deaf in one ear, she had a lumbar puncture and had to lie flat for twenty-four hours. When I arrived, she was lying quietly on her back and smiled cheerfully at the ceiling, moving only her eyes in my direction as she addressed me.

I said, "You seem in good spirits."

"Yes, I was so afraid of the puncture that I was awake last night until four a.m. The last time they did it, it was done badly. They were careful this time and used the X-rays."

"I don't know how you stand it," I said, shaking my head.

Anne smiled even wider. "Today's my birthday."

"Many happy returns," I said, kissing her on the cheek. "So that makes you ... "

"Yes, forty-five. And the good news is that I have no cancer. Only three cells of the meningitis remain."

"How encouraging!" I said, though it didn't exactly seem like good news to me. "Is Doug coming later to celebrate your birthday?"

"No—he left for Europe yesterday, so we celebrated my birthday on Saturday. I was allowed to go home last weekend. I was so happy to be there."

"How was the weekend?"

"Doug was much nicer to me. He washed my hair. He gave me a beautiful cashmere coat. I so wish he hadn't left."

It was hard for me to believe this was the same woman who had been ready to leave him months before. It struck me again that we never know the reality of another's marriage.

"I'm glad he was good to you," I said.

Anne reached an arm behind her for the water glass, and I said, "Here, let me help." I held the glass, but it was impossible to drink from her supine position.

"Don't you have any straws that bend?"

"I don't know why I don't have one. And the last night at home, my hot water bottle broke."

"Aren't you using the electric blanket?"

"I am, and it's wonderful. I don't know why we never had one before. I had the hot water bottle for my head. I woke up when it broke and the bed was soaking. So I went to Sandy's room. Marie, I wasn't able to walk. I literally crawled to Sandy's bed."

"Anne, I simply can't imagine it." That was a lie: I imagined it exactly. Her bed was to the left of the bedroom door. I could see her crawl on the carpet to the doorway, past the circular stairway leading to the first floor, and across the open hall to Sandy's room. It was pitiful and horrifying.

"Sandy's gerbil was using the treadmill," she said, "and the noise kept me awake. So I crawled back to my room and wrapped myself in towels."

"Anne, it's too hideous."

Shaken, unable to lose the image of my friend crawling across the floor, all I could do was drive to the store to buy flexible straws.

———

THE PREVIOUS SUMMER I had invited Anne to visit my in-laws' cottage on her way to her own. My cousin and two friends were visiting for our annual golf and bridge week, my favourite week of the year. I wanted my cousin Doris, who lived in the U.S., to meet Anne, and I wanted to spoil Anne, to give her a complete respite from the demands of her life. I was delighted that she'd agreed to sleep over for one night of her journey.

Anne arrived in the late afternoon, ready for a swim after the hot, muggy day in the city. The cottage sits atop a high bank leading down to the sandy shores of Lake Simcoe, a large, shallow lake one hour north of Toronto. Anne held the railing as she made her way down the steep stairs to the beach. Fearful she might trip on the wooden steps, I followed close behind as she made her arduous way to the shore.

When she reached the beach, there was a row of stones to cross before getting to the sandy bottom again. I reached out to her, saying, "Take my hand."

I guided her as she walked unsteadily over the rocks and then swam in the warm, waveless water. There was no wind, and the air was lush. I kept her in sight as she swam easily in the shallow water.

Later, the three of us had cocktails on the deck and ate grilled salmon and salad at the white dining-room table with views of the lake waters sparkling between the cedars. Bright red geraniums adorned the window boxes on the decks. I could see Anne taking in the quiet beauty, looking totally relaxed.

"The watercolours on the walls are exquisite," she said.

"Yes—they're painted by my mother-in-law. She's eighty-one and graduated from the Ontario College of Art almost sixty years ago, after defying her father to go there."

"She reminds me of my Aunt Jim. She was a famous Olympic figure skater."

"Anne's become quite a watercolourist," I boasted to Doris.

Anne smiled. "I enjoy it. I began after I was diagnosed, as a form of therapy. I wish I had more time for it."

We continued chatting as the dishes were cleared for dessert.

"We're so glad you're here," Doris said. "Now, do you play bridge?"

"Yes," said Anne. "I had to play a rubber of bridge every evening after dinner with my parents."

"Great. If you're up to it, we can play a little bridge after dessert," I said. I could hear someone whipping cream in the kitchen. "Doris and I are fanatics. One time, Doris stood on a table at the Brunswick Tavern after singing on amateur night and said, 'Sixteenth for bridge.' In no time, sixteen of us proceeded to my little apartment—remember the 'monette,' Doris?—and we kept the game going for two weeks."

"Marie and I taught six people to play bridge just to keep the game going," Doris added.

"We even taught my Newfoundland cousin. God, remember when he wouldn't bid for the longest time? We said, 'Michael, what is it? You know, you can open if you have thirteen points.' He continued to stare at his hand, finally saying, 'Did you ever notice the hair on the Jack of Diamonds?'"

After the strawberry shortcake, we sat on the lakeside deck. Through the clearing in the cedars, we watched a scarlet sun slip slowly into the water.

Later, after we'd played a little bridge, I took Anne upstairs to the main bedroom. "I hope you don't mind sharing a room with me. We have a full house."

Anne looked into the large bedroom with windows facing the lake and high windows above the two double beds with fluffy white duvets. The old bureaus and vanities were painted white, and there was minimalist art on the walls. "It looks lovely," Anne said, opening her bag.

I showed Anne where to put her things and pointed out the bathroom. "I have a treat for you. I've brought everything to give you a body facial. You'll be asleep in no time." As she undressed, I put my jars on the nightstand. I wanted to do something special for Anne alone—not just something to make her everyday life easier, like bringing a casserole or having the boys over, but something personal for her. I'd been waiting for this opportunity and had brought a lightly scented oil and lotion. I pulled back the bedding and put a large, soft towel on the sheet.

As Anne removed her dressing gown, I said, "Face down first." She lay down, turned her head to the side and closed her eyes as I covered her with another bath towel. I was careful to keep her buttocks covered while I cleansed and moisturized her back. My aesthetician had no such concern for modesty and included my derrière in the body facial. Though I would have liked to do the same to Anne, I didn't want her to feel uncomfortable.

When it was time for her to turn over, I kept her hidden under the towel.

As she lay quietly breathing, I applied the cream to her face and upper chest, careful to be gentle around her ears, and using both hands to reach behind her neck. I rubbed her arms and held each hand, massaging one finger at a time. I massaged her shoulders where there'd been punctures, and smoothed her arms as if I could take away the hundreds of needles that had jabbed her, and I put sweet oil on her chest where the Hickman line had been. I couldn't help noticing her body, and her breasts looked so beautiful, I wanted to touch them too. Once, I allowed only the soft underbelly of my arm to graze them as I massaged her shoulders. The sensation surprised me—so soft and warm—and I quickly returned my attention to the massage.

I draped a second towel around her shoulders as I rubbed her stomach and hips. She stayed warm under the towels as I massaged her legs, remembering how burnt they'd been, trying to wipe out the pain of the past.

I wanted the pricking, tapping, and sticking to stop. I wanted to run my hands over every part of her and seal it so nothing would ever again invade her. I touched her with a passion I had not felt since my sons were small—that need to hold, nestle, protect. I couldn't love her enough.

My desire for intimacy surprised me. Other than lovers and children, I didn't care to touch anyone. I'd never had the slightest desire to be a nurse or doctor, or do any work that required touching those I didn't know. With Anne, there was no recoil, only affection, no matter what her condition.

I wanted this to be Anne's treat, as it was. In truth, however, it was also my treat—to have Anne with me, in my space, in my room. It probably meant more to me than to her. It was real, immediate, connected. Judging and its aloofness seemed a long way off.

Anne had been long asleep when I eased the towels off the bed and covered her with the comforter. A wind had come up and I hoped she heard the sound of the ocean-like waves of the lake lapping the shore.

The next morning, Anne left early after breakfast. We all stood on the front deck to say goodbye. "We loved having you," I said. After kisses and hugs, I walked across the lawn to put Anne's bag in her car.

"It was a wonderful break," said Anne, and she did look refreshed. "Is there a place I can pick up some raspberries on my way?"

"Yes, there's a nearby vegetable market. Wait a sec and I'll get my keys and you can follow me. That way you won't get lost."

I led the way to the market, got out with her, and made sure she was on the right road again. I watched her head down the rural highway, hating to see her go: I wanted to spoil her forever. I all too well imagined the hectic cottage life awaiting Anne—dealing with demanding children and animals, supervising meals, organizing activities, entertaining guests. Would she be happy?

Gertrude Stein rightly observed in *The Making of Americans*, "It is hard to know of any one whether they are enjoying anything, whether they are feeling something... It is a very difficult thing to know the being in any one." Yes, and it was becoming hard to know the being in myself.

Week One
Wednesday

LUNCH

Peanut butter & banana on white bread—cut
in half—cut off crusts

Bottle of fruit punch

Small container of 2% cottage cheese with
lettuce at bottom

Bag of popcorn

Chapter 8

JANUARY 23

THE CASE ON my docket that Monday morning was *Regina v. Marsh*, in which Dean Marsh was charged with two counts of sexual assault. My deputy knocked on my door shortly before ten and entered my chambers with a neat step.

"Good morning," I said. "Is the case proceeding with a jury?"

"So far as I know, Your Honour."

After he led me solemnly into the courtroom, everyone rose and then sat again, and as usual I bade everyone a general good morning.

"Good morning, Your Honour," counsel and staff replied.

"I understand this will be a jury trial."

"Yes, Your Honour."

"Are there any issues on which counsel require pre-trial rulings or assistance before the jury panel is brought in?" Advance rulings are made so that the jury is not kept waiting during the trial while lawyers argue whether certain evidence is admissible or not. The U.S. "sidebar" where lawyers approach the judge in court but out of earshot of the jurors is unknown in Canada, where jurors leave during such arguments.

"No, Your Honour. As you can see, my client, Mr. Marsh, is a person of colour and will be challenging the jury 'for cause' on the grounds of race." Defence counsel, Adrian Smith, spoke with a slight Dutch accent.

The accused sitting in the prisoner's box appeared to be a person of mixed racial ancestry. His "challenge for cause" meant that prospective members of the jury would be asked if they could set aside any prejudice they might have on account of the accused's colour and decide the case on the evidence.

"How long do counsel anticipate the trial will last?" I asked.

"About five days, Your Honour," Crown counsel replied. Defence counsel nodded in agreement.

The crime of sexual assault ranges from an unwanted touch to rape; their estimate of five days pointed to the more serious offence.

"Please bring in the jury panel," I instructed my deputy, who left the courtroom to assemble the panel. Members of the public who report for jury duty become part of a panel that is herded from court to court as needed over a one-week period. Some may never be selected to sit on a jury. Although jury duty is an inconvenience, many who have served on juries tell me they find the experience rewarding and enlightening.

The participation by members of the community in the criminal justice system is vital. Without juries, all aspects of the adjudication of guilt would rest entirely with lawyers and judges, and only the legally trained would determine that another should be deprived of liberty. Criminal justice requires the broader interface.

About seventy-five people from the panel entered the court-room from the rear and sat in the pew-like benches behind the prisoner's box, where the accused was. Care is taken so that jurors do not see an accused being escorted to or from the court-room in handcuffs or leg irons. Handcuffs are usually removed, but security concerns may result in some accused persons remaining in leg irons that are not visible while the accused is in the box.

Jurors' awareness of the fact that an accused is in custody is considered prejudicial to the presumption of innocence, although in high-profile cases, the fact that a person is in custody may be widely known. Judges, on the other hand, know in all cases whether an accused is or is not in custody pending trial.

Most persons charged with offences are not in custody pend-ing trial and simply step into the prisoner's box as the trial is about to begin. However, those who have been determined to be at risk of not appearing for their trial or of committing further crimes are kept in custody pending trial. Marsh was not in cus-tody. "Madame Registrar, please arraign the accused."

"Dean Marsh. Please rise," began the Registrar.

A slender, dark-haired man of medium height rose from his seat in the box.

"You are charged," continued the Registrar, "that you, on or about the month of February in the year 1994 at the Munici-pality of Metropolitan Toronto, unlawfully did commit a sexual assault on David Byrne contrary to the Criminal Code. How do you plead: guilty or not guilty?"

"Not guilty."

"Dean Marsh, you are further charged that you, on or about the months of April and May in the year 1994 at the Municipality of Metropolitan Toronto, unlawfully did commit a sexual assault on David Byrne contrary to the Criminal Code. How do you plead: guilty or not guilty?"

"Not guilty."

"Good morning, members of the jury panel," I began, slowly and emphatically. "We are about to start a criminal trial. You have heard the clerk of the court read the charges against Dean Marsh, and you have heard him say he is not guilty. We will now select a jury who will determine if Dean Marsh is guilty or not guilty.

"It is essential that every juror be a Canadian citizen, be able to hear the evidence, and be able to understand the English language. If any of you have any difficulties with this, please come forward."

I waited a moment before continuing but no one moved.

"It is also essential that every accused person have a fair and unbiased trial. I am Judge Corbett; Crown counsel is Jane Carr; defence counsel is Adrian Smith; the accused is Dean Marsh; and the complainant is David Byrne. Ms. Carr will now read the names of the prospective witnesses."

I turned to the Crown, a slender woman in her early thirties with an earnest expression, who read seven names, slowly and distinctly.

"If any one of you is related to or connected to any of the parties in this case," I continued, "whether the accused or the complainant or the prospective witnesses or counsel, or if there is anyone who has personal knowledge of the facts in this case, please come forward."

As expected in a large city such as Toronto, no one came forward.

"I am advised by counsel that this trial is expected to take about five days. If any one of you has any particular difficulties or personal hardships as a result of the anticipated duration of the trial, please indicate that to me when your name is called.

"The clerk will now proceed to draw twenty names at random. When your name is called, please come forward.

"Members of the jury panel, each counsel may challenge ten prospective jurors without giving any reason. These are called 'peremptory' challenges. If you are challenged, do not take it as a personal affront. The Criminal Code provides for this procedure, and counsel are doing their job in the best interest of their respective clients.

"In this case there will be another kind of challenge, called a 'challenge for cause.' The accused, Dean Marsh, is a person of colour." I looked at the accused again. There was some colour, though not much. "We are all aware that we may have some ingrained prejudice or bias against people of colour that might affect our ability to decide the case based on the evidence. It is essential that a juror act without bias and decide the verdict only on the evidence at trial. Therefore, defence counsel Mr. Smith will ask each of you whether you are able to decide the case on the evidence without being prejudiced by the fact that the person charged is a person of colour.

"The first two of you whose names are called will listen to the answer given by the third person and decide if that person is acceptable as a juror. If acceptable, this person and the next acceptable person become jurors and take their turn deciding if the next person called is acceptable as a juror. The procedure sounds complicated, but you will soon understand the process."

I scanned the uncomprehending faces. The theoretical under-pinning of this unusual procedure is that whether a person is biased is a question of fact, and questions of fact, as opposed to questions of law, are for the jury to decide. Therefore, the poten-tial jurors could determine each other's bias or the lack of it.

The Registrar reached into the drum containing the name cards of the panel members and removed two, then called two persons to the front of the court. They were sworn by the Regis-trar and took seats in the jury box. A third name was called, and a tall woman nervously came forward, was directed to the wit-ness stand, and was sworn.

Defence counsel then asked her, "Would your ability to judge the evidence in this case without bias, prejudice, or partiality be affected by the fact that the person charged is a person of colour?"

"No, it wouldn't," she replied.

The question invites a "yes" or "no" answer, and the over-whelming majority of people answer "no." In Canada, counsel have limited rights to question potential jurors. Juries selected after a challenge for cause tend to be a particularly cohesive group, as each of them has been determined by the others to be unbiased.

The Registrar asked the two 'triers' in the jury box if the pro-spective juror was acceptable or not acceptable. They responded affirmatively based on their conclusion about the spoken avowal. The Registrar then continued to ascertain if either the Crown or the defence wished to use one of their peremptory challenges.

"Juror, look upon the accused; accused look upon the juror," the Registrar stated, turning to counsel, each of whom said, "Content."

As the juror was acceptable to the triers and to both counsel, she was then sworn as a juror. "Do you swear that you shall well and truly try, and true deliverance make, between our sovereign lady the Queen and the accused at the bar, whom you shall have in charge, and a true verdict give, according to the evidence, so help you God?" I listened, yet again, to the archaic formal language, concluding, yet again, that modernizing the language in the interest of comprehension could be achieved without diminishing the power of the oath.

"I do."

"Please be seated in the juror's box, seat number one. You are now juror number one." Juror number one took the place of one of the two persons in the jury box, and the slow process continued until twelve jurors were sworn who were acceptable to the other sworn jurors and to both counsel.

Peremptory challenges, when they are used, are made on extremely limited information, namely, the appearance of the prospective juror and his or her stated occupation. Crown counsel prefer those who appear more likely to uphold law and order. Defence counsel prefer those who appear more likely to uphold individual freedoms—that is, the defence favours a little scruffiness.

My mother, who would love to be a member of a jury, is dismayed that she has never been picked. I tell her, "It's simple, Mother. You look too respectable and well heeled. The defence will challenge you every time, even if you don't wear all your rings."

In this case, the Crown challenged an educator (prosecuting counsel generally challenge teachers), a child education worker, two students, an engineer, a letter carrier, a clerk, and a technician. The defence challenged two nurses, a health care aid, a homemaker, two clerks, a technologist, an office manager, and a compensation programmer.

The five men and seven women eventually selected as jurors were a customer service representative, two homemakers, a restaurant owner, a bookkeeper, a design engineer, an unemployed man, a pilot, a benefit specialist, a lounge singer, a collection clerk, and an administrator. The jury, like most juries in Toronto, was ethnically diverse.

After the twelve jurors were selected, the Registrar instructed the remaining members of the jury panel to leave with the constable. The Registrar repeated the charges, and Dean Marsh again pleaded not guilty.

"Members of the jury," continued the Registrar. "Look upon the accused and harken to his charge. For his trial he hath put himself upon his country, which country you are. Your charge therefore is to enquire whether he be guilty or not guilty and harken to the evidence."

This outmoded, effete language always embarrassed me. Much of it, like "oyez, oyez, oyez," is incomprehensible. What institutional insecurity resists using words the public can understand? When my colleague Justice Donna Haley changed "oyez" to "Please give your attention" and updated and clarified the phrases like "whose country you are," the Chief Justice compelled her to stop and directed her to use the traditional language.

After twelve jurors were selected, I addressed them. "Members of the jury, you have been sworn in as jurors and you are now the judges of the facts in this case and the judges of whether Dean Marsh is guilty or not guilty. You are judges for twenty-four hours of the day while the case is proceeding. I mention this for several reasons.

"First, do not let anyone speak to you about this case. If anyone approaches you to talk about the case, tell that person you cannot discuss it. If they persist, report it to me and I will take appropriate action. The law provides severe penalties for interfering with a jury.

"Second, do not seek any evidence or information yourself outside the courtroom. You are judges, not investigators.

"I also ask you not to discuss the case with others during the trial, and I recommend that you not discuss the case with the other jurors during the trial." While jurors might refrain from discussing the evidence with each other, I was never convinced that jurors would not discuss the case with others outside the court, such as family members. Still, I hoped my exhortation had some inhibiting value. "It is only when you have heard all of the evidence, the addresses of counsel, and my instructions to you on the law that you will have the necessary perspective to consider your verdict. If you have expressed an opinion during the trial, it may be difficult to change your position once you have stated it. Keep an open mind until you have the whole picture.

"I will outline for you the procedure the course of the trial will take. When I have finished these opening remarks, Crown counsel may make an opening statement to you. What she says in her statement is not evidence: it is an outline of what she hopes to show. Crown counsel will then call her witnesses and ask each witness questions in what we call 'examination in chief.'

"When the Crown has finished questioning the witness, defence counsel may cross-examine the witness. The purpose of cross-examination is to assist the memory of the witness by suggesting more facts that the witness may have forgotten, to bring out evidence favourable to the defence, and to test the credibility or truthfulness of the witness. When defence counsel has completed cross-examination, Crown counsel has a limited right to ask further questions in re-examination.

"When all of the witnesses have been called by the Crown, the defence may make an opening statement and may call evidence. Defence counsel may choose not to call evidence. If he does, the process I have described is continued with the defence witnesses." I tried to speak slowly and clearly, aware that little of this was clear. I also knew it would become clear when the evidence began.

"When the evidence is concluded, each counsel will address you, making submissions on what conclusion you should come to on the evidence. This will be followed by my charge to you, in which I will give you instructions on the law that applies to the facts as you find them. When I have completed my charge to you, you will retire to consider your verdict. At that time, you will not be free to disperse until you have concluded your deliberations.

"Please pay close attention when witnesses are testifying, and have regard to their demeanour. If you have any difficulties hearing a witness, or any other problems, please let me know.

"The court will commence each day at ten o'clock. There will be a morning break about eleven-thirty. The luncheon recess is from one o'clock to two-thirty. I usually do not take an afternoon break, as I like to adjourn for the day promptly at four-thirty, if possible.

"Finally, I warn you that it is a criminal offence to disclose any information relating to your deliberations in the jury room. That does not mean you cannot discuss any problem you may have with me. Apart from that, any information as to how you voted must never be disclosed.

"We will now listen to the evidence.

"Do counsel wish an order excluding witnesses?"

"Yes, Your Honour."

The Registrar read the order, and those who would be witnesses left the courtroom. This way, witnesses would not hear what the other witnesses said.

"Ms. Carr, are you ready to make an opening statement?" The Crown attorney rose and stood in front of the podium on which her binder sat. She was a big woman, one strand of her bounteous hair curling next to her cheek. She spoke earnestly with an air of conviction. "Thank you, Your Honour. Members of the jury, the first witness will be David Byrne, the victim and the most important witness. He befriended the accused and his stepson. While visiting, when he was twelve, the accused, Dean, would grab David and suck his earlobe. David pushed him away.

"Once in April or May of 1994 at a get-together, where alcohol was consumed, Dean lay behind David on the couch and fondled his crotch over his underwear and asked him if he would like to have sex. David said no, and after a few minutes, Dean left. When confronted by David in the morning, Dean said he did not remember because he was drunk. Others will tell you about this party. Your Honour, I call David Byrne to the stand."

This was the first time I heard the allegations. Was I to endure a five-day jury trial on charges of sucking an earlobe and fondling over underwear?

A tall, plump teenager wearing a pale pink shirt ambled toward the front of the courtroom, entered the witness box, and was sworn. He turned to face the body of the court. His blond hair was sheared at the sides, giving him a slightly more adult appearance. He testified that he was fourteen, in grade nine, and lived with his mother, her boyfriend, and her uncle. He met the accused when he befriended Stephen White and went to his house. The accused was often at Stephen's house, as he was Stephen's mother's boyfriend and lived at the house. The Crown asked David to tell the court what the accused, Dean, had done in relation to the charges before the court.

"About two months after I met him, he'd pull me over and start sucking in my ear."

"Did he say anything at those times?"

"No."

"What did you do?"

"I tried to get away." He grimaced. "Like it was disgusting."

"Did this happen again?"

"It happened about three times."

"Were others there?"

"They were there but not around. It happened between the kitchen and the rest of house. The others were in the living room or out back."

"What else happened?"

"Once I was spending the night. We all went to bed and I went to sleep in the living room on the couch. I took off my shirt and this guy, Ron, who was on the other couch getting ready to go to sleep, made a comment."

"What was the comment?"

"He said, 'Is that all it takes for you to take off your clothes, just a couple of drinks?'"

"What happened next?"

"Dean came in behind me and I moved to the end of the couch. Ten minutes later, he asked if I wanted to have sex."

Maybe we'd learn later what went on in *that* ten minutes, I thought.

"I said no," the boy continued, his tone straightforward. "He was touching me when he was asking me."

"Where was he touching?"

"He was touching my genitals and my bum."

"What was he touching you with?"

"His hand."

"What were you wearing?"

"My underwear."

"Was he touching you under your underwear?"

"No, over my underwear."

"How long did it last?"

"About two seconds."

"What did you do?"

"I moved away. Ten minutes later he got up and moved away."

Another ten minutes?

"Where was Ron?"

"He was asleep."

"Were you drinking?"

"Dean got a mickey of Southern Comfort for me. I had one and a half drinks."

"Did you ever go back to the house?"

"No."

"No further questions, Your Honour."

"Cross-examination, Mr. Smith."

Defence counsel rose and walked to the other side of the courtroom to approach the witness. Sliding my eyes to my watch, I noticed that it was almost time to adjourn.

"Was Dean drunk?" he demanded.

"Yes."

"When this happened on the couch, did you scream?"

"No."

"Did you yell?"

"No."

"Did you jump off?"

"No."

"Did you leave the house?"

"No."

"Did you call your mother?"

"No."

"You did none of those things?"

"I said 'no' four times, and that was the end of it."

It was almost laughable, as if the most egregious acts had occurred and the teen should have been yelling and running home to mother.

"You were called a queer after that, weren't you?" Ms. Carr jumped up and before she could say "objection," the witness had replied, "Yes."

He was a squishy-looking teenager. I felt sorry for the softish boys that were teased and bullied as queers, sissies. Girls who didn't fit the mould had it a little easier, as they could be known as tomboys.

"That disturbed you?"

Ms. Carr rose again. "Your Honour, what is the relevance of this line of questioning?" Mr. Smith for the defence relished expounding that it went to the question of motive. I quickly ruled he could proceed.

"Yes."

"You were concerned about loose talk?"

"Yes."

"You told your mother after that you were mocked by your peers?"

"Yes, I wanted him away from me because of what he did."

"You made no complaints until the rumours started?"

"I was called names two days after, and I complained to my mother about the name-calling about a week later. I told her Dean was the source of the rumour."

"And you went to the police three weeks after that?"

"Yes."

"You made no complaint to anyone after the earlobe incident?"

"No."

I looked at the jury. Blank looks everywhere—the earlobe incident?

"And you went back to the house after that?"

"Yes."

I interrupted the cross-examination. "It is now four-thirty, Mr. Smith, and the court will adjourn for the day." I was happy to rise for the day, as Adrian Smith was well known for his tedious questioning. The jurors appeared to share my relief.

I turned to the witness.

"Mr. Byrne, your cross-examination is not concluded. I am instructing you not to discuss the evidence or this case with any-one, including Crown counsel, during the break. Is that clear?"

"Yes, Your Honour," he replied.

"This court stands adjourned until tomorrow morning at ten," I said and watched the constable lead the members of the jury out through the rear exit of the courtroom, behind the witness box. After the members of the jury had left, I rose and my deputy preceded me through the other exit.

———

BY THE TIME I'd changed and gone to the basement parking garage to get my car, I had successfully relegated the court case to a secure portion of my mind. Turning my thoughts and attention to my friend, I drove to Wellesley and Church streets to pick up the milkshake Anne had requested, then drove the short distance to the hospital.

When I entered Anne's room, she was smiling, obviously in a bright mood. Her son Duncan was sitting beside her on the bed.

"Hi, Marie. We're having such fun! Duncan came home from boarding school, and I'm so happy to see him."

"Wonderful!" I said, and meant it. Tired as I was, I offered to let them visit alone and come back later.

"You don't have to go," Anne said. "Duncan is being picked up soon for dinner."

I gave Anne the milkshake and tidied up a little, letting her enjoy her visit with Duncan. After Duncan left, I helped her freshen her face. She looked in a mirror and dabbed on a little lipstick. "My brother offered to take the boys," she said.

"I'm glad," I said. "I know you don't get along with him, but you must feel better that he offered."

"I talked to Duncan about my brother's offer. He said it was okay with him." She set the mirror down and looked directly at me, seeming lighter that she'd been in days, though I couldn't tell if it was her son's visit or her brother's offer. Maybe both.

As I was thinking this over, another friend arrived, and our chance to pursue the subject further was lost. I told Anne I'd see her tomorrow, and as I walked down the wide green hall, I found it macabre to be talking about who would raise Anne's children when she was no longer there. We were talking as casually as if we were discussing what she wanted for dinner, veal piccata or sole florentine.

Everything I knew had turned inside out or upside down. *Pixilated*, I thought again. The power and majesty and authority of the criminal justice system—a jury trial in a superior court, with challenge for cause—was dealing with earlobes and underwear, and my friend and I were casually discussing what would happen when she died. How had all this become normal? I went out the hospital door and looked at the dark, shifting clouds, wondering if a storm was on the way. My sense of who I was and what mattered was shifting, as unsettled as the evening sky.

DINNER

Tossed green salad with dressing—save
some but don't put dressing on that part

Put-back mashed potatoes (*Kids' Cooking*,
p. 53)—suggested toppings: shredded
cheddar or coleslaw (buy creamy coleslaw)
or crumbled fried bacon

Hidden hot dogs (*Kids' Cooking*, p. 18)

Milk

Lemon rice pudding

Chapter 9

JANUARY 24

AS ALWAYS, shortly after I'd donned my gown, my deputy knocked on the door of my chambers and entered. "Good morning. Is everybody ready?" I asked.

"Yes, Your Honour. One of the jurors was a little late, but we're ready now."

I followed the deputy into the courtroom, dreading the prospect of the continuing cross-examination. I knew it would be tedious. Every statement this teenager had ever made to anyone in authority would be brought out, no matter how miniscule.

David entered the witness box, the Registrar reminded him he was still under oath, and defence counsel rose, ready to pounce. He was holding the transcript of David Byrne's testimony at the preliminary inquiry. And so it began. "You told the court yesterday that you first met my client in February 1993. Is that correct?"

"Yes."

"You recall giving evidence at the preliminary inquiry on September twenty-ninth, 1994?"

"Yes."

"I'm reading from that transcript where you testified you met my client Mr. Marsh at your friend Stephen's house in January, February, and March?"

"Yes, I did."

"And you were at the house about ten to fifteen times in January?"

"No, not that much."

"I'm referring to your evidence at the preliminary inquiry at page 45, where you said you were at the house about ten to fifteen times. Was that answer true?"

"Yes."

Ms. Carr for the Crown could no longer contain herself and rose to object to the relevance of how many times it had been. I didn't need to hear from the defence, quickly ruling that while it may not prove to be relevant, it went to the issue of credibility. Ms. Carr sighed, her shoulders slumping.

"And in February, you were there every day?"

"No, about five to ten times, not every day."

"I'm referring to page 45, again, where you testified you were there all the time in February. So that would make it almost thirty times. Were you lying when you said that under oath?"

"No."

"Now, you arrived at the party at five o'clock?"

"Yes."

"So you wanted to arrive for dinner?"

"I'd already eaten. It's not often I'm getting a second supper."

I was becoming peevish. "Counsel, what does it matter if he wanted to arrive for dinner? Please move along."

"Your Honour, with respect, the witness's familiarity with my client and his household is relevant," replied defence counsel.

I resisted the temptation of saying that while the witness's familiarity with his client is relevant, whether he wanted to arrive for dinner was hardly material. But the presence of a jury tends to encourage better behaviour on the part of judges and counsel alike. Resigned, I said, "Proceed, Mr. Smith."

"Now, Mr. Byrne," continued defence counsel, "you brought hashish to the party, didn't you?"

Ms. Carr was on her feet again. I raised my left hand to encourage her to reseat herself, and she did.

"Yes, but I didn't want it and I offered it around."

"My client, Dean, told you not to bring drugs to the house."

"Yeah, but there was already dope in the house."

"And you drank two to three inches of Southern Comfort?"

"No, not that much."

"I'm referring to your testimony at the preliminary inquiry at page 18, where you were asked if you drank two to three inches of Southern Comfort and you replied, 'Something like that.' Was that answer true?"

"It was one to two inches. I gave most of it away."

"You told the court that Dean tried to touch your genitals?"

"Yes." He paused and stared at defence counsel. "He tried to touch my genitals and then moved to my bum."

"At the preliminary inquiry you testified he touched your bum when trying to touch your genitals?"

"Yes. I sat up after he touched me."

"You didn't tell the police you sat up. You told the court the incident occurred between midnight and three a.m.; you told the police officer it was between one and three a.m. Which is the truth?" The jury looked as disgusted as I felt. What earthly differ-ence did it make?

"I can't remember."

"You testified that you never went back to the house?"

"That's right."

"I refer you to your testimony at the preliminary inquiry at page 22, where you said you walked your friend, Stephen, to the house and went in for two minutes and left."

"Basically, I'd go to the door."

The questioning droned on at the same maddening pace for most of the day as the defence asked in detail about the descrip-tion of the house, what each person at the party had to drink, and each person's state of intoxication. Any tiny discrepancy between David's testimony in court and his earlier statements to the police and each line of the transcript of his prior testimony at the pre-liminary inquiry was brought out. The minutiae were deadening. My own fatigue was reflected in the demeanour of the jury: mem-bers were fidgeting, sighing silently, rolling their eyes.

However much I sympathized with their boredom or frustra-tion, there was nothing I could do. Whether the statements made by the witness are directly relevant or not, counsel has the right to elicit any inconsistencies in cross-examination. Counsel's aim is to show that because there are so many discrepancies, the wit-ness is not credible. Even if these discrepancies are insignificant, it is hoped the jury will think that the sheer number of them impairs the witness's credibility. However, I'd observed that such nitpicking often leaves the jury more sympathetic to the witness. The Supreme Court of Canada described cross-examination as the "ultimate means of demonstrating truth." I wasn't convinced.

Admittedly, withstanding verbal attack is a step up from "trial by ordeal," the most ancient form of trial in the Anglo-Saxon tradition. The ordeal by fire required holding hot irons or walking on red-hot plowshares. Ordeal by water required plunging the arm in boiling water to the elbow. Those who were unhurt obtained the "judgment of God," as God was believed to have intervened to rescue the innocent. In effect, the physically weak were considered proven liars.

Like their physically vulnerable predecessors, in modern times the psychologically vulnerable are most at risk of being found liars in the ordeal of cross-examination. The legally sophisticated and the shrewd prepare to avoid inconsistencies. As for ultimate tools in the search for truth, give me physical evidence: fingerprints, blood, or DNA, any day of the week.

Finally, the blessed words: "No further questions, Your Honour." Adrian Smith turned and went back to his counsel table.

"Your Honour, the next Crown witness is Yvon L.," said the prosecutor. A dark-haired young man came forward, with a lilt to his walk. His shirt hugged his chest, and he looked handsome and serious. After he was sworn, Crown counsel began her questioning, drawing out the facts that Yvon was a nineteen-year-old studying gym and religious business. He'd met the complainant about eleven months earlier. He remembered the party, describing it as "in late April. It was late in the month around the time of the welfare cheques." He went with the accused in a taxi to buy liquor: "Forty ounces of rye, a case of beer, champagne, Irish cream, and a mickey of Southern Comfort."

"Did you see David drink?"

"He drank Southern Comfort. He shared it, too."

"Was everyone drinking?"

"All except Ashley. She was pregnant."

"What was Dean's condition?"

"He was a bit fizzed."

"Fizzed?"

"Bubbly, intoxicated."

"Did you see signs of intoxication on David?"

"He only drank a little."

"Did you see the accused and David together?"

"They sat beside each other."

"Did you see anything else?"

"David was in the living room. I went to bed at two or three."

"No further questions."

"Cross-examination," I said, turning to Adrian Smith, who rose.

"You said my client was intoxicated. How much did he drink?"

"I don't know, but he's a two-beer drunk."

"What did you have to drink?"

"I had six beers and two or three shots."

"You told the police it was in mid-June?"

"I made a mistake and called the police back. The weather was warm. I thought it was later."

"No further questions, Your Honour." That had been blissfully short, especially for Mr. Smith.

Crown counsel called another person who'd been to the party. Ashley B. walked nervously to the front of the courtroom. She had large fuzzy hair with bangs. She was chewing gum with one finger in the side of her mouth.

"Ashley, would you please remove your gum?" I asked when she stepped into the witness box. Gum-chewing is my biggest pet peeve, in court or out.

The jury constable hastened to provide a tissue so Ashley wouldn't have to keep the gum in her hand or stick it with the rest of the gum under the top of the witness box. Ashley testified she was "just a mom." I groan inwardly every time a woman describes herself as "just a housewife" or "just a secretary." Why do we describe ourselves with the word *just*? "It's just me." I catch myself doing it too. Women can't seem to get past diminishing who we are and what we do. I don't recall ever hearing a man describe himself as "just a mechanic." I try to avoid using the word except as a synonym for *fairness* and for time, to describe events that "just" occurred.

Ashley was a twenty-year-old with a son aged four years and a daughter aged four months. I mentally calculated: she'd had a child at sixteen. Stephen, who had become friends with the complainant, David, was her brother. She told the court who was at the party: "My mother; Dean, the accused; my brother; my common-law husband, Yvon; Marcy and her son." Ah, so the handsome Yvon was her partner.

"Were people drinking?"

"Yes, everyone but me."

"Did you see anyone drunk?"

"Only my brother was really affected. He got sick in the bathroom and bedroom and passed out on the couch."

"Did you see anything unusual?"

"No. I went to bed at one or two and everyone was still up."

"Did you see David drink?"

"He drank Southern Comfort. Dean bought the liquor."

"What did your brother drink?"

"He drank rye and beer—a little of everything."

"No further questions. Your witness."

"Cross-examination, Mr. Smith."

"Thank you, Your Honour."

"Ashley, you told the police it was at the end of March, and now are you telling us it was in April?"

Here we go again. Was Smith indefatigable?

"I thought about it after and realized I was away at the end of March."

"No further questions, Your Honour."

All eyes were on the large courtroom clock as the minute hand reached thirty. I groaned silently with relief. "Members of the jury, it is now four-thirty. Please return tomorrow morning at ten o'clock. This case stands adjourned."

I RETURNED TO my chambers and heaved off my robe, then removed my vest, shirt, tabs, and skirt. Anxious to leave, I changed as fast as I could into my purple suit with the pencil skirt. The prospect of three more days of this picayune trial was defeating me, and I was irked at the waste of time.

I drove up University Avenue to Wellesley, parked at Wellspring, and walked back to Church Street to pick up a milkshake at Yogurty's. When I arrived at Anne's hospital room, her friend Joanna and her daughter were leaving. I looked inside and glimpsed Anne hunched in bed, holding her sides, obviously in severe pain. "Joanna. What's wrong? Anne looks so uncomfortable."

"Yes. She's having a terrible time with her kidneys." Joanna looked disturbed, and I was sure she wanted to get her little girl out of the hospital. She departed, and I went in to see if I could help.

I walked to the bed and kissed Anne on the forehead. "I have a banana milkshake for you."

Anne looked up, smiling slightly with mournful eyes but still holding her sides. "I'll keep it for later. I have no appetite now."

I took off my coat and pulled up the chair next to the bed. There was bright blood in Anne's urine bag. "I have to use the potty," said Anne. "I know it doesn't do anything, but I have such an urge to try."

"Let me help you." I put an arm under her shoulders so she could sit up, and we moved her legs over the bedside. Carefully, we stepped over to the portable toilet, manoeuvring around the protruding tubes and IV stand. She sat for a while, exasperated, very uncomfortable, and forlorn. "I'm sorry to be like this."

"I wish I could do something to help you, Anne." I felt utterly helpless.

"I know nothing will happen, but I feel better."

Keeping my eyes averted to give her a modicum of privacy, I wondered how I would handle such indignities. My tendency would be to hide—to leave the unpleasant exposure to the professionals. Yet I felt no awkwardness witnessing Anne's piteous bodily intimacies, and felt no diminishment of the desire to touch and soothe her. Her grace and beauty remained.

She looked up, her head in her hands, her elbows on her knees. "Duncan was in today."

"I'm glad. How is he?"

"It was so nice. He lay beside me for an hour before going back to school." Duncan's need to be close mirrored her own, and mine too. Anne gave up after a few minutes and we made the torturous journey back to bed, where she repositioned herself. "I couldn't sleep all last night," she said. "Finally, they gave me morphine and I slept in the afternoon."

"Is there anything I can get for you, Anne?"

"I'm so very cold. Will you fill the hot water bottle?"

I filled the hot water bottle and placed it close under her feet, to warm them. I put fresh socks on her and tucked her blankets around her shoulders, but she still seemed tense and chilled.

Sandy arrived, looking dismayed at his mother's apparent discomfort, and then Anne's cousin Cecil arrived and I took my leave, not wanting too many people crowding around her.

Later that evening, Cecil phoned me at home. "I'm so worried about Anne," she said. "She needs extra help at night. Will you call Marte and arrange for private nurses to come in at night? I'd call myself but I have to leave for Montreal in the morning."

"Of course I will." I was glad she'd suggested it. "Anne could really use the extra care, but she's been so worried about the expense."

"I'll make arrangements," she said. "Her aunt's estate will pay for it."

When I called Anne at ten-thirty that night, the phone in her room was turned off and her calls were being routed to a nurse who told me Anne had "settled down."

"Settled down"? I bristled at the expression, which made Anne sound like a difficult child, but I realized that Anne had likely been sedated so that she was comfortable.

I do not accept that pain cannot be managed. Is there an unspoken rule that if you're sick, you have to suffer? Earlier in the year, a friend had died of prostate cancer in a general hospital. His terminal condition was known to everyone—himself, family, friends, and hospital staff—and in his final days, he was in severe pain. When his brother asked for additional pain medication for him, the nurse refused, muttering about the risk of addiction if he didn't wait another two hours.

I hated the thought of Anne being denied relief for her suffering because of one or another institutional constraint. I wished Anne had someone staying by her side to rant and rave for her like Shirley MacLaine in the movie *Terms of Endearment.* I went to bed and dreamed the dreams of the helpless.

Week One
Thursday

BREAKFAST

Vitamin pill

Honey-nut cornflakes with brown
sugar and bananas

Small jug of milk

Orange slices

Toasted crumpets with honey or
raspberry jam

Chapter 10

JANUARY 25

WEDNESDAY, AND ANOTHER early morning. Edward was leaving the house by seven to go skiing with the school team. I made
scrambled eggs with cheese and filled his thermos with sweet,
milky tea. We sat companionably on two of the three bar chairs
at the blue granite island that dominated the kitchen.

We used to be three at breakfast, before Darrell went to
boarding school at fourteen. I loved to pamper my sons in the
morning, and delighted in varying the menu and watching them
come to life as they ate. After they were off to school, I would
indulge myself for ten minutes—read the paper and finish my
coffee before dressing to go to work.

Those minutes of luxurious idleness were not an option
this week. After Edward left, I couldn't relax enough to read the
paper, so I went upstairs to dress. I was living by rote: the good
mother feeding her child, the professional woman making sure

the accessories—shoes, purse, jewellery—matched the tailored suit. I drove the same route I always took to the courthouse, prepared to perform my judge's role by rote.

Though I would perform my professional duties impeccably, the underwear-fondling trial irked me. I couldn't make sense of my sitting in a courtroom listening to where the sofa had been placed in someone's living room when a friend I loved was so ill. I couldn't make sense of being a judge when I felt powerless to find truth, to do justice. Had all those years of feminism and social justice activism come to this?

My commodious chambers, the place I loved that was all mine, gave me no solace that day as I removed my street clothes and dressed for court. My deputy arrived; all players were in place; I entered the courtroom and took my seat.

"Good morning, Your Honour, members of the jury," said Crown counsel. "The next Crown witness is Darren Fowler."

A teenager slunk through the courtroom and took the stand. Baggy clothes hung on his thin frame. He was fourteen, and a friend of the complainant, David. He was called as a witness because he'd talked to the accused, Dean, on the phone. In that conversation, he told the court, "Dean told me to say that nothing happened and he would pay me back big time." After that, the Crown had no further questions.

Even Mr. Smith's cross-examination was brief. "How often did you stay at the house?"

"I slept over several weekends."

"Did Dean make any advances to you?"

"No."

"Were you at the party?"

"I was there for twenty minutes. I left at eight."

"No further questions."

Interesting. The only relevant statement made by the witness was that Dean told him to say nothing, yet Mr. Smith did
not cross-examine on it. The witness was obviously being consistent with his prior statements about it and there was nothing to
be gained by questioning him. No point in boosting a witness's
credibility when your aim is to discredit him.

"Your Honour, the next witness is Ron Dewey," said Crown
counsel.

Ron also wore oversized baggy clothing. The lower half of
his hair had been shaved all round and, oddly, both his hands
were in splints. Though curious, I didn't expect to be told what
had happened to his hands. Ron was sixteen and knew the
accused from being at the house. He was asked about his Young
Offender record, which comprised theft under, fail to appear,
and a fine for smoking. When Crown witnesses had a record,
they were always asked about their records, in order to show
that nothing was being concealed, and it was a better tactic to
have the questions on a record come from the Crown than to
have them elicited in cross-examination. Ron knew David, the
complainant, but hadn't known him for long. Ron, too, was
staying at the house at the time of the party. As he recalled
the get-together, "Everyone was sitting around and everyone was drinking. Stephen got drunk and was throwing up all
over the place."

Though these young, laconic guests had little to offer, I knew
the Crown was calling those at the party who might have witnessed some relevant behaviour. It was part of the onus on the
Crown to prove the case. As well, in this way, the defence could
cross-examine the witnesses, as opposed to the defence sub-

poenaing the witnesses, who would then be cross-examined by the Crown.

"Cross-examination, Mr. Smith," I said.

"Your friend, Stephen, and Dean asked you to stay in the house, didn't they?" began defence counsel.

"Yeah, I was in a group home before."

"You said you saw David at the party?"

"I saw him on the couch by himself in the living room. Everyone was crashed out. I looked in and went to the bedroom."

"Were his clothes on?"

"Yes."

"Had David stayed overnight before?"

"Yes, about three times when I was there."

"Did you see David in the house after the party?"

"A couple of times."

After protracted questioning, defence counsel concluded. Only that lawyer could have taken the entire morning to cross-examine the two teenagers.

"Do you have another witness before the luncheon recess, Ms. Carr?" I asked Crown counsel.

"Your Honour, I am requesting an adjournment until tomorrow morning. The next Crown witness had child-care problems today and is unable to attend. My learned friend has no objection."

"That is agreeable to the court. Members of the jury, you are free to go at this time. This court stands adjourned until tomorrow morning at ten o'clock."

Smiles all round showed that the jurors felt exactly as I did—sprung.

———

BACK IN MY CHAMBERS, Anne's cousin had left a phone message that she had received permission from all the lawyers to engage private nurses as required. This would be a gift from her aunt's estate. She asked me to tell Anne so she would not be inclined to grit her teeth and do without in order to leave more money for the boys.

The adjournment would give me the opportunity to buy a flannel bed jacket. Anne constantly complained of being cold, saying, "I never get warm enough. Wool is too heavy, and the cotton hospital blankets are cold." Although she hadn't asked for a warm cover-up, I liked to bring her things that might make her more comfortable.

Back in my suit, I walked down the back stairwell to ground level. I ignored the "alarm will sound if opened" sign and walked out the door and across Nathan Phillips Square in front of City Hall to the large Bay department store.

In the well-stocked lingerie department, the selection of flannel was limited. I selected one garment in bubble-gum pink and white plaid. It was nothing like the pale lace and satin gowns Anne liked to wear in bed, but it would be warm.

I drove to the hospital, picking up a yogurt shake on the way. When I arrived at three, Anne was feverish and in severe pain. Her face was yellow and the urine bag contained blood.

"What happened, Anne?" I asked, trying to keep the panic out of my voice and face.

"It's the chemo. The worst time is always ten to fourteen days after." She spoke drowsily.

I offered the yogurt shake. "Do you want this?"

"... love it, but I can't drink. My mouth and throat are burned. All I've had is half a popsicle." I put the shake on the side table, worried, and asked if she'd been given something for the pain.

"I had morphine at two-thirty...," she murmured. "Doesn't seem to help. I have a pain in my back where the chemo is hitting the bone marrow." Anne's somnolent face looked ravaged.

"I have a present for you," I said, opening the plastic bag. "Not very elegant, I'm afraid." After wrapping the pink bed jacket around her, I sat close and held her arm with mine. "The drugs should kick in soon. What can I do?" I asked.

"Talk to me."

I considered what might make her feel better, feel as far away from the misery of the hospital room as possible. She had always loved to hear the story of the time I met Princess Diana, so I asked if she'd like me to tell that again.

"Oh, yes," she said, her voice tight with pain. "Wasn't that wonderful!"

"It was. Remember the picture from the newspaper I showed you? Her gown was a deep green colour, very unusual. She's very tall and incredibly gorgeous."

"Mmm," she said, nodding slightly.

"The area in front of the ballroom at the Royal York Hotel was cordoned off to make a corridor. We were there, waiting for her to arrive. We were instructed not to speak unless spoken to. The guests waited behind the cord and, as you might expect, we were most genteel. I manoeuvred my way to the front and waited with the others. And you won't believe it, but Princess Diana shook my hand as she passed by."

"And to think she picked you!"

"Yes, I made sure to focus on Diana's eyes as she approached and then on Prince Charles. Diana kept walking after shaking hands, but Charles stopped. I told him my two sons were the same age as his. He was so smooth! He said I didn't look old enough to have two young sons—a forgivable gallantry.

"During dinner and dancing, I couldn't keep my eyes off Diana. I made sure Alex and I danced near the Princess, and it was comical to watch her jitterbug with the Premier. He's about a foot shorter than she is!"

"I wish I'd been there. Didn't you have dinner with Margaret Thatcher? Tell me about it."

"Yes, my friend Jean Wadds was the High Commissioner to England and invited Alex and me to London. We stayed with her when she hosted a dinner at the official residence for the Prime Minister."

"How many were there?"

"About twenty. Alex and I were the least significant guests, so we sat farthest from Mrs. Thatcher and her husband. I learned something fun about official dining: you talk to the person on your one side during each course. They tell the story of Prince Philip saying to the woman on his left, 'I'll finish the story during the fish course.'"

Anne smiled slightly. "Tell me more."

"After dinner we all gathered in a salon. Until Jean was appointed—the first woman to represent Canada in London— men and women separated after dinner. Of course it wouldn't do to do that: the woman Prime Minister and the woman High Commissioner would remain with the ladies. So the social rules evolved. I thought it terrific that the monarch was a woman, the Prime Minister was a woman, and the High Commissioner was a woman."

I liked reliving the memories of Jean, a consummate politician, at the time of the repatriation of the Constitution, and I was glad to distract Anne from her pain. "After dinner," I continued, "Jean took me by the arm and led me to the sofa where Margaret Thatcher was sitting. She whispered, 'I want you to sit beside the Prime Minister.' On her right was Monique Bégin, a Quebec cabinet minister and on her left was Gilles Loiselle, the Quebec Agent-General. I started to say 'But... ,' and there I was directly in front of Mrs. Thatcher. Immediately, the Agent-General rose and offered me his seat, though I could see his annoyance. You see, Jean didn't want him bending the Prime Minister's ear as Quebec was opposed to the new Constitution, and she knew he had to offer his seat to a woman. Jean was always *politique*."

"What was Margaret Thatcher like?"

"We discussed being women in law, and the three of us talked about our struggles to be taken seriously as women. I had no doubt Margaret Thatcher was a feminist, but not a seventies-style feminist. She didn't appoint women to her cabinet—or, actually, only one, for a short time. I think she didn't want to have any female competition or any comparison with other women."

"How lucky you were," Anne breathed. It was good to see her caught up in something outside her pain and way beyond the hospital room.

"And you too," I reminded her. "Remember your times with Mila Mulroney, Queen Noor... You'll have lots more splendid occasions when you get home."

Anne was breathing easier and the drugs seemed to be kicking in.

I stood up and went around to the other side and sat on the bed so I could drape my arm around her shoulder. Speaking very slowly, I began to take her back to the beach at Lyford Cay, where we had gone the previous April, after Doug's death. "Anne, remember, you are walking on soft white sand... The sun is warming all of your body... " Anne sighed softly. "You're walking slowly... Feel the sand in the curl of your toes... The water refreshes your feet... You're in no hurry... The sun dances on the water in rainbows, and the gentlest breeze nudges the waves to shore." Anne's eyes closed and her body went limp.

I returned to the chair by her bed, and while Anne slept, I remembered our trip, the year before, to the Lyford Cay Club. Anne was glad she could still be a member of the club after Doug died, and she'd taken me there for a week.

———

ANNE AND I had risen at four-thirty for our morning flight to Nassau. Notwithstanding the hour, Anne was impeccably turned out, in navy Escada slacks and a matching cardigan over a white silk shirt with a tennis motif. Even the black cane did not mar her elegance.

As we boarded the plane, Anne said, "If you don't mind, I'd like to have the inside seat. I only hear out of my left ear now. It was that bout of spinal meningitis last year. I think they used an experimental antibiotic."

Though I had wondered before whether Anne felt she was a guinea pig, I knew that, experimental or not, she'd try whatever the doctors recommended.

When we landed at the Nassau airport, the club's limousine awaited. Fifteen minutes later, we passed through the access control gates to the club property and then drove another five minutes to the townhouse where we were staying. Lyford Cay Club, in its own words, offers "total privacy, security and natural beauty... magnificent homes within the 1000-acre estate... a half-mile private beach... The Club has grown to embody a spirit of luxury."

It was luxurious, yes, yet sterile, in the manner of such private clubs. The trappings of the lifestyle of the respectable rich are notably homogeneous. I prefer a measure of eccentricity.

Still, I was glad to be with my friend in the place she loved, and it wasn't difficult to appreciate and enjoy its comforts and service. The chauffeur let us out at a spacious pink two-storey house with balconies front and back. Tall royal palms, coconut palms, and flowering bougainvillea abounded. Each unit had a golf cart for transportation on club grounds.

At the front door, a smiling maid welcomed us and offered to unpack our suitcases. Anne discussed supplies and cleaning with her.

As soon as we could get outdoors, we walked along the beach, and Anne swam a little. We hadn't yet begun the series of activities Anne had scheduled in advance: water aerobics and two "playing" golf lessons and tennis lessons for her. Anne's momentum and organization had not faltered, even in planning a holiday. Like me, she never relaxed.

After our walk, we stopped for a while to sit on the thickly padded chaises nestled in the beach's cove, protected from the sun by yellow and white striped canopies. The indigo waters turned to an inviting turquoise over the coral reefs. No one else was on the beach, as the March-break crowd was gone.

Anne talked about how she loved the beach and treasured her memories of the family's vacations at the club. "And," she added, "Simon told me I'll have to go south next winter for my health. Toronto is too cold for my damaged lungs."

"Where would you like go?"

"Actually, I was thinking I'd like to come here, to Lyford Cay. Sandy could go to school on the property. There's a school in town for Duncan, though I don't know how good it is. I'm also thinking about boarding school for him next year.

"Duncan has refused to study French and even refuses to go to French class, but do you know what he did? He decided he'd learn by himself, using Doug's old set of tapes. The funny thing is, they're the type a businessman might study before going to France."

We laughed at the thought of young Duncan learning to negotiate business deals in French. "It's fabulous he's motivated, and he's so bright," I said. "I've tried and tried to encourage Darrell and Edward to learn French. I took them with me on all the judges' French-immersion courses. No luck. I probably should have told them not to bother learning French. Then they might have taken an interest."

"Maybe! It's nice your boys get along so well." She sounded envious; I knew her sons didn't always get along.

"I'm grateful for it," I said. "Darrell once told me that having Edward as a brother was like having his best friend sleep over every night. I hope Edward appreciates it."

After a brief rest in our rooms, we dressed for dinner. Anne looked exquisite in a long navy silk blouse printed with bold pink hibiscus. We went to the yacht club at Lyford Cay Harbour for the seafood buffet. We walked along the docks looking at the sailboats and yachts, some like small ocean liners, and Anne pointed out the yacht belonging to President Eisenhower's granddaughters.

After a sumptuous dinner, the first of our mega-meals, we stayed to watch the floor show with limbo dancers. Brightly dressed West Indians bent back low, inches beneath the flaming rod. I enjoyed the show, but Anne stared at the flickering fire, apparently uninterested. "I'm worried about money," she said suddenly. "I think I have to sell the cottage. And I'll need to fix it up first."

We discussed Anne's woes handling Doug's estate while still looking after her aunt's. "My aunt's butler just quit because my aunt burned the TV. She was cold and went downstairs to light a fire in the fireplace. I don't know how she managed it, but she lit the fire in the TV by mistake."

"I shouldn't laugh," I said, laughing. "But it's funny."

"Her estate's been a lot of work for me. She has so many properties and so many staff. She has a huge property in Palm Beach. You'll have to come with me sometime." I relished the prospect.

Anne insisted I take the larger bedroom at the front of the house and, after the long day, I quickly fell asleep to the soft sound of waves. Anne slept in the bedroom down the hall. Around midnight, I was awakened by the sound of Anne steadily moaning. I walked quietly to her room, where I saw that she was asleep, groaning in pain even though unconscious. I thought it best to let her sleep, and she continued to moan periodically during the night. I wished I could hold her.

At 9:45 the next morning, Anne was still asleep, and I couldn't imagine her doing the aerobics she had scheduled or even thinking she could. But right after breakfast, we were headed for the pool for water aerobics.

"I won't be able to go in, Anne," I said. "I can't swim."

"You don't have to swim to do aerobics."

"I'll stay in the shallow end."

"Why can't you swim?"

"I wish I could. I'm a Cancer, a water sign, and I've taken five swimming courses without success, including the Red Cross. I even selected swimming as my mandatory sport at McGill. Darrell and Edward tried to teach me, too. When Darrell tried, he stood beside me in the lake saying, 'Repeat after me, Mom: The water is my friend. The water is my friend.'"

Those water aerobics classes that Anne pushed me into were a lasting gift. The instructor used aquatic fitness gear that included special adult water wings, which enabled me to stay up and move in any deep water. I ordered a set for each of us and have used mine ever since.

We played golf in the afternoon with the club pro, Jack Kay, formerly of the Rosedale Golf Course in Toronto, where my husband and his parents were members. Our golfing ability was unremarkable, but Jack was an old hand at flirting with matrons. We played behind Sean Connery, who was by himself although his wife is an accomplished golfer. Alas, he did not invite us to join him for the round, but we certainly enjoyed watching his famous backside.

For dinner we were joined by David, a family friend of Anne's. He'd flown in from Chile on his way to New York. It was typical of Anne to make social arrangements wherever she might be, nothing I was ever tempted to do. She would have been a perfect diplomat.

As always, that evening in the restaurant her appearance belied her physical condition. With gleaming blond hair, wearing a pretty blouse with pale pink roses, blue cornflowers, and baby's breath on a dark background, she was a gracious, attentive host. Only close examination revealed the weariness in her eyes.

———

WEDNESDAY AFTERNOON, in the hospital, I was roused from my reverie when Anne awoke in a heavy sweat. The private nurse entered the room at that moment and Anne looked up, relieved to see her.

She took Anne's temperature and reported, sympathetically, "She has a high fever. This is the point of the lowest resistance from the chemo."

She called the nursing station to cut off telephone access and refuse visitors. I was allowed to stay, though the nurse directed me to put on a face mask. Together, we bathed Anne's pale yellow face and body with tepid cloths.

After the nurse stepped quietly away, I stayed by Anne's side, softly singing the hypnotic refrain of "An Irish Lullaby" through my mask. By six-thirty, the pain seemed to subside, or else the drugs were working more effectively. When she was calmer, Anne looked at me with fear in her face. "Marie, I'm afraid. I'm afraid to die."

"Oh Anne, don't be afraid. You'll feel better soon. You know this is the worst time after chemo. Things will get better." My heart hurt so, I could barely breathe.

"Yes, I'd forgotten that."

Though Anne seemed a little better, her temperature continued to rise, reaching 104 degrees. Anne's nurse called the doctor,
and around seven-thirty, he entered the room and I left to call
home as I was unusually late. There was no answer at my house,
which worried me. I didn't want to leave Anne, but I didn't know
where Edward was and felt I had to go home to sort things out.

When I went back in the room, Sandy had arrived with his
stepbrother.

"Anne," I said, "I've got to leave to check on Edward. Call me if
you feel anxious and want me to come back."

I left feeling a bit chaotic, and worried about more than one
person. To my relief, Edward arrived home soon after I did.

When I called Anne's room later, her nurse answered, telling me Anne was sleeping and her temperature had at last gone
down to something closer to normal. I asked her to call me if
Anne needed me. "I will. Don't worry. She'll be fine. I'll be here
until eleven-thirty and another nurse is coming in after."

I slept a little better than I had in days, knowing the nurses
were looking after Anne.

Week One
Thursday

LUNCH

Crispy oven-fried chicken
(*Creative Cooking*, p. 2)

Carrot raisin salad (*Creative Cooking*,
p. 47)

Frosted chocolate conecakes
(*Kids' Cooking*, p. 66)

Chapter 11

JANUARY 26

THE NEXT MORNING, I was back at the interminable trial.

"Your Honour, the next Crown witness is Martin Snider," said Crown counsel.

A burly man with neatly groomed hair and a black beard walked smartly past the jury to the witness box. He wore a grey suit and pink shirt with a matching handkerchief. The jury and I perked up, looking forward to hearing from the natty dresser. Crown counsel began her examination, eliciting the information that Martin was thirty years old with three children and lived with his mother. He was a carpenter, he said, adding that he was "unemployed right now."

"Did you go to school for that?"

"No, I have a grade-three education. I spent a lot of time in group homes when I was young."

"Do you have a criminal record?"

"Yes."

The Crown took him through his criminal record dating from 1979: theft over, two counts, and theft under, two counts—

sixteen months; escape lawful custody—thirteen months; theft over, two counts, and theft under, seven counts—thirteen months; uttering and forgery—six months; wilful damage, theft under, possession of stolen property—six months; possession of an unlawful weapon—two years less one day. The amount of time was significant, as it meant the witness had not served a penitentiary sentence. Any sentence of two years and over is served in a federal penitentiary rather than a provincial institution.

The Crown continued listing the offences: break and enter, three counts—two years.

It finally caught up with him, I thought, listening to the grim recital.

Still the Crown continued: theft over, dangerous driving—two years; break and enter and theft—twenty-four months; attempted theft, mischief, fail to appear—seven months; indecent act, failure to comply—two months; indecent act—ninety days...

I bit my lip to stop myself from smiling at the astonished expressions on the faces of the jury as this dapper man responded "yes" to each conviction. He must have spent most of his adult life behind bars. The fact that a witness might have a criminal record is usually not directly relevant to the issues, but it is introduced in regard to whether the witness is credible. You bring your character as it relates to truthfulness and honesty into the witness box—as we say to juries, it's not left at the courtroom door. A witness's record is introduced by the Crown because the defence will invariably ask about it in cross-examination to show that such a person cannot be or ought not to be believed.

Finally, the Crown got to the matter at hand. "Do you know the accused before the court?"

"I was acquainted with him for three to five days."

"Did you have a conversation with him?"

"Yes. He told me about his charge. He said it was made by a young boy about fourteen."

"What did he say?"

"He said he can't be charged with sexual assault unless he makes penetration. He said it only happened one time. He placed his hand on his crotch area and tongued his ear."

"Did he say anything else?"

"He said he could discredit the young fellow by saying he was about to break into a shed in the back. He told me he'd say the boy did it even if he didn't."

"Did you initiate this conversation?"

"No, he brought it up."

"No further questions," concluded Crown counsel.

"Cross-examination, Mr. Smith," I said.

Mr. Smith rose and began questioning with obvious relish. "Did you tell my client you were in custody on a charge of committing an indecent act?"

"Yes, we were in the same cell. I got ninety days and had thirty-three days left on the sentence."

"Where did the indecent act take place?"

"About two hours outside of Toronto, I urinated outside. I pleaded guilty."

"And you were transferred to Toronto's East Detention Centre?"

"Yes."

"You spoke with the police?"

"Yes."

"And you were given Dean Marsh's statement to read?"

"Yes, but I can't read that good. The officers talked about it and read parts."

"At the time, you were facing other charges?"

"Yes."

"Two charges of possession of stolen property?"

"Yes."

"What was the property?"

"Licence plates."

"You were facing three charges in Nova Scotia: fail to appear, mischief, and sexual assault?"

"Yes."

"After you spoke with the officers, the Ontario charges were withdrawn?"

"No, they weren't withdrawn. They were dismissed for lack of evidence."

I looked at the faces of the jury, noticing the odd wry look. That a person had a criminal record was often of little import for me, but evidence from someone who could have been co-opted by the authorities merited careful scrutiny.

"But you are still facing the Nova Scotia charges?"

"I don't know the status of those charges."

"I put it to you, there is a province-wide warrant in Nova Scotia for your arrest?"

"Yeah, maybe, but they don't want me back."

"Do you know what deals are?"

"Yeah, I've made deals. I'd plead guilty to a lesser charge, but I never made a patched deal before. I told the police what Dean told me and that was it."

"You were put in his cell to get a confession, weren't you?"

"No, it was the only empty cell. It was all he talked about, the charge and his home life. He talked about it every day, constantly. He showed me letters. He read parts to me that the fourteen-year-old lied in court."

"You know what a rat is?"

"Sure. A rat is a stool pigeon."

"You know what happens to rats?"

"Rats can choose to be in protective custody."

"You were promised a deal with your outstanding charges if you got a confession?"

"Nothing was promised to me."

"But you know there are brownie points involved? You know you could be sent back to Nova Scotia? You know the score."

"Yeah. Basically, I've been a criminal all my life."

Some jurors seemed taken aback by the statement, likely never having encountered a self-described career criminal. I'd encountered so many in the courtroom, I'd become inured to such assertions. As a lawyer and as a judge, I'd learned that there is more interface with the police among lower-income people than higher-income people.

Early in my career, I was asked by the Legal Aid Director to act for a seven-year-old boy at a time when such representation was uncommon. The boy lived with his grandparents in public housing, and his mother was a drug addict. He'd stolen two dollars from his grandmother's purse, and she called the police—to teach him a lesson. Once the police were involved, Children's Aid was called because of the extreme physical limitations of the grandparents. It grieved me that after all the difficult interactions with the law and the courts, the boy was eventually taken into foster care. I knew that in middle- and upper-class families, the police would rarely be the first recourse to help discipline a child.

I felt the same about this case. Would the parents of a teenager in Rosedale call the police if their son said such acts had occurred? I suspected other avenues of redress or investigation would be used in the first instance. Yet for all I knew, other avenues might have been taken in this case but had failed.

In some ways, there was so little a judge knew. I never knew all the facts of a case—only the facts that the lawyers adduced in evidence. There were always many factors that I never heard about.

Defence counsel concluded his cross-examination, and I granted his request to address the court in the absence of the jury. After the jurors left, he moved to dismiss the charges because there was no reliable evidence of the age of the complainant. The age of the complainant was an essential element of the offence. If David had been under age fourteen, it made no difference if he consented or not. If David had been over age fourteen, the Crown would have to prove David did not consent to being touched.

"Your Honour," he argued, "the only evidence was David's statement that he was fourteen and would be fifteen in August. David's evidence is hearsay, and his mother should have been called or his birth certificate should have been produced."

It was a cute argument, and almost supportable on an unduly literal interpretation. David obviously didn't remember being born and must have been told by his mother how old he was. She hadn't been called as a witness, so there was no direct evidence of the teenager's age. Still, in the ordinary case, a person's statement is some evidence of age.

After I dismissed his motion, the defence elected not to call any evidence. A person is presumed to be innocent until proven guilty. A corollary of this presumption of innocence is that a person charged with an offence need not take the stand or give any evidence to defend himself or herself against the charge. At the end of the Crown's case, the lawyer for the accused will assess whether to call the client or not and whether to call for other evidence. The decision to call for more evidence is that of the accused person, who generally follows the advice of counsel.

If the case for the prosecution is weak, defence counsel may conclude that the prosecution evidence standing alone will not be sufficient for proof beyond a reasonable doubt and may decide to call no defence evidence. Further, if the accused person has a significant criminal record, defence counsel may be reluctant to put the accused on the stand.

In this case, however, the prosecution case was strong and I inferred that the defence did not want to call the accused because he had a criminal record or would otherwise not be a good witness.

I called the jury back to court, told them the evidence had been concluded, and excused them until the next morning when counsel would address them.

BACK IN MY CHAMBERS, I sat at my desk to prepare the jury charge. The first part of the charge needed no special preparation, as it is boilerplate text used in every criminal trial. In the next part of the charge, I would set out the relevant law and review the evidence. I concluded with an outline of the positions of each counsel and the possible verdicts.

After working on the charge to the jury, I left the courthouse and bought another nightshirt for Anne. However, when I arrived at the hospital at four o'clock, no visitors were permitted. I looked in the small window to Anne's room and saw that she was sleeping. Hoping she was all right, I decided to go home.

After dinner, I called Anne's friend Fran to tell her I was going up north to our ski cabin on Saturday and gave her the telephone number in case Anne needed me. Fran noted the number, sounding tense, and then burst out, "Mary told me that Anne ripped me out of her black binder. I'm no longer appointed as guardian."

"Fran, she did not rip you out. She didn't know what to do about Duncan and Sandy and finally decided to leave it to the person who wanted to do it."

"I cried for five days."

"But Fran, she thought it was too much for you to take on."

"She tore me out on her deathbed. I can't believe it. I've known her for a hundred years."

"Fran, it's not like that at all." Silently, I took a deep breath. "It's not a black and white situation. The papers in the binder are copies. They're not the originals."

Despite my insistence, Fran kept complaining.

"It doesn't mean you and Tim can't be guardians or that Anne does not want you," I repeated, trying to suppress my impatience at Fran's self-preoccupation.

Fran went on about Anne putting her in an untenable position. I was aghast—she thought *she* was in an untenable position!

I repeated that nothing was final and all would be consulted, especially the boys.

"Her brother could take the boys," Fran said, "and I heard Jessica wants them."

"It's not like that: the boys are not up for grabs."

"I feel terrible about it."

"We all feel terrible," I said. "You're being too hard on yourself." In fact, I was politely lying; her self-indulgence disgusted me. "The important thing now is to do what we can for Anne."

We ended the conversation and, though I was drained afterward, I continued to work on my jury charge and helped Edward type a school paper.

The phone rang just before eight o'clock. "This is Anne's nurse. She asked me to call to see if you would come see her."

"Of course. I'll go right down. Is she okay?"

"She's not too bad. Her brother's with her now."

"I'll be there in fifteen minutes."

After giving Edward the number of Anne's room, I drove straight to the hospital, arriving at the same time as her son Sandy and Lisa, Anne's "cancer twin." Anne said she still had a fever but was freezing. Quickly, I helped her change and wrapped the fresh bed jacket around her shoulders. Over her feet I spread the light comforter.

Warmed, Anne seemed a little better, and she clearly rallied for Sandy. "Tell me what you're doing, darling." Sandy sat beside his mother on the bed on the other side of the IV drip.

"Lisa knows the neatest mind puzzles," he said, bouncing lightly. "Listen to this, Mom. You are trapped in a room with only two doors to get out. Behind one is a room made of magnifying glass, right? And the blazing sun will fry you." I could see Anne was struggling to pay attention. "Behind the second there's a fire-breathing dragon. How do you escape?"

Anne looked quizzical. "Well, I wouldn't want the dragon."

"That's right, Mom. You wait for nightfall and when it's dark, you go through the room made of magnifying glass."

"That's a good one, Sandy."

"Yes, Lisa knows lots of them."

I smiled, thinking how Anne must know what it felt like to be fried by hot waves.

After they left, Anne collapsed into the bed, saying, "I'm completely exhausted."

I held her hands for a while and then gently rubbed her head. She vomited suddenly and violently. At the same moment, diarrhea flooded the bed. Gagging, embarrassed for my friend, and trying to hide both reactions, I removed the fouled bed jacket and blanket and called the nurse for fresh clothes.

While the nurse changed the bedding, I spoke with Anne's friend Marte in the corridor. She'd had a lot of experience with death, and in the course of our conversation she told me, "At some point, people have to be given permission to die."

"Permission?" The notion shocked me. I didn't doubt that Marte knew a lot about dying. She had her own health care business and was the current chair of Wellspring, which Anne had founded. Still, the idea of giving Anne permission to die was horrifying. Marte must have read the confusion on my face. "Yes, Marie, people facing death need to be told that it's not necessary to hang on at all costs."

I looked at her, unable to answer. Was *I* supposed to give Anne such permission?

"Well," she said, retreating slightly, "perhaps this isn't the time for Anne."

Until that night when Marte talked about Anne facing death, the imminence of Anne's death hadn't seemed real. My love for her had clouded the reality of her condition. How could I give Anne permission to die when she wanted to live, when I wanted her to live, when everyone wanted her to live?

When I entered the room again, Anne was clean and calm. Valiantly, she said she felt better. Before leaving that night, I kissed her goodbye and told her I loved her, adding that things would get better.

Even the weighty job of deciding guilt or innocence for a stranger accused of a crime seemed easier than telling Anne it was okay to die. In court, there were rules, laws, and precedents, which, however flawed, were based on goals of truth, fairness, and justice. In the room of my dying friend, there were no guidelines. But Anne looked so forlorn, and in many ways *was* so forlorn, that I began to think seriously about the wisdom of Marte's advice.

Week One
Thursday

DINNER

Alpha-Getti

Small salad from Wednesday dinner

Two sticks of cut cheddar cheese

Two brownies from Tuesday

Oranges from Wednesday

Chocolate milk

Chapter 12

JANUARY 27

FINALLY, IT WAS FRIDAY, and the end of the crotch-fondle case was in sight. I went into court to hear counsel address the jury. Ms. Carr looked haggard, her hair messier than usual. Adrian Smith could wear anyone down. Crown counsel's twenty-minute address was understandably uninspired. She asked the jury to find that the two incidents, ear tonguing and genital touching, occurred as described by the complainant, David Byrne. She noted also that his evidence was uncontradicted, was supported by the evidence of a witness to whom the accused admitted he had done it, and was supported by the evidence of a witness whom the accused had asked to lie.

I enjoyed observing the interface between male and female lawyers. Men and women alike have had to learn to interact with each other in a professional environment, and in a male-dominated profession. Such interaction is recent, dating from the second half of the twentieth century. Men have had hundreds of years of socialization and bonding both in and out of court and have developed familiar ways of dealing with each other in public arenas. It's a big adjustment for men—relating to women professionally and not sexually. To ensure that professional boundaries are maintained, we have had to enact laws against sexual harassment in the workplace.

It's a big adjustment for women too. Not only do we have to learn to interact with men in the workplace, we have to learn new ways of relating to each other, professionally. I've heard complaints that women don't support other women; that women are their own worst enemies; that they don't like working for a woman boss. I caution such speakers that we need patience—women are new to the scene. We need time to acquire the ease with which men bond. We are learning how to interact with each other in the public domain. It's as if evolutionarily we have not yet acquired the necessary interplay and social veneer.

When I was appointed a judge, women were a mere three percent of the judiciary. In my law-school class, the number of women students was the largest in its history: nine of us. We were misfits—freaks, even. Some male students objected to our taking the place of breadwinner males. Adjustments were large and small. When I was appointed to the Ontario Municipal Board (the second woman ever to be so appointed), the chairman would not stay in the same hotel as the woman member he was travelling with, lest someone suspect hanky-panky. Another member would not let me pay for a meal in a restaurant while we were travelling because it reflected poorly on him that a woman had to pay for her meal in his presence, though we were both on expense accounts. The chairman of the Pension Commission of Ontario opened the meeting of members and, looking directly at me, said, "Good morning, gentlemen." Even when present, we were invisible.

On a personal level, our emotions may be more evident. We tend to be more serious, more earnest, even more rigid, and we often seem more involved in our cases. I remember as a young lawyer prosecuting a *Construction Safety Act* case for the City of Toronto against a large demolition company; the case alleged that safety standards had not been upheld, resulting in the death of a worker. I wanted to adduce a critical statement by an employee of the company and expected to face an argument that it was hearsay. I prepared for the objection and had my authorities that the statement was an admission by an agent and not hearsay. When the judge refused to let me adduce the statement, even after I cited the proper authorities, I was so frustrated, I didn't know what to do, and I started to cry. At that point the judge didn't know what to do either, and he called for a recess. No doubt, seasoned lawyers learn it doesn't always go as it should, whether there are legal authorities or not. There's definitely a social learning curve for women in the courts. So I sympathized with Ms. Carr's frustration with Mr. Smith.

Mr. Smith strode to the front of the jury box and began with references to the origins of our system of law and the Justinian Code of 800 BC. Ms. Carr rolled her eyes and shook her head slightly. Only in extreme circumstances does counsel interrupt another counsel during jury addresses. I made notes as usual, taking down his sweeping rhetoric: "We still rely on you, the community, for common sense." "The complainant now appears like one of Raphael's angels." "These false charges are now rampant against men." "I remind you members of the jury how hard it is to defend against such charges. But don't think that I am unsympathetic to young people."

On and on he droned, reviewing the molehills of evidence and the faint inconsistencies in an effort to discredit the complainant's testimony. No one could fault him for not being thorough. He asked the jury not to believe an unsavoury character such as Martin Snider, who had everything to gain by disclosing the confession to the police, and he asked the jury to find that the Crown had not proved the charges beyond a reasonable doubt. After two full hours, he finally concluded.

Rising from my slump, I turned to the jury. "Members of the jury, you have now heard the addresses of counsel. I would normally charge you now, but it is not my practice to charge a jury on Friday afternoon. If I did, you would be required to stay together until you have concluded your deliberations. I do not want to risk your deliberating into the weekend. I propose, therefore, to charge you first thing on Monday morning. You are excused until Monday morning at ten o'clock. Have a pleasant weekend." The members of the jury beamed at me, stood quickly, and gathered their things, apparently grateful for the adjournment.

After the jurors had filed out, I discussed the content of my charge to the jury with counsel. Defence counsel requested the "unsavoury witness" caution, and I had planned to include it anyway. Then I adjourned the court until Monday morning.

I was glad of a short respite that afternoon, as Monday would be a busy day. As well as delivering the charge to the jury, I had to deliver reasons for sentence in a lengthy drug-trafficking trial. After that, the biker trial was scheduled to continue.

It was one o'clock, time for my weekly French lesson. This was the last thing I felt like doing, but dutifully I returned to chambers to pick up my French exercise book and took the stairs to my teacher's small office on the fifth floor.

Over years of instruction, Denise, an attractive woman of indeterminate age—or more precisely, a woman who never discussed her age—and I had become friends. She attributed her still unlined face to heeding her mother's exhortation: "Never frown." She smiled as I entered the small office and welcomed me warmly. *"Bonjour, Marie. Ça va bien?"* All I could manage was to describe my sorrow in halting French. *"Je suis très désolée,"* I began. *I am very sad.*

After the class, I returned to my chambers and changed into street clothes for yet another trip to the Bay to purchase another bed jacket and a lightweight duvet. I then returned to my chambers one last time to pick up my files to prepare for Monday, which I was dreading.

I carried the files to my car and drove up Yonge Street to the video store to pick up movies to watch at the cabin on the weekend. I bought the usual banana milkshake Anne liked and drove to the hospital. However, when I arrived at the hospital with the large shopping bag, the cold shake dripping onto my hand, there was a sign on the door to Anne's room that no visitors were permitted. Disappointed, I walked to the nursing station and asked if Anne wanted to see me, and the nurse said yes, but I had to take precautions. I washed my hands and put on the face mask.

An awful sight awaited me. Anne was shaking uncontrollably and vomiting into a dish. She had been vomiting for hours, the nurse told me as she tried to comfort Anne and at the same time take away the soiled sheets and clothing. Diarrhea had plagued Anne all morning as well; she couldn't control herself to reach the potty in time. No sooner had the nurse changed the bedding and left with the soiled bundle than I had to call her back to change it again. In addition to the misery of throwing up and losing her bowels, Anne was freezing and shivering.

As calmly as I could, I filled her hot water bottle and placed it at her feet. I covered her with the fresh jacket and placed the new duvet on top of the other blankets. She was limp, barely able to move her body or respond at first, but after a few minutes she was warming up. As I laid the fresh bed jacket over her shoulders, she was able to tell me that there'd been a mix-up with the private nurse. "My nurse came to the room and saw another nurse with me and thought she wasn't needed, but it was the hospital nurse. So she left."

"Oh Anne, I'm so sorry." More than sorry—I was aghast. "I'll call her right now to make sure about tonight."

As I rang her nurse, I could hear Anne's steady moans behind me. After I hung up the phone, I took her hand, which was as cold as if she'd been outside in wintertime. Her breaths were fast and hoarse. She looked despairingly at me from deep, circled eyes. "Marie, I can't go on."

"What does your doctor say?"

"Simon said I would feel better on Sunday."

Even if Simon were right, that meant two more days of intense misery. As we spoke, Anne's hand shook in mine: she was still shivering.

Unable to speak, I sat on the edge of the bed and leaned to hold her close, manoeuvring my limbs around and inside the tubing. With Anne's face close to mine, I started to cry, and couldn't stop. I pulled my surgical mask higher to cover the stream of tears and began to sing very low the Irish ballad "If I Were a Blackbird." I'd sung it to my sons for years. Its soothing properties didn't fail; Anne closed her eyes and became calm. I sang the three verses I knew until we were both less upset, then wiped the tears, resettled my mask, and returned to the chair on the other side of the bed.

Moments later she opened her eyes, asking, "Do you think Jackie Onassis had an assisted death?" From her tone, she could have been asking about Jackie's cosmetic surgery. However, I knew that beneath the casual attitude and the simple, lucid question lay a deep and dreadful question.

"Probably," I replied carefully. "I'm sure she was made as comfortable as possible." She left the subject there, and I had to go home.

I was annoyed at myself for agreeing to meet a friend at my house for tea. Here I was doing it all, again. I apologized to Anne and offered to cancel my other engagement and stay with her.

Ever gracious, Anne replied, "No, you go. I feel better now."

She did seem slightly better—at least she'd stopped vomiting and the diarrhea had ceased for a few minutes. Yet I knew Anne wouldn't have asked me to cancel even if she'd wanted to. Why didn't I cancel on my own? My friend would have understood if I'd rearranged the visit. It was my well-established habit of fitting everything in, doing it all, not wanting any one of my juggled balls to drop.

As I walked out, the nurse at the station stopped me. Putting a hand on my arm, she told me that the nurses had heard my singing, and that Anne always settled when I sang to her. I felt more tears coming, and quickly thanked her and moved on.

I arrived at the house shortly before Chaviva's taxi arrived. We sat in the living room and chatted over cucumber sandwiches, sweets, and tea. I'd married Chaviva and her husband, and we reminisced about the wedding reception at my home. We talked about her work for the Prime Minister, and she asked how being a judge was going after nine years.

"It's been really exciting," I said, not sounding excited at all. "But lately, I don't feel challenged. I used to think being a judge was such a powerful position. Now I'm becoming aware of how little real power I have. I feel confined, after so many years of social activism, of trying to change things."

Chaviva nodded. "Maybe our goals don't have the same appeal once achieved."

"Or else we're just *driven*. I mean, as if I don't have enough to do, I've founded—now this is a mouthful—the Canadian Chapter of the International Association of Women Judges."

We talked easily together, having shared a history of feminist activism in the seventies and eighties, and I found myself sharing my sorrow about Anne. Then, inevitably, as mothers do, we talked about our families, my sons and Chaviva's stepson.

"Can you believe when I was appointed a judge, Darrell and Edward were only six and three years old?" I spoke lightly, remembering a time when my life had seemed good, full of exciting challenges and worthwhile activities. "And at that time, women were a mere three percent of the judiciary, and almost all women judges were childless or had become judges after their children were older. At least now there are more of us. I guess I'm my own role model."

Even as I spoke, though, images of Anne in the hospital remained vivid, and I was not sorry when Chaviva said she was leaving. She wrapped her scarf around her neck, gave me a hug, and said, "I won't keep you. You'll be going back to the hospital, and I have to think about dinner. Let me get a taxi home," she said.

"Of course not! You're only ten minutes from here—I'll drive you." And of course, I did, taking the shortest route, making sure she got in safely before I went on to my next task and the next and the next.

As soon as I returned home, I put on some casual clothes and Edward and I had dinner. He left to meet his girlfriend to go to a movie. He agreed to be home by eleven, and I reminded him to make sure Veronica returned home safely. "You can't just leave her on a street corner or at a subway station."

"But she's being picked up at the bus stop by her father," he said.

"It doesn't matter—you stay till he arrives." It wasn't a lesson in politeness I was teaching him: I wanted my sons to be considerate of women and never let their girlfriends be unsafe.

When Edward left, I called the hospital, and the nurse said Anne was up and wanted to talk to me. "Will you come down?" Anne asked.

"Of course."

When I arrived, her son Sandy was standing at the foot of the bed staring helplessly at Anne, who was lying on her side, throwing up. I gave him a quick hug. He looked so frightened, and I wondered if he'd seen his mother like this before, given how Anne hid her pain in the presence of her sons. When Anne's heaving slowed and stopped, I wiped her face. The cool facecloth immediately turned warm.

"Are you okay to stay, Sandy?" I asked, worried about his seeing his mother so wretched. "It's fine if you're ready to go home now."

"I want to stay," he said, stoutly.

I told him that Marlene, my housekeeper, had made a lasagna for him and dropped it at his house. Anne took her son's hand, promising, "I'll have it with you on Sunday. Simon said I could go home for a visit. We can eat dinner and watch movies."

Sandy seemed a little relieved. I was glad when his stepbrother Mark arrived and took him home.

As they left, Anne grimaced with pain. She was still lying on her side, in case she needed to vomit. I massaged her back a little.

"Oh Marie," she said, rasping, "I don't want to live this way."

"Anne, it's so horrible and unfair. I can't bear to see you suffer. Is there anything you can do?"

"Simon talked about another bone marrow transplant—I simply can't do it."

Although Anne's diarrhea had stopped for the time being, she continued to throw up every few minutes, and her urine, clearly visible in the catheter bag, was dark red.

Even worse, she had pain in her chest. I pressed the button for a nurse, and Anne asked for more Ativan.

"It's not time yet for the next one," the nurse explained.

I took a sharp breath in. "I don't see why Anne can't be made more comfortable," I said.

"I'll see what I can do," she said, whisking away. She was a relatively young nurse, perhaps in her thirties, and I sensed that she had not had as much experience as some of the others.

A few minutes later, the nurse brought more Ativan and helped Anne take it. I knew that the nurse was glad to give her the medication, probably wishing she were not so bound to the strict dosage timetable that she had to get permission to vary it.

Then the nurse and I removed the soiled top sheet and replaced it with a fresh, clean one.

When the nurse left, I sat close beside Anne and asked her if she wanted me to sing or to talk.

"I'd like you to talk," she said, her voice faint. "I still remember the story you told at your swearing-in."

Anne had often expressed her enjoyment at the story I told at the ceremony for my appointment as a judge. To recognize my Newfoundland roots, I'd asked my uncle to find a story with a legal twist, and at the swearing-in ceremony, I told the anecdote in a resurrected Newfoundland accent.

Holding Anne's hand, pausing occasionally to wipe her forehead or to help her rinse her mouth, I told it again.

"At Twillingate Harbour, the late winter fishery is pursued by inserting a herring net through a hole in the bay ice. Simeon Squires, my ancestor, spent two full hard-working days making a proper hole. He cut through the shell ice, the new ice, the old ice, and the ballicaters —"

"The what?"

"Ballicaters. That's the ice formed in winter by waves along the shoreline. Like frozen waves, if you can imagine." I continued: "... the ballicaters, which had rafted offshore the previous fall driven by a northeast wind. When he went back with his net next morning, lo and behold, it was occupied by another net, belonging to Norman Nippard. My ancestor thought about it and decided to make a legal complaint to the judge, simply stating that Norman Nippard had stolen his herring hole."

Anne suddenly spit up slightly, and I wiped her face. She told me to go on and I continued telling the story as I had memorized it for my audience all those years ago. "The judge, Solomon Gosse, arrived on his annual circuit in July. The first case on the docket was *Squires v. Nippard*. Nippard had obtained the services of lawyer McGillicuddy from across the bay. Simeon Squires —"

"Is the name really Squires?"

"Yes, it's a very common name in Newfoundland. Anyway, Simeon Squires said he would act on his own behalf, as what could be clearer? He'd made a hole and Nippard had stolen it for his own use.

"McGillicuddy opened his questioning by asking Simeon what a hole was. Simeon replied that it was a space with nothing in it, as he had removed the ice. The lawyer then stated that a hole was really something that did not exist and therefore could not be stolen. He then asked Simeon if he could produce the stolen hole or a similar item, in whole or in part thereof, to prove it existed and could be stolen. Simeon had to admit that this being July, the hole had drifted out of the bay long ago. McGillicuddy thus offered the conclusion that there was no case as the stolen item never existed and could not be produced.

"His Lordship, Solomon Gosse, thought hard and heavy on the matter and after a difficult night handed down his decision. The hole, even though it was the absence of matter, did exist in relation to its surrounding ice. He found Norman Nippard guilty as charged and instructed Constable Doyle to have the said Nippard produce an equivalent hole in the following March and deliver it to Simeon Squires in good order."

Anne smiled widely, her pale face looking bright for a minute. "I love that story," she said.

And I love you, I thought. I asked her again if she wanted me to talk about anything special.

"Yes," she said. "Tell me about the O.J. trial."

I told her the recent developments, the latest witnesses. Anne lay on her side, her face turned toward me. After I'd brought her up to date on the trial, she smiled, saying, "You always settle me down."

"I'm glad. Listen, Anne. I told you I was going to the cabin in the morning for Edward's ski class, but I don't have to go. I can stay in the city."

"You go. I'll be fine. I remember when I went to that ski event with the boys."

"I've given Fran and Sue the number. I can come back at any time. It's less than two hours away."

Anne breathed heavily again and something went across her face. She was quiet, and when I looked into her eyes, I knew she was miserable. "You go now," she said softly.

"I don't have to go now. I can stay with you," I said.

"I know, but I'm too sick."

Overcome with sorrow for her pain and for my inability to do anything more than comfort her, I wished the unwishable, I craved the impossible. I wanted her to be free of the cancerous marauder.

"I love you, Anne." I stroked her face and kissed her cheek once before leaving.

I took the elevator and left the hospital emotionally drained, bereft of hope, despairing at the prospect of life without her.

Not wanting to go back to my empty home, I dropped in on family friends two blocks away. After checking to make sure there were no extra cars in the driveway—I certainly didn't want to see or be seen by a group of people—I rang the bell, and then asked if I could come in for a glass of wine.

I enjoyed the drink and my friends' kind, supportive company, but I couldn't keep my grief over Anne at bay. Unable to stop crying, I left after twenty minutes.

The house was still and silent, my husband away, my son still out on his date. In the kitchen, I poured another glass of wine, put on Rod Stewart's *Greatest Hits* CD way too loud, played the song "Sailing" over and over and over, and waited for Edward.

Week One
Friday

BREAKFAST

Vitamin pill

Pancakes with fruit (batter from Tuesday)
and warm maple syrup

Slice of back bacon

Sliced peach

Milk

Chapter 13

JANUARY 28

AFTER FIVE HOURS' SLEEP, I staggered out of bed at five-thirty to take Edward to his racing class at Osler Bluff Ski Club, over two hours away. I'd considered turning off the alarm and going back to bed, sure that Edward would be happy to sleep in after his late evening instead. However, Edward had signed up for the team, and I was a stickler for honouring commitments.

At that time, I didn't realize that I had the right to change my mind. I'd do what I said I'd do, not distinguishing between those undertakings that could be changed and those that couldn't. I'd keep social engagements I didn't really want to keep—I was teaching my sons by example that if they'd said they were going to participate in a sports event, they would participate, regardless of whether they felt like it on any given day.

That morning, the fact that my best friend, Barbara, agreed to join me made my own commitment more bearable. As I pulled out of the driveway to pick her up, a large, old-model Cadillac drove by at about five miles an hour. The man in it seemed to be casing the houses. I got out of my car—or "exited my vehicle," as police officers said in court—and approached, asking if he needed help. He said he was a new limousine driver and that he was learning the area. I thought, *Sure, you are*. Still, I didn't bother to note the licence number.

By the time Barbara, Edward, and I arrived at the ski club, the morning was filled with sunshine, reflecting hot off the white snow. Barbara and I dropped Edward off then went to my family's log cabin, which was on the club's property. Settling in for the day, I turned on the water and heat and lit a fire in the large stone fireplace. After making sure the flames were burning well, I turned to Barbara and said, "I'm exhausted. I'm going upstairs to rest for a while. Would you mind unpacking the rest of the food?"

"Happy to. It's gorgeous to be here."

Not long after I lay down, Barbara answered the ringing phone and called me downstairs to talk to Anne's friend Joanna.

Weary, I sat at the breakfast counter and tuned in to Joanna's soft voice.

"Hi, Marie. I'm calling to say Anne can go home for a visit. I'm helping her get ready."

"I'm so glad," I said, wishing I could be at the hospital to help pack Anne's few things. "How is she?"

"She's weak but so happy to go home."

"Okay, good. Give her my love." As I started back up the stairs to resume my nap, the phone rang again. This time it was Simon, Anne's doctor.

"Anne asked me if she could go home for a few hours," he said. "She wants to be home and she wants to see her mother."

He sounded cautious. He knew I was one of Anne's attorneys, and I had the sense he was making sure I agreed. "Is there any reason why she shouldn't go home?" I asked.

"Medically, no. I told her that she could go home on the understanding that her nurse would be with her and that she would return to the hospital after the visit. She agreed." My tired brain tried to process his words. What did that mean, "medically, no"? And if it was okay for her to go home, why did she have to return to the hospital?

"How is she now?"

"Her condition is becoming critical. It is unlikely that the cancer can be controlled." What did "unlikely" mean? *Tell it like it is.*

Simon continued. "She's suffering from the disease and from the treatment of the disease."

Yes, and she always has been.

"The decision," he said, "is whether to continue with intensive care now. The level of care in intensive care is not a huge amount more than what's she's been getting. This is a normal decision at this point. Even if Anne is in intensive care, major problems may develop and she may die anyway."

I was trying to take all this in. I still didn't really think that Anne would die, certainly not very soon, yet Simon seemed to be implying that death was closer than I'd thought. "What kind of time are we looking at?" Reflexively, I started making notes on the little pad by the phone.

"Three or four weeks is a realistic estimate."

"I see. And if she stays at home and doesn't return to the hospital, what time are we looking at?"

"It could be two to five days."

I was grateful that at least Simon answered direct questions with candour. I said, "Does Anne know this?"

"No," he said.

"You didn't tell her?"

"No."

"Shouldn't she be told the truth?"

"It's not really a lie. Anne needs to believe there is a reasonable possibility of good things, and always has."

Oncologists certainly walk a fine line in determining how much to disclose, I thought. I persisted: "Anne was very ill yesterday and told me emphatically that she didn't want to live this way."

"Yes, Anne is adamant. She doesn't want to continue treatment if there's no medical merit. She can make the decision about returning this afternoon, when she's at home. When will you be back in the city?"

"I'm too exhausted to return today." I wanted to return but couldn't muster the energy to pack everything up again and drive back. Besides, I still had a sentence to prepare. "I'll come in the morning. Thank you for telling me this."

I hung up the phone and slowly rose, feeling a pain in my back from all the hours of sitting on the bench, sitting in the car, and not doing my usual exercises.

Edward had skied back and was sitting in the large chair near the fireplace looking at me, his cheeks rosy.

Feeling shaky, I sank down on the sofa beside Barbara. "Anne may die within two to five days." Tears streamed down my face. I was inconsolable even though I still didn't quite believe what the doctor had said.

Mid-afternoon, I called the hospital to see if Anne had left and was surprised when she answered the phone, sounding sanguine. "Hi, Marie. How is the snow?"

"The snow?" I didn't know what she was talking about.

"The snow. Aren't you skiing at Collingwood?" Her question didn't strike me as rote politeness, that formalized thoughtfulness toward others. Many people have good manners but lack genuine regard for others. Even as she was dying, Anne thought of others before herself.

"Oh, yes," I said. "At least, Edward is. It's great, thank you. And you?"

"Simon said I could go home! I'm waiting for my ride."

"I'm happy for you."

"I'll still have to come back here after the visit," she said, her voice flat.

I took a deep breath. "Anne," I said slowly, "If you don't want to go back to the hospital, you don't have to."

"What do you mean?"

"I mean, if you don't want to leave home, you don't have to." I spoke slowly. "You can see how you feel, once you're there."

"Here's Joanna now."

"Anne, I'll come down tomorrow morning."

After I hung up, Barbara said, "You did the right thing. Not many people would have the courage."

After the phone exchange, I wondered how much Anne had understood of what I'd said. Barbara and I ate lunch, and then I dragged myself to the black dining table to work. I sat looking through the large window past the shining snow piled high on the deck, out to the cobalt blue of Georgian Bay.

I opened my bench book to review the *Lam* case, a trial that had concluded three months earlier. It was the last thing in the world I wanted to do, but the sentencing was scheduled for Monday morning at ten. The trial had been lengthy, and I had to sentence four men. If it had been a judge-alone trial, I would already have reviewed the evidence in my reasons for judgment. However, as it was a jury trial, I had only the verdicts. I took a long look outside before I started making notes.

———

SIX ASIAN MEN had been charged with conspiracy to import and importing six kilograms of heroin with a street value of $13 million. The jury trial had lasted six weeks, with forty witnesses and over 150 exhibits. My charge to the jury took a day and a half. The nature of the case and the amount of money at stake brought out the legal heavyweights, and that, in turn, generated every conceivable legal challenge. The complex pre-trial motions alone had taken four weeks, including rulings on wiretaps and motions to quash the search warrants.

In addition to the usual legal procedures and complications, the trial had presented serious logistical challenges in order to accommodate the eleven defence counsel, six accused, and six Cantonese interpreters. The prisoner's box was too small for six, and it wouldn't have been fair to have some sitting inside and others out, so we'd used the largest courtroom, where all of the accused could sit in the grand jury box opposite the jury. In preparation, I had requested a particularly large jury panel to ensure the selection of twelve jurors able to serve for six weeks.

This case wasn't going to be as exciting to the public as a murder trial, and I wanted to be sure of having enough in the panel. Consequently, we began jury selection with 270 people crammed into the courtroom, some trailing into the hall and straining to hear. I spoke loudly and clearly.

On the first day, 140 prospective jurors were excused from jury duty because of lack of English language comprehension, health problems, or other hardships. As I usually did, I excused those required to care for others and those who would not be paid during jury duty by their place of employment. Employers must permit employees to be absent from work in order to serve as jurors, but the law does not require them to pay for lost wages. The province compensates jurors only after the tenth day of jury duty, at the rate of $40 per day, rising to $100 per day after ten weeks of service.

Remarkably, twelve persons willing and able to commit to a long jury trial were selected on the second day of the trial, after the challenge-for-cause procedure, undertaken by the lawyer for Chan to ascertain if prospective jurors were biased against Southeast Asians from Hong Kong. Strangely, that lawyer used his peremptory challenges to challenge prospective jurors who were Asian, as if they might be biased against Southeast Asians.

For six weeks, the court was an intense bustling community unto itself. With the accused, counsel, jury, interpreters, reporters, and court officers, a minimum of forty people were in attendance daily. Witnesses, police officers, and members of the public came and went constantly.

When the trial began, a lead counsel and an interpreter wearing a headset stood beside each of the six accused men. When the jury entered, the throng in the courtroom rose. I sat on the dais peering at all of them, thinking, *This is as good as it gets.* I'd worked hard to become a lawyer, and I'd clawed my way to do criminal jury work because I was a woman and because I'd had no criminal law experience before becoming a judge. In fact, I'd begun by sitting in criminal trials only four weeks a year.

Now I was a member of the "murder team," a select group of judges who could authorize after-hours wiretaps, and I had been a criminal-team leader. As well, I sat in the Divisional Court, an appellate and review court composed of three members of the Superior Court assigned at the pleasure of the Chief Justice. At the top of my game then, I knew the law and how to use it—the more complicated the better. I trusted my own judgment over any other.

These days, that sense of rightness and empowerment was gone, and my work, good as it was, no longer sustained me. I turned my attention back to the current afternoon, the work ahead of me, and my bench book.

The first two accused, Lam and Chan, had flown from Hong Kong to oversee the delivery of the heroin in Canada; the third accused, Kar Tat, was their agent in Canada who recruited the fourth accused, Ko, who in turn recruited two students, Eddie and Patrick. The last two—the mail drops—provided their addresses for delivery of the mailed packages of heroin.

To avoid confusion, I had directed that the accused men would sit in the same order every day and that counsel would sit at the counsel table in the same order as their clients. In this way, the jury had less difficulty differentiating between the accused men and their respective counsel. All the accused and some of

the lawyers were clean-shaven young men in their early twenties—except for Lam, the overseer, who was about thirty years
old. I vividly recalled his slender, elegant companion from Hong
Kong, and I easily remembered Ko, who'd recruited his student
friends; he had a forlorn, hangdog expression of gloom every
minute of the trial.

The investigation of the crimes began when a Canada Customs enforcement officer had examined a package containing
heroin that arrived in Canada Post: its value was declared to
be about three times higher than the usual HK$200. The feisty
RCMP officer-in-charge, Gagnon, a well-dressed Jacqueline Bis-
set look-a-like, ascertained that Eddie resided at that address
and was in Canada on a student visa. That evening, a second,
similar parcel, mailed to the address where Patrick lived, was
intercepted by another Canada Customs inspector.

The discovery of the second parcel pointed to a large scheme
of conspiracy to import drugs, and the police operation became
full-scale. Wiretap authorizations were obtained and surveillance of the two addresses began. Having substituted innocuous
powder for the heroin, officers posing as postal employees made
a "controlled delivery" of each parcel. On delivery day, everything was in place to follow the two students to whom the parcels
were delivered: to determine where the heroin was going and
who would pick up the parcels. Earlier surveillance and wiretaps
had elicited that while waiting for the deliveries, the students
had contact with Ko, and that Ko had contact with a fourth man,
Kar Tat. As a result, he was also followed after delivery. Ko was
followed to a downtown hotel, where he met Lam and Chan, the
two overseers from Hong Kong. The four men were then followed,

and when they came to a stop at the parking lot of Kar Tat's place, the takedown occurred. All four were arrested at the scene. The two students, Eddie and Patrick, were arrested later.

Officer-in-charge Corporal Gagnon—soon to be Sergeant Gagnon—was given the card-key for room 709 at the hotel where Ko met the two overseers. The key had been found in Chan's wallet. The next day she went to the room and seized travel documents, IDs, and the like. When she told the manager about the arrests, he asked her about the other room. "Other room?" she asked. The manager showed her into room 710, where another package containing heroin was found in a suitcase.

Eddie and Patrick gave evidence. Eddie testified that he was doing his friend Ko a favour by letting him use their addresses for mailing packages to lower the import duty. Patrick testified that he too was doing a favour for Ko but thought the package contained fake credit cards. Both claimed no knowledge of heroin in the packages. The jury gave them the benefit of the doubt, and they were acquitted.

Of the others, only the forlorn Ko gave evidence. The jury didn't believe him and had little sympathy. It cost his taxi-driver father $20,000 a year for him to stay in Canada, and he "guessed" the packages contained something illegal, but not heroin. Each of the four accused was to be sentenced on Monday for conspiracy to import heroin, importing heroin, conspiracy to traffic in heroin, and possession of heroin for the purpose of trafficking.

Finished with my summary of the facts, I reviewed the submissions made by counsel on sentence, decided on the sentences, and began preparing my reasons. When the room grew chilly, I rose to put another log on the fire.

Barbara, hearing my movements, leaned in to say, "Good, you're finished."

"Another half-hour should do it," I confirmed, hearing the tiredness in my own voice. I couldn't imagine Monday and how I was going to get through it all: charging the jury in the crotch-fondling case, delivering this drug sentence, and then continuing with the rose-tattoo case, all before going to see Anne at home or in the hospital, wherever she was by then. Still, I knew I would get through it, relying on something inside myself that I had always relied on.

The sun was setting when I closed my bench book, and Barbara had a martini ready.

Later in the evening, Anne's friend Susan called to say that Anne had decided to stay at home. Both Anne's sons were there with her. I told Susan I would return on Sunday, but it wouldn't be early as I was still exhausted.

I then called Simon to say the same thing, and he told me Anne was resting and could go back to the hospital tomorrow.

"Do you think she *should* go back?"

"It's okay if she wants to."

"Simon, if death is imminent, I feel she should die at home with her boys beside her. They're the most important thing for her. They shouldn't think their mother died somewhere else with strangers. It would be wrong for her to be in the hospital alone."

When Simon said "I agree," I closed my eyes and sighed. I felt calm, though the relief was dark and heavy.

Week One
Friday

LUNCH

Chicken sliced in a croissant with
lettuce & Miracle Whip

One hard pear

Two devilled eggs (*Fannie Farmer*, p. 102)—
make ten

Three peanut butter cookies, from recipe
box—make enough for weekend, freeze half

Drink

Chapter 14

JANUARY 29

BY THE TIME Barbara, Edward, and I had eaten breakfast on Sunday and packed up, it was ten-thirty. After dropping Edward at home, I drove to Anne's, and arrived in the early afternoon.

Anne's friend Fran answered the door, not smiling, and announced, "I'm exhausted. I haven't had any sleep in forty-eight hours. I slept beside Anne all night."

Despite her haggard look, jealousy cut through me. It should have been me. "How's Anne?"

"I'm getting things organized with her nurse for Anne to return to the hospital. Anne wants a massage before she goes back, and I'm calling the masseuse she likes."

I was surprised that Anne had changed her plans and wondered what else I'd missed in my short absence. Upstairs, Anne was lying in her bed breathing through oxygen tubes. An IV had been inserted, and she seemed to be surrounded by nearly as much equipment as she had been in her hospital bed. Still, here she had her dogs at her feet and her own things around her, and I thought she looked peaceful. She seemed to be in and out of consciousness, opening her eyes briefly and closing them again. I sat on a chair beside the bed until she stayed awake.

"Hi, Anne, how are you?"

Her eyelids fluttering, she smiled weakly. "It's so good to be home, to be back in my own bed."

"I'm sure it is. What have you decided to do?"

"I'm going back to the hospital."

"What does Simon say?"

"He guaranteed there would be an improvement."

I couldn't believe what I was hearing. How could he make such a promise? "When are you going?"

"When is the masseuse coming?" she asked. "I'll be able to handle going back if I have a massage. When can she come?"

"Fran's calling her. I'll give you a facial while you're waiting, if you like."

"Yes, yes. Your hands are wonderful. And I'd like to put on a fresh nightgown." She pointed to a drawer. I showed her two, and she pointed to the white silk one with small pink flowers and a matching bed jacket.

I lifted the sheet and blanket, eased her nightgown up, and saw that she was wearing an adult diaper. Careful not to move the Hickman line, I gently lifted her forward to raise the old nightie over her head and out of the IV line. Very carefully, I helped her into the delicate nightgown she had selected. Then I covered her with a soft towel and gently gave her a facial. When her mouth relaxed, I saw that her tongue was covered with white pustules.

She couldn't support herself, and every movement, even lying still and awake, was an effort. Exhausted by the facial and the movement, she fell asleep. I stayed beside her and quietly hummed, watching her breathe slowly and heavily.

Once, she opened her eyes and looked around her bedroom as if to get her bearings, and she smiled contentedly. Tiger Lily, one of the little dogs at the foot of the bed, saw that she had awakened, and walked to her head and licked her on the lips before returning to nestle by her leg. I watched with trepidation as the Siamese cat, which I hadn't seen under the bedclothes, emerged and did the very same thing. Anne looked warm and at ease as she slipped back to sleep. *Could she die now?* I wished her a peaceful passing.

Duncan came and sat on the other side of the bed. He held his mother's hand and cried as she slept. Later, Susan and Fran entered the room and also sat on the big bed. The group on the bed started chatting, at first quietly and then more noisily, and as everyone engaged in an animated conversation about Disney World, Anne became alert. Though I had no interest in such places, I enjoyed seeing Anne lively again.

When Anne drifted back to sleep, we tiptoed downstairs to the living room, where Fran announced, "I'll go back to the hospital with Anne."

"What was Anne told about going back?" I asked.

"Simon said that Anne would have two to six days if she stayed at home and perhaps three months in the hospital. He didn't tell Anne about the three months."

If he hadn't told Anne she'd have months more in the hospital, why was she returning? It made no sense to me. "I don't think she should go back to the hospital. There's absolutely no hope. And besides, she's suffering so," I said.

"I agree with Marie," said Anne's nurse, Marie Samuels. "She's more comfortable here."

"I disagree with both of you," said Fran. "She should go to the hospital, where she can get the best treatment."

Treatment? I thought. How absurd.

Simon came to make a house call, and I asked him what he had told Anne.

Looking downcast, he said, "I told her it was her choice. She could stay home and have a better quality of life, or she could go back to the hospital and continue treatment. She wouldn't go back to intensive care. The treatment would be continued, and then she had a chance of containing the cancer. She chose to go back to the hospital."

So, I thought, she was doing all that just for a chance. Yet I didn't think she had much chance, and I felt that Anne would not go if she knew how small that chance was.

Preparations continued for Anne's return to the hospital. Her nurse repacked her bag of medicines and clothing, and someone called for medical transport. I went upstairs, to find Simon, Susan, and Marie Samuels sitting and standing around Anne. In the middle of them, Anne looked small and overwhelmed. "May I stay another day?" she asked Simon.

"Yes, you can. You can also revisit your decision to return to the hospital. But you have to know what the choice means."

Anne turned to Susan and me. "What would *you* do?" she asked.

"It's up to you, Anne," Susan replied from the edge of the bed. "I can't give an opinion."

"Come on, you high-powered ladies. You always have an opinion!" Anne said to encourage us.

"I don't think you're strong enough for further treatment," I said quietly.

"I can't say," said Susan.

"Anne, are there any questions that you have for Simon?" I asked, hoping she would ask precise questions about timing and chances of recovery.

Anne turned to Simon. "What are the prospects for the future? For example, do I need platelets?"

"Yes, you do. I can tell from the sores on your tongue."

"I'm afraid of the side effects."

"Will Anne have the same symptoms she's been having?" I asked Simon.

"Some of them, yes."

Anne paused, absorbing this information. "Can I be cured?"

"We cannot cure the cancer," said Simon.

"If I couldn't be cured, why were you so aggressive before?" Anne asked.

"Then, there was a realistic chance of beating it."

"What are the chances that further chemotherapy will contain the cancer?" Anne continued. It was rugged, but I was glad she was asking clear questions and getting good information.

"About twenty-five percent. If you go back, you would slowly improve or you would decline. We would know one way or the other on a daily basis."

"Then I don't want to leave."

For Anne's benefit, I asked Simon a few more questions. "If Anne wants to return to the hospital, can she refuse any treatment?"

"Yes."

"If Anne goes to the hospital, can she return home any time she wants to?"

"Yes," he said. Anne was paying close attention.

"Could Anne postpone this decision until tomorrow?"

"Yes."

"Anne, do you want to talk about this anymore? Do you want more time to think?"

"No." She paused. "I'll rest now."

Marie Samuels stayed back with Anne, while Simon preceded me out of the room. He turned toward me before heading down the stairs and spoke quietly. "I concluded Anne didn't want to go back today," he said. There were tears in his eyes.

"I agree. She doesn't want to leave home." I squeezed his hand and added, "It was the right decision. It's the right thing to do."

That decided, we continued downstairs, where Fran said, "What's happening?"

"Anne is staying home today," I replied.

"How did all this change so fast?" Her own questions mirrored my own of an hour earlier. How we both wanted to know what was going on! How we both wanted to be the one at Anne's side!

"Anne discussed what she wanted to do upstairs with Simon," I said. "She wants to stay home."

Anne's brother arrived to take Duncan and Sandy to dinner, but Sandy didn't want to leave.

"You can go with Murray or, if you want, you can come to my place," Fran told him.

"You can come to mine too, if you want," Susan said.

"And to mine," I added. "Sandy, your mother is staying at home today."

"But," he said, wide-eyed, "shouldn't she go to the hospital?"

"She is sick," I agreed, "but she wants to stay home today. I've got two movies in the van that I rented for Darrell and Edward.

You can watch them if you like." It was a small comfort but all I had to offer. He nodded, and I went to my van to get the videos.

When I brought them into the kitchen, I met Simon's wife, who had accompanied her husband. "There are too many people here," said Margaret. She had a soft, gentle voice, but her manner was grave.

"It goes with the territory," I replied. "There's no husband. Anne's mother is in the basement suffering from a stroke, with her own nurses. The executors aren't family members. Anne doesn't really care for her brother, who is the closest next of kin, or he would probably be in charge."

"It's such a commotion."

"Yes, but there's always a lot of commotion."

About five o'clock, I returned home to have dinner with Edward. We were having some soup at the kitchen counter, and I was grateful for his company, thinking again how shocking it would be for me to have to give him and Darrell up, as Anne was giving up her boys. That made me wonder how aware Duncan and Sandy were of how soon their mother might die.

"Edward," I began hesitantly. "You know I'm thinking about Anne. I want to ask you something. If it were me dying, would you want to know about it? The details, the time frame, I mean?"

He answered immediately. "Yes. I'd want to know."

"And would you want to be there when I died?"

"No, because I'd want to remember you looking well and not sick." He paused and reconsidered. "Actually, yes. I would want to be there."

"Why?"

"In case there was something we wanted to say or wanted to do."

I knew then what I had to do. As soon as we'd finished eating, I called Simon to ask if Duncan and Sandy had been told their mother might die and that it might happen soon. He said the therapist had told them.

"Have they been told Anne could die right now?"

"No, not that she could die now."

"Should I say something to them?"

"Yes, they should be told."

I returned to Anne's, thinking hard about how to tell the boys and dreading the prospect. They knew I would be returning to pick up the movies, and they were comfortable with me, but of course they had no idea of the news I had to break to them. Anne's friend Joanna was there, and as we talked about the situation, we agreed to try to involve Anne's brother more in what was going on. That decision was relatively obvious; my next duty was far more subtle and difficult.

I joined Sandy on the sofa, where he sat staring at the last minutes of *Wolf*, starring Jack Nicholson.

"I like this movie better than the other movie, *Shadow*," Sandy said.

Just then, Marie Samuels, the nurse, beckoned me into the hallway. She wanted me to go get an ointment to put behind Anne's ear because she was having much difficulty breathing and the ointment seemed to help her congestion.

Taking the moment alone with her, I asked, "Will you know when Anne is going to die?"

"Yes."

"If you know it's time, I think the boys should be there."

"I agree."

Sandy and I watched the end of the movie together, and I told him I'd be back after returning the movies and getting some medicine for his mother. I was glad of the errands: I felt better to be doing something concrete that might help Anne, and it also postponed talking to Duncan and Sandy. I drove to the drugstore at Church and Wellesley, but it had none of the ointment. Frustrated, I continued on to the drugstore on Yonge Street near College, which also had none. The dark evening was cold, and it was hard to find a place to park. Driving through the night traffic, I was becoming frantic. I felt foolish, as if it were a waste of time, yet I continued on to the Shoppers Drug Mart at Bay and Gerrard streets. There, at last, a pharmacist handed me the right box. "It's no longer being manufactured," he said. "This is the last package."

I took the movies back to the video store and returned to Anne's with the precious ointment.

I went upstairs again, wondering what I'd find. Joanna was lying on the far side of the bed. Anne was alert, petting the cat and a dog that lay on top of the blanket that stretched between Anne's legs like a little hammock. She was chatting, not always lucidly. She spoke about not everyone liking wedding bells. It took us a minute to realize Anne was talking about the movie *Four Weddings and a Funeral*. She talked about the new tennis instructor at the Toronto Lawn Tennis Club. Anne and Joanna got into some light chat about titles—*marquis* and the like. At one point Anne said, "Well, I really should go now."

Joanna and I froze, taken aback, until we realized the phone was ringing and Anne meant she should answer the phone.

It was someone calling to confirm that a minister should come over, in response to Anne's request for Doug Stoute. Joanna made the arrangements, as Anne couldn't talk on the phone.

Anne was breathing heavily. Her throat was dry and I gave her a little water, after which she looked relieved, closed her eyes, and seemed to go back to sleep .

No longer able to postpone my discussion with Sandy, I went downstairs and found him in the hall. I walked close to him and put a hand on his arm, saying softly, "Sandy, your mother's condition is critical."

"She'll get better when she goes back to the hospital." He seemed sure of this.

I stifled a gasp, feeling worse by the minute, but forced myself to go on with the information I had to impart. As gently as I could, I said, "Sandy, there is now no real chance of recovery. I'm sorry, but there's no real chance even if your mother goes back to the hospital."

Sandy had a hard time taking this in. I waited a few moments. "You could sleep with her this evening if you want. Or the nurse could call you if things got bad."

Sandy began to cry. I hugged him closely, holding him as long as he'd let me, for a full minute before he pulled away. He walked into the living room, then back and forth behind the sofa. "Do you want me to go or to stay here with you?" I asked.

"Stay."

Together, we paced back and forth, back and forth. As we paced, I spoke from time to time, slowly, watching Sandy's silent face. I told him, "You have your mother's and your father's spirit and resources to count on ... It's all so sad ... You can cry all you want. You can mourn all you want ... You will have so much grief, so much pain. Yet I know you will eventually find the strength to get through it."

Sandy cried silently, tears washing down his face as they did mine.

"Your mother loves you so very much," I said, wondering if he could understand how much. "You and Duncan kept her going through everything. She tried so hard to be well for you." I could only imagine the anguish inside him as we walked back and forth, up and down the polished floorboards.

After several silent laps, Sandy asked, "What's going to happen to me now?"

"I don't know. I wish I could tell you. One thing I know is that nothing will happen overnight. You'll be consulted and other people will be consulted. You'll be able to give your views. Where you want to be will be important. You'll be listened to. If something happens and you don't like it, it can be changed."

Sandy moved to the sofa and sat down. I sat beside him. "I know it's not fair, Sandy. We want life to be fair, but it isn't. I'll help you in any way I can. I love your mother, and I'll love you."

"Does Duncan know?"

"I'm going to tell Duncan now. Will you be all right? I know how awful this is. I'm so sorry."

Sandy looked utterly forlorn, much how I felt as I stood up to look for Duncan. Flattened by sorrow, I left the living room. From the hall, I saw Duncan in the kitchen talking excitedly to Reverend Stoute, and I was relieved to see Joanna join Sandy in the living room.

I stood in the hall, hoping to get Duncan alone. Not wanting to interrupt, I waited several minutes, until I decided that perhaps it was best to tell Duncan in Reverend Stoute's presence;

that way he would be with Duncan after I left. I walked into the kitchen and leaned on the counter.

"Duncan, I'm leaving soon," I said. As Duncan looked up, I drew a deep breath. "Before I go, I have to tell you that your mother's condition is critical at this time. There is now no real possibility of recovery."

Duncan's eyes widened as he began to understand what could happen.

"Your mother will be in and out of lucidity," I continued, "but she will know you. You can be with her. If anything happens, the nurse could call you."

Duncan absorbed each statement—panic, fear, and grief showing all at once.

"I've just told Sandy." I kissed Duncan and hugged him, murmuring the best encouragement I could give: "Duncan, you have your mother's and your father's spirit inside you. It will help you through." Reverend Stoute and I made eye contact over Duncan's head, and he nodded at me. I left them together.

I walked back to the living room and hugged Sandy again. When I left, Sandy was sitting on the sofa holding his old ragged bunny from when he'd been a toddler.

I went upstairs one last time before going home, to find Anne awake but breathing heavily. She opened her eyes and looked at me, with something vacant in her expression.

"Do you know me?" I asked.

"Yes, Marie."

"You are a truly good person, Anne," I said. "You have done so many worthwhile things in your life. You have given of yourself to everyone."

Anne looked deep into my heart. "Marie, I thank you for all you have done for me."

"I love you so much, Anne."

Anne went back to sleep. I kissed her goodbye, hating to leave but feeling I'd done all I could do. I had nothing left in me, and the next day, Monday, would be demanding and brutal.

Week One
Friday

DINNER

Broiled veal chops (*Fannie Farmer*, p. 193)—don't overcook

Applesauce from a jar

Sweet and sour beets
(*Fannie Farmer*, p. 238)

Scalloped potatoes
(*Fannie Farmer*, p. 265)

Pineapple upside-down cake
(from Tuesday)

Chapter 15

JANUARY 30

I WAS WIDE AWAKE at six a.m. and rested enough to enjoy having breakfast with Edward. Over boiled eggs with "toast fingers" for dipping, we talked about the snow, the weekend, and Anne.

Alex had returned from his business trip late the night before and had gone straight to sleep without a chance for us to talk, but I was driving him to work so I could keep his car for the day. I hoped I might have an opportunity to see Anne later, although I doubted it. Alex and I drove down Yonge Street, blinded by the brilliant sun that beamed back from the glassy office buildings on this crisp, clear morning. "It's a good day to die," I remarked to Alex, not believing it. I brought him up to date, though he seemed unaffected by my friend's critical illness. I finished by saying, "You wouldn't believe what I have to do today. I hope I can make it through."

"You'll be fine," he said. I knew Alex had complete faith in my abilities, professional or otherwise. I knew he took them, and indeed me, for granted.

I arrived at the courthouse at eight o'clock. My docket listed the drug sentencing at nine, followed by the charge to the jury in the fondling case, and then the resumption of the rose-tattoo trial. With one hour before the official day descended, I first called Anne's brother, Murray. His wife answered the phone and told me he was at work. I told her that because Anne had decided not to go back to the hospital, it could be a matter of days before she passed away.

"Oh, no." She sounded shocked, as I supposed she was. "What about Duncan and Sandy?"

"I told them their mother might die soon. It was unbearable."

"I'm so worried about them," she said. "And what about Anne's mother?"

"I don't know what will happen to her." I hadn't been able to think about that at all, and I felt I couldn't be expected to. "Murray will have to look after his mother."

"Do you know what funeral arrangements Anne made?"

"I really have no information about that," I said, feeling besieged by her questions. "Anne didn't bring it up. It's not something I would ask about. I expect she's left instructions."

Realizing that I didn't know what would happen, in a practical sense, when Anne died, I called Donna Haley, a close friend and judicial colleague who was also an expert in estate law. She explained to me that because Anne was at home, a doctor would have to be called to sign the death certificate. Then the funeral home would be called to take charge of the body. I told her Anne had a will, and then suddenly remembered that the black binder was still at the hospital. Donna reminded me that the executors would have the final say about the body and then they would take charge of her estate.

One of the first things we learn in estate law is that there is no "property" in a dead body. A person may request burial or cremation, but the executors are not legally obliged to carry out those wishes.

After talking to Donna, I called Anne's brother at the office and brought him up to date.

"How are the boys?" Murray asked.

"Sandy was fine—well, as fine as he could be. He was sad, but his responses were appropriate. He seemed upset, but calm too. Not hysterical. I don't know about Duncan because I had to leave not long after I spoke to him. I was glad that he was with Reverend Stoute."

"I've already talked to Duncan about his mother dying. Duncan mentioned something about summer plans. I told him it wasn't going to happen."

I winced, imagining Duncan's disappointment and distress at that news, but I was glad Murray was stepping up to the task. "I think it's important that a person like yourself take charge. I'll support you in this," I said. I didn't want to be the one making arrangements after Anne's death, and I passed on to Murray the information that Donna had given me.

It seemed as if much less than an hour had passed when my deputy knocked to summon me to court. I was glad to see Frank, the chubby, ruddy-faced deputy who wouldn't chat me up.

"Your Honour, the accused have not yet arrived for sentencing. Counsel and the interpreters are in court."

"Would you make inquiries in the cells to see what happened?"

Paddy wagons transport prisoners from various detention centres throughout the city to the cells in the basement of the courthouse. It's often difficult to ensure that those in custody arrive at the cells in the courthouse for an earlier-than-usual nine-o'clock start. The logistics of this trial were going to be difficult right to the very end.

A colleague called to discuss a retirement dinner I wanted to arrange to honour Mabel Van Camp, the first woman appointed to the Supreme Court of Ontario and the fourth federally appointed woman judge in Canada. I'd been trying to arrange this event for some months, as I felt strongly that women should celebrate the achievements of those women who went before us. Mabel had resisted being singled out, and kept insisting, "There are others more deserving."

Trying every tack, I finally said, "Mabel, it's not personal. You just happen to be the first federally appointed superior court judge. It's important that we honour whoever was the first." On those grounds, she agreed. With my friend, we arranged a date for the dinner and a possible venue.

As soon as I hung up, the phone rang again. It was nine-thirty, and my housekeeper was on the line. "Madame," she whispered, "Mrs. Gibson has died."

The loss didn't register. I didn't let it sink in, knowing that if I thought about Anne, I couldn't get through the day. Even as I refused to feel, I continued to do what needed to be done for Anne—for her family. I listened to a voice-mail message from Anne's cousin; she was on her way to visit Anne at home. How devastated she would be when she arrived!

I called Murray again, but he had left the office. Then, remembering the black binder, I called Susan in her chambers. She was my colleague and Anne's close friend. I told her about Anne.

She was shocked, adding, "I'm glad I dropped in to see Anne on my way to work."

"How was she?" I asked. For a second, I let myself think of my friend.

"She was peaceful."

"Susan, I have to be in court any minute. Would you be able to go to Anne's room in the hospital to pick up the black binder containing Anne's papers?"

"Yes, I can go."

"Can you go now? I don't want the nurses picking everything up and keeping them."

"I'll go right now."

Manic, I continued phoning. I called each of the executors. I called Jessica, who wanted to adopt the boys, and I called two more of Anne's friends. Next, I called the Order of Canada office and the YWCA Women of Distinction office to advise them of Anne's passing. I had submitted applications for each of these honours on Anne's behalf. As I picked up the phone to continue making calls, my deputy returned, saying, "Your Honour, the prisoners have arrived."

At ten o'clock, I entered the courtroom. It was crowded with people involved in three trials. Not wanting to keep the jury waiting, I decided to handle the crotch-fondling case first.

"Good morning," I said. My mind was in Anne's bedroom, picturing the doctor and nurse with Anne's body. "I wish to advise those who are present on the *Lam* sentence proceedings that I have a jury to charge at this time. The *Lam* sentence proceedings will be adjourned for one hour. For those who are here on the *Davidson* trial, I can only say that the trial will resume after these two matters. I apologize for the inconvenience. Please let the deputy know where you can be reached."

I pictured Anne's cousin being let into the house, hearing the news. When those involved in the drug sentencing and the *Davidson* trial had left the courtroom, counsel in the fondling case took their seats at the counsel table. The jury was brought in. Anne was dead. I addressed the jury.

"Good morning, members of the jury. You have now heard all of the evidence and you have heard the addresses of counsel. It is now my privilege and my duty to speak to you about the law that applies to this case.

"As jurors you have a direct and deciding voice in the administration of justice. We are both judges, but our roles are quite different. I am the sole judge of the law; you are the sole judge of the facts. You must take the law as I give it to you now." Although I was reading the standard part of the charge on automatic, I spoke slowly, solemnly, as if I were saying it for the first time.

"I tell you as a matter of law that an accused person is presumed to be innocent and that presumption of innocence remains unless and until the Crown has proven the guilt of the accused beyond a reasonable doubt. This is not a charity given to this accused. It is an important legal principle that is applicable in every criminal trial. An accused person is presumed to be innocent until the Crown has satisfied you of his guilt beyond a reasonable doubt.

"The onus or the burden of proving the guilt of an accused person beyond a reasonable doubt rests upon the Crown and never shifts. There is no burden on an accused person to prove anything. The Crown must prove beyond a reasonable doubt that Dean Marsh is guilty of the offences with which he has been charged before he can be found guilty. If you have a reasonable doubt as to whether he committed either of these offences, then it is your duty to give him the benefit of the doubt and to find him not guilty. There is no burden on an accused person to prove his innocence.

"What is meant by 'reasonable doubt'? Use the words in their ordinary, natural meaning. A reasonable doubt is an honest and fair doubt based on reason and common sense. Proof beyond a reasonable doubt will be achieved when you are sure of the guilt of the accused person. It is not a doubt based on sympathy or prejudice or emotion."

I pictured Susan going with the nurse to Anne's hospital room and taking the heavy binder from the cupboard under the bedside stand. I could still see Anne in her hospital bed.

"I instruct you that in order to return a verdict in a criminal trial, it is necessary that all twelve of you be agreed on your decision. On occasion, this proves impossible, since jurors have the right to disagree. Disagreement, however, is the most undesirable result at the conclusion of any trial. No jury will be in any better position than you to determine the case right now.

"Members of the jury, your verdict must be unanimous. However, you may arrive at your verdict by differing views of the evidence. You need not agree on any one single piece of evidence, only your ultimate conclusion.

"In this case, you will have to determine, as every jury does, the credibility or truthfulness of the witnesses and the weight to be given to the testimony of each of the witnesses. How do you assess a witness's evidence to determine the credibility of the witness? The best advice I can give you is to use your own common sense. When you become a juror in a court of law, you do not leave your common sense at the courtroom door." As I spoke, I looked into each of the twelve faces before me, seeing their sombre, responsive eyes. Although I was barely aware of the words I was speaking, some of the emotion I was feeling carried into the charge. Although Anne was dead and I longed to be out of my robes to grieve for her, it was no less important that day than any other that the jury understand its role and perform it well. I was doing my duty, as a judge and as a friend—that would get me through the day.

"In weighing the testimony of the witnesses, there are some matters which may appeal to your common sense in determining how much reliance to place on any particular witness's evidence. It is a common occurrence that witnesses see and hear things differently. Discrepancies do not mean that testimony must be wholly discredited. Discrepancies may easily and innocently occur, particularly with the passage of time. A deliberate falsehood, on the other hand, is a different matter and may taint the rest of a witness's testimony.

"Some of the factors you may wish to take into account are: How did the witness testify? Did the witness seem sincere and forthright, or was the witness evasive and argumentative or not responsive to the questions that were being asked? Was the witness convincing? Did the witness's evidence make sense? Was the witness's evidence consistent within itself? If there is an inconsistency, is that because of a lapse of memory, a misperception of events, an honest mistake, or a deliberate lie?

"You may wish to consider whether the witness has an interest in the outcome of the case. Even though a witness may have an interest in the outcome of the case, that does not necessarily mean the witness is not telling the truth. Common sense, however, tells you to consider that witness's evidence carefully.

"When you are assessing evidence of the witnesses, bear in mind that you are not here to pass judgment on the lifestyle of any of the witnesses. The accused is on trial, and he is on trial only in respect of the offences with which he is charged."

I went on, explaining the difference between direct evidence and circumstantial evidence, and that circumstantial evidence is not second-class evidence. As I'd observed with other juries, their concentration was waning at that point.

I'd said all that boilerplate information so many times, I barely looked at my notes. Today, though, I was afraid not to be grounded or to lose my place, and I followed the text more closely. At the same time, I kept picturing the upheaval at Anne's house. What were Duncan and Sandy doing? I felt sure Reverend Stoute was there. After the general instruction, I went on to the offences charged.

"The indictment against this accused charges him with two counts of sexual assault. Members of the jury, I will first define assault and then sexual assault. The Criminal Code provides that an assault is the intentional application of force to another without the other's consent. A punch, a slap, a shove are all acts that are frequently assaults. No particular degree of strength is required. Mere touching is enough.

"The word 'sexual' in the context of sexual assault means anything involving or connected with sexual gratification.

"Members of the jury, age fourteen is the legal age for consent for sexual activity as alleged here. You will recall that David Byrne testified that he was fourteen years of age and would be fifteen in August. If you are satisfied beyond a reasonable doubt that these acts occurred when the complainant was under fourteen, then you do not have to concern yourselves with consent. Consent is legally irrelevant in respect of persons under the age of fourteen. In this case there is evidence on which you can find that the incident occurred when the complainant was under fourteen.

"In respect of each charge, the Crown must prove beyond a reasonable doubt, first, that the accused committed the offence at the time and place charged; second, that the accused intentionally applied force to the complainant; third, that these applications of force were sexual in nature.

"There is evidence on which you can find that the offences occurred at the time and place charged. David Byrne and several witnesses described David Byrne visiting their residence at the time charged.

"With respect to whether the applications of force were sexual in nature, if you are satisfied beyond a reasonable doubt that the acts occurred, you will have little difficulty finding that the acts were sexual in nature.

"I will now review some of the evidence." I summarized the evidence for the jury, though I was sure they had no difficulty remembering it. I told them they had to determine the credibility of David Byrne, a "youthful witness, testifying about matters that occurred almost two years earlier. As with any other witness, you must carefully assess the evidence of David Byrne. He was cross-examined at length with respect to inconsistencies in his evidence at the preliminary inquiry and his evidence at trial. You will consider any inconsistencies in determining the truthfulness of David Byrne. There was evidence that David, like others at the party, had been drinking, and you will consider what if any effect that alcohol may have on his ability to recall what occurred.

"There is some evidence that David may have a motive to fabricate because he was called 'a queer' after the party and he attributed these rumours to the accused. Members of the jury, motive is a factor that you may have regard to. It is for you to determine if the complainant told a deliberate falsehood because of the name-calling. The Crown does not have to prove motive and a witness does not have to prove or disprove motive; it is simply one factor you may take into account in determining the credibility of a witness.

"In this case, there is not only the evidence of the complainant; there is the evidence of Martin Snider, which is capable of supporting the evidence given by David. He testified that Dean Marsh told him he placed his hand on a young boy's crotch area and tongued his ear.

"Martin Snider has a lengthy criminal record. The fact that a witness has a criminal record doesn't mean that he's not a truthful witness. It is a factor you may take into account in determining credibility. You will assess his testimony as you would any other witness. He was cross-examined as to a motive he may have had to fabricate his testimony, namely, that he would receive favourable treatment in relation to his own outstanding charges. You must examine Martin Snider's evidence with great care.

"Members of the jury, you must deal with each charge separately. If you find the accused guilty or not guilty of one charge, you must not assume he is guilty or not guilty of the other charge.

"This is the end of my charge to you. When you go into your jury room, it is your duty to consult with one another and to deliberate with a view to reaching a just verdict based on the evidence. At the outset you will select a foreperson who will preside over your deliberations and who will see that your deliberations proceed in a calm and orderly fashion. Keep an open mind, listen to what is said by your fellow jurors, and put your views forward in a reasonable way. It is not your function to be a lawyer to argue one side or the other. You are judges. You will approach your deliberations calmly, put forward your own views, and listen to the views of others. If you have any questions, I ask you to put them in writing and I will reconvene the court for your assistance." I concluded then, and took a deep breath.

I expected that the jury would find the accused guilty as charged. I rarely disagreed with a jury verdict. Only once had I not agreed with a verdict. Notwithstanding considerable evidence, the jurors were unable to convict a hard-working religious black mother of welfare fraud. That was okay with me. It was their job, not mine.

I left the courtroom so that counsel could leave and the next group of counsel and parties could arrange themselves. I returned to my chambers and for ten minutes sat still in a chair, without moving, hardly breathing. I wondered if Anne's body was still at her home. Susan must be there by now, looking at Anne's final instructions.

My deputy arrived again and told me that all the prisoners were in court. I entered the courtroom and saw the four now-familiar prisoners in the dock. "Order, all rise." I sat at the dais and asked if all counsel were prepared to proceed with sentencing.

"Yes, Your Honour."

I turned to the lengthy notes I had prepared at the cabin on Saturday—what a long time ago that seemed! I began by outlining the charges and the verdicts found by the jury against the four accused men. I found that the relationship between the accused was hierarchical. Lam and Chan were overseers who came from Hong Kong to supervise the movements of the heroin when it arrived in Canada. The person responsible for the Canadian side of the importation was Kar Tat, who took instructions from these overseers. Kar Tat recruited Ko, asking him to provide addresses of others. Ko followed the instructions of Kar Tat. These four persons were arrested at the point when the heroin was to be turned over for further distribution. I found that the scheme was highly organized and that the four accused acted in concert, knew there was heroin in the back of Ko's vehicle, and knew the heroin was about to be turned over for further distribution under the direction and supervision of the overseers. Including the package found in the hotel room, the heroin amounted to about 5.5 kilograms and had a street value of $1.3 million.

I outlined the principles of sentencing. "The principles of sentencing require me to have regard for the need to deter others from engaging in the trafficking and importation of heroin and the need to deter these four accused from doing so again. I must also consider the seriousness of the crimes, the individual accused, and the possibility of rehabilitation in respect of each accused." I also took into account that Canada is a party to a number of international commitments respecting narcotics. I said, "I also have regard to the following: First, the importation of heroin is an offence of the utmost gravity. Heroin is a deadly drug, and this large amount of heroin could have devastating effects for thousands of people. Drug sentences, particularly for importing heroin, are harsh and rightly so for the protection of the public.

"Second, the importation was part of a sophisticated international scheme.

"Third, there is no evidence that any accused is an addict. The activity was engaged in for profit, which is an aggravating factor.

"Fourth, general deterrence is the prime sentencing factor in these cases."

I reviewed the sentences given in other cases involving similar crimes and continued, "In my view, a term of seventeen years imprisonment is appropriate for Lam." I applied the customary rule of giving credit for incarceration before trial by doubling it. Pre-trial custody is served in detention centres, which are maximum security facilities, and the detention there is known as "hard time." I gave Lam credit of nine months for his pre-trial custody of four and a half months. "I, therefore, sentence Lam to a further period of incarceration of sixteen years and three months."

I sentenced the nineteen-year-old Chan, who had no record and was in a subservient position to Lam, to fifteen years, which meant a further period of incarceration of thirteen years.

Evidence was given on sentence for Kar Tat, aged twenty-one, and a pre-sentence report was prepared. His father, who lived in Kowloon, Hong Kong, with his wife and three children, testified on behalf of his son. Kar Tat came from a close, supportive family. He had arrived in Canada on a student visa, failed his courses, and dropped out of school. I found that he was the chief organizer in Canada, and recruited and directed others. I sentenced him to a further period of incarceration of eight years and eight months.

Evidence was also adduced on behalf of Ko, aged twenty-one years, who came to Canada from Hong Kong on a student visa. He was a good friend of Kar Tat, whom he'd known in Hong Kong. Like Kar Tat, Ko had no criminal record and came from a stable and supportive family. He too did not complete his courses at school. After his arrest and obtaining bail, he had completed five courses. Ko had developed a relationship with a young woman in Canada, with whom he had a child.

"Ko enlisted two friends in a criminal endeavour who had to face criminal charges as a result. The Crown has not proved that Ko knew the precise amount involved. However, I find that he knew it was substantial, having regard to the sophisticated nature of the operation, the need to recruit two addresses, and the size of the packages. The Crown has not proved that Ko knew or was involved in the importation of heroin in the hotel room, and I am sentencing him on the basis of the two parcels that were in his car.

"Ko is an unfortunate young man who, like Kar Tat, engaged in criminal activity and failed in his duties to his family, to his friends, and to his host country by engaging in serious criminal activity on a large scale. He does appear to be genuinely remorseful. Indeed, he has looked downhearted and distraught throughout the trial. In my view, the appropriate sentence is a period of incarceration of seven years. I give him nine months credit for pre-trial custody of four and a half months. I therefore sentence Ko to a further period of incarceration of six years and three months.

"That concludes these proceedings. I thank counsel for their assistance throughout these matters."

The clerk intoned "All rise" as I left the courtroom and returned to my chambers.

———

IN MY CHAMBERS, I found that Susan had left a message: she'd arrived at the house and was asking me to help with the obituary. When I phoned the house, Anne's lovely voice answered, and for a moment, I thought, *Oh, you're not dead after all!* Then, in a flash, I realized it was her pre-recorded telephone greeting. I called again, and Susan answered.

"We're drafting the obituary," she said. "The problem is Anne had left instructions for a very sparse obituary."

"That wouldn't be right," I said. "She's being modest." *Here we go again*. I was all too familiar with women of achievement who were loath to acknowledge their accomplishments. Likewise, I had little patience with the women who say "I'm *only* a housewife," "I'm *just* a secretary," I had even less when successful women found it so hard to take a bow and say "Yes, I did it." Our achievements weren't because of our mothers, our families, our mentors, or a heavenly god. Why is it so ingrained for women to diminish what we do and who we are? Why would or should a woman like Anne request a brief obit? *A man takes a piss somewhere, and they put up a plaque.* The vulgarity of my thought shocked me: *piss* is my least favourite word. Yet I recalled the frustration that had earlier given rise to the sentiment.

When Mabel Van Camp, the first Superior Court woman judge retired, I asked the Chief Justice to offer her chambers in Osgoode

Hall to the most senior woman judge. When Mabel was appointed, these chambers had been fitted with an adjoining washroom, as hardly any of the Osgoode Hall chambers had private washrooms and all the other judges' washrooms were for males. Over the years, Mabel always had shared her chambers with visiting women judges. I thought it would be fitting that her chambers be preserved in some way in memory of Mabel, such as with a commemorative plaque.

My request to have the chambers continue to be occupied by a woman garnered little support, was assigned to two supernumerary male judges, and finally was refused by the Chief Justice. I had no luck either with my request to the Chief Justice and two successive treasurers of the Law Society to hang a portrait of the first woman judge in Canada, who presided in Ontario.

"Susan, I'll bring over my Order of Canada file at the luncheon recess," I said. "It has a lot of biographical information with dates."

I drafted a covering memo for Susan, Libby, and the others and attached it to the file:

I favour adding something like the following:

Anne was as warm and luminous in life as the clear brilliant sunshine on the day she parted. Anne's spirit and courage will warm all who knew and loved her and all whom she has helped. Her sons, Duncan and Sandy, sustained Anne throughout her illness and her love will nurture them always.

P.S. I think there should be a special acknowledgment for Duncan and Sandy.

P.P.S. Change voice message on phone.

My deputy entered the room. "Your Honour. The court is ready." At 12:20, my head reeling, I returned to the courtroom to resume the biker trial. Despite my determination, I could barely focus. The last Crown witness took the stand. The fifty-six-year-old woman was Kathy's mother, apparently very close to her daughter. "We talk three times a day," she said. Kathy had told her what happened in her apartment. "My daughter is very tiny and finicky," the mother went on. "She used to be happy. Now she just stares and gets grumpy."

Her daughter had told her she saw a rose tattoo on the man's arm. She'd begged Kathy to tell the police about the tattoo. Her daughter had refused, saying if she did, she'd be killed. Her mother turned her head to me, as if seeking validation. "I told her the system doesn't fail you all the time." I thought Kathy was lucky to have such a supportive and wise woman as her mother.

At one o'clock, I recessed for lunch and asked my secretary to drive me to Anne's—I couldn't concentrate enough to drive. Inez, my perfect secretary, agreed. While Inez drove I made myself eat a tuna sandwich, knowing I would need every ounce of energy.

At Anne's, the house was chaotic, filled with distraught people making various funeral arrangements. Everyone seemed to be on a phone, talking across a room, and making notes. I dropped off the file and returned to my chambers. I was back in court at two-thirty.

The Crown's case was concluded, and defence counsel called his client to the stand. A fair-haired, clean-shaven man walked from the prisoner's box to the witness box and was sworn. He was thirty-one years old and his girlfriend of seven years was in court. He was a millwright and had been in the union for six years. He'd been a member of Satan's Choice for three years.

At this point, the deputy assigned to the jury who were delib-erating in the fondling case brought me an envelope, saying, "The jury has a question, Your Honour." *Oh good grief! This day will never end.*

"I'm sorry to interrupt this trial," I said. "As you know, I have a jury deliberating in another trial, and they have asked a question. This trial will be adjourned. When I have answered the question, the Registrar will advise you and we will resume. I apologize for the inconvenience." Those in the biker trial cleared the court-room for the next set.

I took the sealed envelope to my chambers and read the ques-tions handwritten on foolscap paper:

1) Can we hear the list of names of witnesses that the defence was going to call if he had presented a defence?

I smiled as I read this question. It seemed it didn't matter how many times we told a jury that an accused person doesn't have to prove anything, they still want to know what might have been.

2) What legal consequences did David face if he decided to drop the whole thing before going to trial?

3) Can we have a copy of the minutes of the trial to look over while we are deliberating?

I was still smiling as I read the last two questions. Small won-der so-called reality television and courtroom shows are popular. People want to know everything.

I used to want to know everything too, I reflected. After I'd first been appointed a judge, I, a voracious fiction reader, had stopped reading fiction: there was no longer any need to, because real life was so varied and compelling. And I'd also wanted to know everything about everybody. But now I'd learned enough about people and what they did to themselves and others. I was sated.

I entered the courtroom and read the questions to counsel. Judges customarily seek the views and guidance of counsel when the jury asks questions. After reviewing my answers with counsel, I summoned the jury again.

I reread each question and answered in turn. "Members of the jury, with respect to the witnesses the defence might have called: Mr. Marsh has the legal and constitutional right to remain silent, and he has exercised his right to do so. He is presumed to be innocent. The Crown must prove his guilt beyond a reasonable doubt.

"Question two is theoretical. Charges are laid and investigated by the police. The decision to proceed to trial is made by the Crown. Persons who bring false charges may be subject to criminal proceedings. There is no evidence David Byrne decided to drop the case.

"You have asked for a copy of the minutes of the trial. There are no minutes of the trial. A transcript of the entire trial would take four days to produce. If there is any particular matter on which you require assistance, please advise the court, and I will provide it for you.

"You may now continue your deliberations."

The constable led the jurors out of the courtroom, I excused counsel, and the court was reassembled with the cast for the continuing biker trial. The afternoon seemed like a series of theatre sets as we assembled and disassembled, trying to make things make sense. Anne was dead and ten things seemed to be happening at once here and, I imagined, in her home.

Defence counsel resumed questioning the accused, Mike. The only way I could concentrate was to take verbatim notes of the testimony, which I routinely did. That afternoon I wrote constantly, fast, whether what I wrote was relevant or not.

The accused spoke confidently and testified that he joined a chapter and participated in the club run to Sudbury on the weekend of the alleged assault. "Club runs are mandatory. If I didn't go, I'd be fined." From where I sat, I couldn't see a tattoo. He acknowledged his criminal record—theft under, possession of a narcotic, failure to appear, possession of a restricted weapon. His longest sentence had been thirty days. At the time of the offence he was five foot eight and weighed 165 pounds.

"Well, I'm still five foot eight." He grinned as he said this. "Now I weigh 160 pounds." His record of arrest showed 176 pounds. He said he'd shaved his goatee in August before the Labour Day weekend run to Sudbury. He denied knowing the complainant, Kathy, or her boyfriend or any debt owed by him.

He described the club run to Sudbury, two hundred miles away. "On Saturday, September fourth, I went on my bike to Barry's house at eight-thirty in the morning. I waited a half-hour while he had an egg sandwich and tea. Then we went to a gas station and met the guys after. Four bikes and a truck were going to Sudbury. There were quite a few bikes on the road. We stopped in Bala for gas. The OPP was following and pulled the truck over. Those on bikes arrived at the clubhouse between three and four-thirty.

"It's a large bungalow on the side of a rock with a four-foot fence around the yard. Vern's got a real beautiful place," he said, moving his head back and forth. "I parked my bike and got a beer. All the Sudbury chapter were there." I looked at the photograph of Vern's. It *was* a bungalow, nestled in a big, bald rock. *Beauty certainly is relative*, I thought.

Noting my interest in the photo, Mike added, proudly, "You can see my bike in the picture. I tried to enlarge the photo, but the plate was blurred."

On that evening, he went on, "we drank beer, went for burgers, partied. At ten, we took a cab to a nightclub, Solid Gold. I was wearing a Choice vest, and they tried to get me to take my colours off. I refused. Everyone else took theirs off. I was slightly drunk and obnoxious. I razzed a management female. She was upset, and I took it off."

They went to another club till four and he was drunk. His friend Barry put him in a cab. Barry's girlfriend, Collette, had somehow gotten two black eyes, and Mike checked to see if she was okay. I wondered to myself why she had black eyes—maybe I'd find out why, maybe not. I'd long ago learned not to interject myself into the questioning. The accused left Sudbury about noon on Sunday and arrived in Toronto about five o'clock. "On the way back, I was pulled over at the French River Trading Post for riding recklessly." He said this somewhat proudly.

Then, finally, the tantalizing question: Do you have a tattoo?

"Yes," he said quickly. "I have the Grim Reaper on my right arm. It has a dagger through a rose and a Confederate flag. It's hard to think of it as a rose. You'd think the most distinctive feature is the dagger."

"Do you have any tattoos on your left arm?"

"No."

"No further questions, Your Honour."

Good, I thought. It was four-thirty, and I adjourned for the day. I retired to my chambers to await the jury's verdict in the underwear-fondling case. The deputy knocked on my door shortly thereafter.

"The jury has a verdict, Your Honour." I appreciated their timing. An earlier verdict would have meant yet another interruption in the court.

"Hallelujah. Assemble the court, please."

A few minutes later, I entered the courtroom for the sixth time that day. "Please bring in the jury."

"Will the accused please stand? Will the foreperson please stand?" the clerk asked. "Members of the jury, have you agreed unanimously on your verdict?"

"Yes," said the foreperson.

"How do you find the accused, guilty or not guilty, on count one?"

"Guilty."

"How do you find the accused, guilty or not guilty, on count two?"

"Guilty."

"Members of the jury, the court has recorded your verdict that you find the accused guilty on count one and guilty on count two. Is that recording correct?"

"Yes."

"So say you all?"

"Yes."

"Is there any reason why this jury should not be discharged?" I asked.

"No, Your Honour," replied both counsel, declining to have the members of the jury polled.

"Thank you very much, members of the jury. I thank you for the contribution you have made to the administration of justice.

I thank you for your attention and your punctuality. You have honoured your oath. You are now discharged and free to go." The members of the jury left the jury box.

"Are counsel agreed on an appropriate sentence?"

"No, Your Honour."

There being no joint submission or agreement on the appropriate sentence, I remanded sentencing till the following morning, and left the room and the building as fast I could.

———

I DROVE HOME, grateful to have Alex's car and looking forward to having dinner with Barbara before I would go to Anne's house to meet with her brother. I told Barbara as soon as she arrived that Anne had died that morning, and thanked heaven for best friends as she hugged me. Then I poured us both a glass of wine, relaxing in her company.

"You don't realize what a great thing you did for Anne," Barbara said, touching my arm.

"What do you mean?" I wondered if she was referring to the time I'd spent at Anne's bedside or to the legal advice I'd offered.

"You expressed your opinion that you wouldn't go back to the hospital."

"I couldn't bear to see her suffer needlessly." I remembered Anne's hollow, burnt face, her weakness and pitiful shaking. How could I have wished her to go back to that?

"When the time comes, I hope you'll do the same for me," Barbara said.

"Absolutely. I know you'll do the same for me."

By that time, we were both in tears.

At seven-thirty, Barbara drove me over to the house, which was thick with people. Gathered in the separate coach house on Anne's property were Anne's doctor, Simon; two of the three executors; Anne's friends Fran, with her husband, and Joanna; her brother, Murray, and his wife; and one of Anne's cousins. Anne's body was at the funeral home, but I wished I'd been able to see her one more time.

I looked at all those present, greatly relieved not to be an executor or a judge in this matter. Libby, Anne's friend and a lawyer, had been a perfect choice. As we settled down, Simon spoke first, saying the meeting was to consider what should be done for Duncan and Sandy. I didn't involve myself in that discussion, though at one point I outlined the legal position in relation to custody: that determination of guardianship came down to the welfare of the children, that any arrangements for custody were always open and could be varied in the best interests of the boys, and that given their ages, their wishes would be taken into account.

There seemed to be consensus: Duncan and Sandy would stay in the house for the short term; their cousin David and their stepbrother Mark would stay with them; and Anne's brother, Murray, would take charge with a view to becoming guardian. All agreed that the boys would be consulted. There was prolonged discussion about the boys, their schools, and the house. Murray asked if there was enough money. The executors replied cautiously, indicating that the house would probably have to be sold.

Bless Libby, I thought. She told everyone, "I don't lie. I won't lie to anyone. And I certainly will not lie to Duncan and Sandy."

As it would soon unfold, the house was sold, and Mark became the boys' guardian and lived with them in a new home in midtown Toronto.

The obituary was read and given to Murray for insertion in the papers. I was happy to see the reference to Duncan and Sandy.

GIBSON, Anne Elizabeth Margherita—At home, on January 30, 1995, at age 46, after a courageous and inspiring six-year battle with cancer. Beloved wife of the late F. Douglas Gibson, mother of Duncan and Sandy, stepmother of John, Jenny, Chris, Mark, Peter and James. Daughter of Nancy McDougald Pollitt and the late Donovan Hoult Pollitt and sister of Duncan and Murray Pollitt. Her sons, Duncan and Sandy, sustained Anne and her love will be with them always. Anne's spirit and courage will warm all who knew and loved her. Anne graduated from Havergal (1966), Briarcliff College (1970), Osgoode Hall (1973). She practiced, published and taught estate law from 1975–1995. She was Chairman and Founder of The Wellspring Centre, a support centre for cancer patients. She was trustee, co-Founder and legal advisor to Genesis Research Foundation. She was a member of the Board of Governors of Havergal College. Anne was the *Toronto Sun* "Woman on the Move," 1993, and the B'nai Brith Woman of the Year, 1994. The funeral service will be held at St. James Cathedral, 65 Church Street (at King and Church Streets) on Friday, February 3, 1995, at 11 o'clock. Charitable donations in her memory may be made to The Wellspring Centre, 81 Wellesley Street East, Coach House, Toronto, Ontario, M4Y 1H6 or to the Genesis Research Foundation, 92 College Street, 3rd floor, Toronto, Ontario, M5G 1L4.

After offering to help in any way, I excused myself at nine. My work was done. As I left the coach house, Murray's wife stopped me and thanked me for calling that morning. I asked how the boys were, and she told me they had spent time with Anne during the night. I was glad to hear that.

I walked over to the house to say hello to the boys. Duncan was in the basement. I hugged him and told him how sorry I was. Upstairs in the living room, Sandy was with the therapist. I hugged him and kissed him, telling I was sorry I could not be there earlier.

"Thank you for being the only person who was honest," he said, his fourteen-year-old voice cracking slightly. "Everyone was in the house and nobody said anything."

"I love you, Sandy. You can come and visit Edward and me any time."

"What's going to happen?" he asked.

"I was at the meeting. Nothing's going to happen fast. You and Duncan will be consulted about what will happen. They're good people. Libby is an executor, and she won't lie to you." Wishing I could give him more, I said, "I'll keep in touch with you."

As I was leaving, the therapist told me how much Sandy appreciated my telling him about his mother, and that Sandy wanted me to stay in his life. "That's the best thing I've heard all day," I replied.

After calling Alex to pick me up—"Watch for me, I'm going to start walking"—I stepped in to the cold air, exhausted in body and spirit, lonely for Anne. I was too tired to cry the tears I knew were soon to come.

Week Two
Monday

BREAKFAST

Vitamin pill

Toad-in-the-hole (*Kids' Cooking*, p. 15)

Welch's frozen grape juice

Slice of crisp bacon

Toast

Chapter 16

JANUARY 31

"ORDER IN THE COURT. All rise." I was so exhausted I could barely remember what case I was doing. I looked out at two sets of Crown attorneys and defence counsel. I looked down at the two indictments the court clerk had put in front of me and opened my bench book to refresh my memory. Then I remembered, and advised those assembled that we would be proceeding with the Dean Marsh sentencing, and then the *Davidson* trial would continue. I waited for the parties to leave and for the court to become quiet.

Ms. Carr, the Crown attorney, rose confidently. "Your Honour, I tender Dean Marsh's criminal record as Exhibit One." I read Dean's criminal record going back some ten years: thirty-five convictions for a number of thefts, being unlawfully in a dwelling, forgery, fraud, theft of credit card, use of stolen credit card, impersonating a police officer, dangerous driving, and then the most recent one, the kicker: abduction of person under fourteen years of age. For that abduction he had been sentenced to two years, which was varied on appeal to twelve months. Given his record, it was easy to understand why he hadn't taken the stand.

"Your Honour," she began, "with respect to the nature of the offences, I acknowledge that the crimes are at the lower end of the scale. As to the nature of the offender, Mr. Marsh is a thirty-five-year-old repeat offender, and—" She paused. "—he has a conviction for abduction. This conviction raises serious concerns in light of his present convictions. He pled guilty to that earlier charge of abduction. I have a transcript of the sentence proceedings in this court on the abduction conviction and the pre-sentence report filed at that time."

I read the transcript and the report. I generally enjoyed reading pre-sentence reports, because they fleshed out the person before the court. Today, I read it twice to make sure I missed nothing. Dean Marsh admitted he had abducted the boy, whom he'd befriended in an empty building and given food and shelter. Three days later, when he saw the television report on the missing boy, he called the police. He'd spent ten months in pre-trial custody in segregation, as opposed to protective custody, which meant exactly one movie a week, no television, no radio. He was locked up twenty-three and a half hours a day and allowed twenty minutes per day in the yard, weather permitting.

At that sentencing, the Crown asked for six to twelve months in addition to his pre-trial custody of seven months. The sentencing judge had rightly observed that with his thirty-five convictions, he was serving a life sentence on the instalment plan. The pre-sentence report further noted that the accused worked sporadically at odd jobs—a caller in a bingo hall and a sandwich-maker at a sub shop. Again, that was not surprising with his record. When that judge had asked Mr. Marsh if he wanted to say anything himself, Mr. Marsh told him: "I lost my sister while I was in jail. I have gone through a great deal of grief and pain for that, and a lot of self-incrimination due to the fact that if I hadn't picked up this child and harboured him for three days, I would have been there for her when she needed me." Then Mr. Marsh had done something he absolutely should not have. He'd baited the sentencing judge, saying, "Well, Your Honour, all I can suggest if you feel that further incarceration is needed and after what I've suffered and gone through, just give me two years."

"I was thinking twelve months in the reformatory," said the judge.

"Two years," Dean Marsh snapped back.

Then the judge did something *he* absolutely shouldn't have: he rose to the bait. "All right. You want to go to the penitentiary. Two years in the penitentiary."

"It's not that I want to. I'm saying I don't understand what further incarceration is going to do for me. What is it going to benefit me?"

"It's going to send a message to society and, hopefully, deter you from getting involved again in this kind of thing."

"It's not in your hands. After what I have received, fuck it."

The sentence was appealed and the Court of Appeal reduced the sentence to twelve months, the same sentence the trial judged had been inclined to impose.

Rereading that sentencing scene reminded me of the time a man trudged past me on his way back to the cells after I'd found him guilty. "Fucking old cow," he fumed as he walked out. His counsel shook his head and rolled his eyes, appreciating that such rudeness was stupid, since I hadn't sentenced the prisoner yet. Crown counsel had leapt to her feet, asking me to find him in contempt of court. As I had another matter at hand, I blithely answered I wasn't sure I heard precisely what he said. Needless to say, at his sentencing, the first words he uttered were an apology. I didn't impose a greater sentence for his outburst, and I was prepared to make allowances for occasional lapses of control. It was one of those rare occasions where justice is better served deaf.

That morning, one day past Anne's death, Ms. Carr submitted that the principles of general and specific deterrence required further imprisonment of Dean Marsh for the protection of the community, and she asked me to take into account that he had elected to have a jury trial.

In mentioning his election of trial by jury, Ms. Carr was asking me to impose a heavier sentence. Every person accused of a serious offence has the right to elect trial by jury. However, as a practical matter, in cases where the evidence against the accused is overwhelming or the charge is trifling, the sentencing judge may consider that the expense of a jury trial is not warranted. On the other side, a person pleading guilty or re-electing trial by judge saves the state the burden of a jury trial and may receive a more favourable sentence, especially if vulnerable witnesses are relieved of the necessity of testifying at trial.

In Marsh's case, I decided not to penalize him for choosing trial by jury. Although the circumstances had been trifling, the possible consequences for this accused upon a finding of guilt were great, given his lengthy record and his prior conviction for abduction. So he'd chosen a jury trial, as was his right.

I turned to defence counsel. "Mr. Smith, submissions for the defence." He rose ponderously, his receding hairline gleaming, and I anticipated another lengthy, extremely thorough oration.

"Your Honour, with respect to the abduction conviction, my client pleaded guilty to that offence. The boy was the same age as his son and had left a group home. He was helping the boy. It was only when he saw the television report that he realized the boy was missing.

"My client is thirty-seven years of age and was born in Toronto. He is the divorced father of three children, aged three, nine, and seven years of age. His mother is a nurse and his father is a college teacher. He has three brothers; one is a guard at Millhaven Penitentiary, one is an executive in California, and the other works at Bell Canada.

"The Crown takes issue with my client exercising his right to trial by jury. It's no fault of my client that we are in this court. We shouldn't have been here. If the Crown had proceeded summarily in the lower court, we wouldn't be here. If he'd been convicted of a summary offence, the maximum sentence would have been three months. My client should not have to serve any more time in custody. As well, Your Honour, there was no need for the Crown to lay two charges for one incident. I suggest to you that the Crown is being homophobic."

I certainly didn't think the Crown was being homophobic. In this case, it had come to the attention of the authorities that sexual fondling of a boy occurred, and they'd investigated it, resulting in the charges. I thought the case would have proceeded in the same way if Dean Marsh had been Diane Marsh.

Mr. Smith went on: "I did not call evidence at trial, Your Honour, because too much damage would have been done by the introduction of his record in evidence.

"As for remorse, hypocrisy takes over substance. Hypocrites leap on the horse of remorse to lessen punishment. My client has been in custody for seven months, which, giving credit, is a sentence of fourteen months."

Mr. Smith had a point. I was required to take in to account whether the accused showed remorse for his crime. It's a catch-22 situation because, first, remorse in the face of a plea of not guilty and before being found guilty makes little sense. Remorse after being found guilty is often construed as, or is in actuality, remorse for having been convicted.

"I don't need to hear from you further, Mr. Smith."

He looked startled. "But I haven't finished, Your Honour."

"Yes, you have, Mr. Smith."

Unaccustomed as Mr. Smith was to being cut off, with a regretful look at his sheaf of papers, he slowly took his seat.

Mr. Smith enjoyed hearing himself talk, but I agreed with his submission that his client had served a sufficient sentence with his pre-trial custody—I didn't need to hear further submissions from him to convince me to do something I was already going to do.

I proceeded to give detailed reasons for sentence, reviewing the evidence at trial and the submissions on sentence. I concluded, "In my opinion, notwithstanding the lengthy record, having regard to the relatively minor nature of these offences, the appropriate sentence is fourteen months." I then addressed Dean Marsh directly, looking him in the face. "As you have spent seven months in pre-trial custody, I sentence you to time served. I am placing you on probation for two years. You shall have no contact whatsoever, directly or indirectly, with the complainant. I am further recommending that the probation officer order you to undergo a psychiatric or psychological assessment.

You will report as required by your probation officer. Thank you, counsel, for your assistance." I declared the court adjourned for fifteen minutes so that the room could be cleared for the ongoing biker trial.

I returned to my chambers and sat at my desk. Anne was dead. What was I? Back at work, alive, functioning, fulfilling my duty; but I'd had enough of seeing and living and working in the sluice of life. I felt I could no longer endure seeing the remains of the legal autopsies, the shredded and rotten detritus of others' lives.

Furthermore, I didn't want to be sitting above everyone. I wanted to be in the fray, in the thick, pulsing, active stream happening in present time. I was tired of examining the second drama, the re-enactment of events gone before. I wanted to be in the first drama. I wanted to be in the heart of life, not removed from it.

After thirteen years on the bench, I seemed to be half-living other people's lives yet not living my own. I was reliving the lives of others—the father who sodomized his stepdaughter on their walks in the local park; the six-year-old on the stand who plaited and unplaited the ears of her worn, stuffed bunny, unable to look at her molester in the prisoner's box; the wife who had allowed her children to be tortured for years by her husband and who now carried a hat pin to stab herself as she crossed the street, lest she begin to go into another personality; the husband and wife who broke every major bone in their newborn's body... The horrors were unending, and too many details stayed fresh. I was always on the outside required to look in, seeing what they did and who they did it to, seeing who they were, all those accused and innocent and guilty and not guilty who lived rent-free in my mind and appeared at will.

Anne was dead. Where was she now? In a freezer? Already in the coffin?

I felt lifeless too. It wasn't only the range of the horrors I witnessed second- or third-hand, or that I wanted to let no more such tenants into the cubbyholes of my mind. Exhausted by being a witness to the lives of others, I wanted to find the energy to live my own life. Of course I knew being a judge was important, relevant, powerful, and prestigious. *I'm a success—and I'm a good judge.* Why wasn't that enough?

Anne was dead. I wanted more from life. I wanted more of that passion and commitment I felt for Anne, passion and commitment that had come from nowhere—somewhere—deep inside me.

I want to live fully in the moment. I don't want a role. I want more immediacy, more directness, more harmony of mind and heart. I no longer wanted to dissect what had gone on before, a robed institutional cog in the machine of justice.

The familiar, discreet knock at the door summoned me back to the courtroom to resume the biker trial. As I took my seat, I remembered where the trial had begun, with Kathy tied to her bed, a knife running back and forth over her arms and legs. The memory morphed into Anne suffering in her hospital bed. With so many threads hanging in my overfull brain, I was grateful for my accustomed position awaiting the continuation of the story that would unfold before me.

"Your Honour," Crown counsel began. "When we adjourned, the accused had completed his evidence-in-chief."

"Thank you. You may cross-examine."

Mike Davidson, the one who'd joked about still being five foot eight, the one who'd said his tattoo was not so much a rose as a dagger, strode confidently to the witness box, where the Registrar reminded him he was still under oath.

"Do you have a motorcycle?"

"Yes, you need a Harley to join."

"Satan's Choice is an outlaw club, correct?"

"Yes."

"You have a one percent patch?"

"Yes."

"That means you are one percent of the population and you are above the law?"

"No." He shook his head vehemently. "It means we're brothers. The rules of the club require loyalty."

"You told the court you weigh 160 pounds. Your arrest record shows your weight at 175 pounds. Does your weight fluctuate?"

I was grateful for the familiar pace of conducting a trial. Writing most of what the witness said absorbed my attention and kept grief at bay.

"No, but I did say that when I was arrested. I like to say I'm heavier than I am."

"Why is that?"

"Because most people I'm around are heavier."

"You've been to Sudbury before?"

"About six or seven times."

"Those photos you produced of the ride could have been taken at one of the other rides?"

"No. I asked around to see if there were any taken for that ride. Anyway, the police were noting plates that day. Mine would be one of the first they'd see."

"This incident occurred on Saturday, September fourth, about ten in the evening. You would have had time to collect the debt and go to Sudbury and return, isn't that right?"

"Well, I didn't."

"No further questions."

The next defence witness was Collette C., a dark-haired woman wearing tight jeans. Realizing that I was looking forward to hearing her, I was relieved that my interest in those who came before me hadn't waned.

Collette testified, with a measure of disdain and in a gravelly voice, that she had gone with a girlfriend on the club run to Sudbury on Labour Day weekend. She corroborated that she and others were stopped on the way and that after they were pulled over, she drove the truck to Sudbury. She also corroborated Mike's attendance at the nightclub, the argument about wearing colours inside, and that Mike had sat with her because she had two black eyes. About that injury, she said simply, "I said the wrong thing to the wrong person." She saw Mike at brunch the next day.

Over the three following days that it took to conclude the trial, I would hear from a motley array of bikers. I was surprised at the number of them called to the stand, knowing how reluctant and unwilling they usually were to testify about each other and about club activities.

The next defence witness, Trevor A., looked like Willie Nelson and smelled of peanuts. He testified that he was a member of Satan's Choice and self-employed. "I rent a tow truck," he said. He had a criminal record for breaking and entering, for which he'd received probation. He'd been stopped many times by the police—"They know me," he said flatly. He'd known Mike, the accused, for five years, and both men had been on the Sudbury run. Mike, he said, was at his side "most of the night" and left for Toronto about one o'clock. He knew Kathy's boyfriend, Fred Clark, "vaguely."

"I met him to discuss the debt," he said. "That was after Sudbury. I asked him to make a payment. He said yes."

Defence counsel asked him how tall he was.

"Five feet ten inches."

"How much did you weigh in 1993?"

"Two hundred and thirty pounds. I was working out."

"Do you look the same today?"

"I had blond hair and a goatee then."

"Do you have tattoos?"

"Yes, on both arms."

"No further questions."

"Ms. Barker, cross-examination."

"Mr. A., do you have a rose and dagger tattoo?"

"No."

"Do you have a one percent patch?"

"Yes."

"What does it mean?"

"It means many things. It's part of the colours. It means one percent that is beyond the law. It means we have loyalty."

"What happens if you are disloyal?"

"The penalty for disloyalty is to be kicked out."

"It means you would lie for a brother, doesn't it?"

"I wouldn't lie for a brother." His neck turned bright red. I agreed with his neck—he was lying.

"Do you know Collette?"

"Yeah. She's been around on other runs."

"Did she have two black eyes?"

"Yeah, it was a love spat." *Sure, it was!*

Next was Barry G., the past president of the Oshawa chapter of Satan's Choice. He had long grey hair that was short on top. Three substantial rings adorned his fingers. He'd been a member of Choice for thirty years and had founded the chapter. As he put it, he "didn't want to hang out with the people who rode Hondas."

He'd had breakfast with the accused and had been in the truck going to Sudbury. In addition to his burly appearance, he had a serious record, including various assaults and a conviction for conspiracy to traffic, for which he was sentenced to twelve years. He'd known Mike for eight years. He acknowledged in cross-examination that before Mike became a member in 1993, he'd been something of an underling. "He had to do what he was told," he said.

The next defence witness, Rick W., in army pants, was beefy and tattooed. He had a short brown goatee and wore an earring in his right ear. He was sneezing and coughing, sick with flu, and I kept my left hand over my nose. A member of Satan's Choice for one year, he was currently out on bail on drug charges. He corroborated that he was in the truck that was pulled over by the police. He didn't go to the strip bar, preferring a country-and-western bar, but he had seen Mike at the hotel.

He was followed by Paul H., who wore his brown hair in what I was concluding must be a favoured biker style—short on top, long at the back. He had a goatee and tattoos. I noted that he had three rings on his left hand and walked with a limp, but by that time I could barely distinguish one biker from the other. As Paul lived in Sudbury, he'd hosted the run, and he testified that Mike had been there till Sunday at two p.m.

The next defence witness, David MacD., also had long hair that was short on the top but he distinguished and differentiated himself by wearing a suit. A foreign exchange broker, he wasn't part of Satan's Choice but had gone on the run with a friend who was a member. He'd seen Mike at the club and at the strip club and met him on the way back to Toronto at a restaurant in Parry Sound.

At the end of the long parade was the last defence witness, François, a tattooed forty-four-year-old with long black and grey hair tied in a ponytail. Speaking with a Québécois accent, he testified that he had a criminal record for obtaining money under false pretences and assault. That couldn't have been too serious, as there was no sentence of imprisonment. He was the owner of DDC, a registered Ontario company, the company said to be collecting the debt, but he'd never employed Mike, the accused. He was familiar with Fred Clark's debt and testified that he owed $46,000, but he denied intimidating Fred's girlfriend, saying, "I just do out-of-town."

The array of witnesses in the formal trial setting was carrying me along through my personal grief. In the courtroom, as the trial's life took over, mourning was at bay. I was grateful for the momentum of the drama before me and for the comfort of the system of justice that almost appeared to be working without me. The system mostly did the job it was supposed to. Yes, I saw its limitations, yet it was more than that. I wasn't sure I wanted to continue to be a part of it, but for that day, the matter at hand grounded me.

Crown counsel did her best to show that each one of the stream of bikers was lying, though each witness essentially corroborated every part of the weekend bike run. In reply to the defence witnesses, the Crown called Detective Sergeant McIsaac, an Ontario Provincial Police officer for twenty-five years, who worked in a special squad dealing with motorcycle gangs. He had done surveillance of the Sudbury clubhouse on the Labour Day weekend, anticipating a possible conflict between Satan's Choice and the Black Diamond club. He noted down those he saw as well as licence plate numbers. Though he knew the accused, he didn't note him on Saturday at the clubhouse or at the hotels. He did, however, see him in Parry Sound—located between Sudbury and Oshawa—between three-thirty and four, at the Trading Post restaurant. "Mike was animated and said hi. Normally he's withdrawn." The inference could be drawn that Mike was drawing attention to himself in front of the officer.

Crown counsel asked him if he made notes of who he had seen over the weekend.

"Yes. On Friday at four o'clock about nine members arrived. I saw Barry G., whom I've known for years. I didn't see Mike at all. I shut down at two a.m. I didn't see Mike at any of the hotels. I saw Trevor A. on Saturday around the clubhouse. I saw Paul H. I saw François S. at the Journey's Inn. I saw Ricky W. David MacD. is new."

Defence counsel rose to cross-examine the officer.

"It was crucial to know who was attending the meet, and that's why you took notes, is that correct?"

"Yes."

"Your notes don't indicate Barry G. was there?"

"That was an oversight on my part."

"No further questions and no further defence evidence." The implication was clear: if the officer had made one oversight of someone he knew, he could have made another. With that, defence counsel returned to his table, and I turned to the Crown and asked for submissions.

"The defence raised is that of alibi. I submit, Your Honour, that the alibi is false. Mike was not in Sudbury on the Labour Day weekend of September. It is the position of the Crown that Mike rode to Sudbury on Sunday. I acknowledge it would be tight, because it is a four- to five-hour ride from Oshawa to Sudbury, but it is possible.

"Seven witnesses testified that Mike was in Sudbury. I ask you not to believe them. There are numerous inconsistencies in their evidence. I acknowledge that many are minor. I ask Your Honour to find that the alibi evidence does not raise a reasonable doubt.

"I ask you to find that the identification evidence is reliable. The accused was identified by the victim in a photo lineup. Three men had visited on an earlier occasion, and Kathy correctly identified them. She correctly identified that Mike had a rose tattoo and told her mother about it.

"I ask you to accept the identification evidence and find the Crown has proved the charges beyond a reasonable doubt."

"Thank you. Submissions for the defence, Mr. Mather."

Mr. Mather, looking serious but calm, began: "There are major discrepancies in the description of the perpetrator. The most glaring inconsistency is that Kathy described the perpetrator as five foot eleven and weighing 220 pounds. My client is five foot eight and weighed a maximum of 174 pounds.

"The photo lineup was not representative because the officer selected photographs of Satan's Choice members and did not match the physical description given.

"The alibi evidence raises a reasonable doubt. The accused was in Sudbury for the weekend. It is entirely unlikely that the accused rode up on Sunday. It's true that Detective Sergeant McIsaac didn't make a note of the accused being on the run, but this is not significant because his notes are incomplete. He didn't note the presence of Barry G. He did not properly do his job, although he is a credible witness.

"The Crown may have proven extortion but no crime has been proven against this accused."

"Thank you, counsel," I said, automatically. "I'll adjourn to prepare my reasons. Please advise the Registrar where you'll be."

As Anne's funeral was the next day, I did not want to carry the matter over. I reviewed the evidence, paying particular attention to the identification evidence and the descriptions of the rose tattoo. Within an hour or two, I wrote an outline of reasons for judgment and returned to court to give them.

I began: "The accused is charged with one count of sexually assaulting Kathy Y. with a knife on August twenty-fourth, 1993, and one count of sexually assaulting Kathy Y. on September fourth, 1993." I reviewed the evidence of the witnesses in detail and continued. "The description given by Kathy Y. is that her assailant on August twenty-fourth was a thirty-six-year-old white male, weighing 210 pounds, with light brown, shoulder-length hair, a goatee, and numerous tattoos on both arms, mainly the left. He had a scruffy, biker appearance and a bad, musty smell. This description does not match that of the accused before the court, who is thirty-one years of age, five feet eight inches tall, and weighs about 170 pounds.

"With respect to September fourth, Kathy Y. testified that one of the two men was the same perpetrator as before. She described him as thirty-three to thirty-six years old, five feet ten or five feet eleven, had a large build, with brown hair, a bit on the shoulders.

"Kathy also testified that the perpetrator had a rose tattoo on the inside of his right arm. The first time that Kathy Y. testified that the perpetrator had a rose tattoo was at this trial. She testified she withheld that information earlier because she didn't want the person caught. She just wanted to be left alone. Over time it came back to her, and she told her mother about the tattoo, three months before the trial. His tattoo was shown to the court. It is difficult to imagine describing it as a rose tattoo. The most prominent feature is a dagger with some rose configuration.

"She recounted a pattern of menacing behaviour arising out of a claim made against her boyfriend, Fred Clark, by his ex-girlfriend.

"Mike Davidson testified on his own behalf. He testified that on August twenty-fourth, he was home all day and his girlfriend arrived in the evening. He testified that on September fourth of the Labour Day weekend, he attended a compulsory Satan's Choice club run. He arrived at the clubhouse in Sudbury between three and four-thirty. He stayed at the Coach House Motel. In the evening, he joined others at the Solid Gold. He wore his Satan's Choice vest and there was a minor incident when he initially refused to remove it. At closing, he went to the clubhouse and left about three or four the next day.

"Several witnesses testified that the accused was in Sudbury for the club run and corroborated the incident at the Solid Gold. Four members of Satan's Choice, who have criminal records, testified that the accused was in Sudbury on Saturday and Sunday of the Labour Day weekend. A girlfriend of a member and David MacD. testified to this effect as well.

"The complainant identified the accused as the perpetrator on both occasions. If the accused was in Sudbury on Saturday, September fourth, he could not have attended at the home of the complainant. If he did not attend on September fourth, the initial identification of Mike Davidson as the perpetrator is undermined.

"The defence evidence of alibi raises a reasonable doubt notwithstanding the unsavoury characters of most of the defence witnesses. Taken together, and having regard to the minor nature of inconsistencies in their evidence, it was sufficient to put the accused in Sudbury at the relevant time. The police officer noting plates of bikers did not note the plate of the accused, but his evidence is not significant in that his notes were incomplete in this regard. While it is possible that the accused could have driven up to Sudbury on Sunday and returned on the same day, such a finding is improbable in the face of the other alibi evidence.

"Kathy's evidence was credible, but not entirely reliable with respect to the description given and the height and weight of the accused, notwithstanding the selection of the accused from the photo lineup, which I find to be representative. Her description of the accused having a rose tattoo was not convincing, having regard to the late disclosure and its actual design.

"There is no doubt Kathy was the victim of assaults and the subject of extortion to enforce a debt, but the crimes have not been proven beyond a reasonable doubt against this accused. In the result the charges are dismissed, and I find the accused not guilty."

The accused beamed and extended his arm in gratitude to his lawyer. I rose to leave the courtroom and the world of that trial. The court clerk said, "This court stands adjourned until tomorrow morning at ten o'clock. God save the Queen."

I departed the courtroom feeling depleted. In my chambers, the judicial robe felt heavier than usual as I lifted it from my shoulders. Still, it protected me, as if the workings of the legal system were a shield, enabling me to perform my duty no matter how I felt.

Week Two *Monday*	LUNCH
	Toasted white bread with butter, peanut butter, and jam
	Banana smoothie
	Apple
	Celery with light cream cheese or chocolate chip cookie

Chapter 17

FEBRUARY 3

ANNE HAD SPECIFIED that her pallbearers were to be women.
It was fitting. The honorary pallbearers, too, were women, and
included Mila Mulroney, wife of the Prime Minister. We agreed
to wear black or navy and to assemble at Anne's house at nine-
thirty. The mass program read:

A Service of Thanksgiving for the Life of
Anne Elizabeth Margherita Armstrong Gibson
March 1, 1948 – January 30, 1995
at the Cathedral church of St. James—Anglican Church of
Canada, Toronto, Ontario
Friday, February 3, 1995, 11:00 a.m.

On the back of the program was a picture of Anne, slightly
puffy-faced, with her two little dogs. I gazed at it for a long time,
with affection and sadness, though I would have preferred a
photo of Anne with her sons. Underneath was a traditional
Gaelic blessing:

May the road rise to meet you.
May the wind be always at your back.
May the sun shine warm upon your face.
May the rains fall softly upon your fields until we meet again.
May God hold you in the hollow of his hand.

Anne's pallbearers were her friends Joanna, Susan, and Fran; Libby, an executor; Simon's wife, Margaret; and me. We assembled at the back of the nineteenth-century Gothic cathedral. It was bitterly cold, but we decided we would not wear our coats in the funeral procession. The funeral-home staff organized us and directed us where to leave our things. There was a tiny measure of comfort in having the formalities arranged; attending to mundane details such as where to put our purses, learning our order of proceeding, and making sure everyone had Kleenex deflected our sorrow as we waited for the coffin to arrive.

The large, elaborate coffin was rolled through the doors of the church, and we stood motionless, overcome by the reality that Anne was finally gone. I saw a clear image of her lifeless body within the thick mahogany. We took our places beside the coffin, trying to control our tears at least for the procession. As suggested by the funeral director, we'd put lots of tissues in our pockets. At the funeral director's signal, we lifted the coffin, sinking slightly—it was heavier that we'd expected. The organ roared triumphantly as we walked down the centre aisle. Pale light filtered through the tall, stained-glass windows.

After we carried the coffin to the front, we sat together in front pews. I looked to my left and was comforted to see Alex, Darrell, and Edward seated in the same row. Duncan, Sandy, and others of Anne's family sat in the first pew on the other side. They looked solemn and serious, much as they had been while sitting in the same pew at their father's funeral a little over a year earlier. They'd been only a little smaller then, yet so much had happened in their young lives since.

The cathedral was filled. The organ continued its thunderous rolls. Six clergy officiated: three Reverends, a Venerable, the Very Reverend Doug Stoute, and the Most Reverend Bishop Edward Scott. Their robes were luxuriant, long gowns with embroidered silk crosses. The vestments and colours of God's choice clashed with my images of Satan's Choice: textured gold silk with wheat sheaves and crucifixes couldn't be further from black leather, daggers, and Grim Reapers.

Anne had selected the exultant music sung by the Choristers of Royal St. George's College and the Gentlemen of St. James Cathedral and of Royal St. George's College. The choirs sang gloriously and richly, and I lost control at the offertory hymn, "Lord of the Dance." With its exuberant theme, I couldn't believe Anne had chosen it:

I danced in the morning when the world was begun
And I danced in the moon and the stars and the sun;
And I came down from heaven and I danced on the earth;
At Bethlehem I had my birth.

Dance, then, wherever you may be,
I am the Lord of the Dance, said he;
I'll lead you all, wherever you may be,
I'll lead you all in the Dance, said he.

Simon and Susan were the readers, while Joanna, a church deacon, read the intercession. Reverend Doug Stoute, a close family friend and the man who had been counselling her son the last night I'd seen Anne alive, gave an eloquent, personal eulogy. After the invitation to receive Communion, hundreds rose and proceeded toward the altar. Although I was neither religious nor a churchgoer and I did not go to the altar, I had grown up Catholic, and I well knew the comfort of ritual, ceremony, and fellowship.

As I watched Duncan and Sandy walk to the altar, I thought how their mother must have passed on her remarkable ability to rally. Yet again her sons were rising to the demands of the grim occasions thrown before them in their young lives. I looked from Anne's sons across the pew to my own sons. How secure they were! They would go home to our orderly household, loved by two parents.

I saw how painful and disorienting it would be when Duncan and Sandy returned home after the interment. They would glance up toward their mother's bedroom and long for her to be there, no matter how sick. And when all the guests left after the reception at the house, what then? No father and now no mother. They were still young enough to need not only parental love and support but the physical intimacy of mothering. I grieved for the past and I grieved for the future.

The priest's final prayer for Anne resounded through the graceful room. *"Into thy hands, O merciful Saviour, we commend thy servant Anne. Acknowledge, we humbly beseech thee, a sheep of thine own fold, a lamb of thine own flock, a sinner of thine own redeeming. Receive her into the arms of thy mercy, into the blessed rest of everlasting peace, and into the glorious company of the saints in light. Amen."*

Bach's Fantasia in G resounded as we carried the coffin through the church and into the waiting hearse. Glancing across the street, I saw Anne's cousin watching the funeral cortège, forlorn in grief.

We drove for the interment to St. James Cemetery, the oldest cemetery in Toronto, located south of Bloor Street and east of Parliament Street. We pallbearers were in the first vehicle to pass through the iron gates, which are curved like open arms and buttressed by four large, square pillars. We passed the chapel of St. James-the-Less, built in 1860 of stone in a high-Victorian Gothic design, and continued up the winding path, which was still showing patches of old snow from the storm a few days earlier, when Anne had been alive. Barren trees bordered the rising incline. The cemetery sloped into a ravine on the east.

One last time carrying the coffin, we pallbearers stepped firmly to create a path across the fresh snow to the gravesite. The grave opened black against the white snow, and freshly dug earth lay in piles with an eerie, coffin-sized mound of dirt on the side.

The bishop and four priests walked toward us, black capes flowing on this grey, sunless day. Save for the high-rise tenement apartments of St. James Town across the street, it could have been the Scottish moors in winter. I stepped back to make room for Duncan and Sandy, who stood close together, not looking at one another—as if a glance might unravel them. After the interment ceremony was conducted, Anne's coffin was lowered to rest beside her husband's.

I imagined Anne's small body inside the wooden box, on a cushion, going into the cold, cold earth. In life, I'd tried to warm her when she was shivering, and in her death, I wished I could crawl into her coffin to warm her again. I finally understood the wailed torment of those "cold, cold grave" songs.

There will be a reception following this service at the Gibson home, 91 Elm Avenue, to which you are all invited.

A great many people attended the reception, but I didn't stay long; I couldn't bear to be in Anne's home without her.

The next day, the first Saturday in February, began as crisp and bright as the day Anne had died. I walked down Yonge Street toward the courthouse. South of Bloor Street, I looked ahead to see the gleaming waters of Lake Ontario, and to myself I sang the Rod Stewart song that, at home, I played over and over at deafening volumes:

I am sailing, I am sailing
Home again across the sea
I am sailing stormy waters
To be near you, to be free

Bleak January was over. Anne was dead at forty-six, having lived as a loving mother, dutiful wife, successful lawyer, and community activist. I was alive at fifty-two—having lived as a loving mother, dutiful wife, successful lawyer, and community activist. Was either of us happy? Everything in the past weeks, months, years—decades, even—had been about achieving, contributing to social betterment, doing for others, doing my duty, making a difference. I was coming to realize that doing what was worthwhile did not always sustain the doer.

January, the end of Anne's life, the first month of the new year, was for me a beginning. My life, enviable though it may have seemed and satisfying as I had once found it, did not fulfill me or make me happy. Starting with Anne's passing, I would examine my unexamined life, assess what mattered, who I was, and how I wanted to live the rest of my years. I could change my life.

It would take three years.

———

ONE MORNING three years later, I rose from my new bed, opened the door of my condominium, and reached for the *Globe and Mail*. I walked to the kitchen and prepared a French press of freshly ground coffee. I poured a glass of orange juice, sat at the small, round kitchen table, and began to read the news. I took my time. I was no longer a judge, I'd ended my marriage, and I could and would go out if, where, and when I wanted. Sitting in the quiet morning, I felt myself smiling, and realized, *I'm happy.*

THE HON. MARIE CORBETT is a retired superior court trial judge. In her thirty-year career, she was a dedicated crusader for social justice and reform of environmental, family, and pension law. She was the first woman president of the Canadian Environmental Law Association, a member of the first Ontario Status of Women Council, and Vice-Chair of the Pension Commission of Ontario. Marie lives in her native Newfoundland and in Florida.